WRITING LESSONS FROM THE FRONT

The First Ten Books

ANGELA HUNT

Hunt Haven
Press

Hunt Haven
Press

Visit Angela Hunt's Web site at www.angelahuntbooks.com

ISBN paper: 978-0692311134
ISBN hardcover: 978-1961394100
ISBN ebook: 978-19613394773

Subscribe to Angela Hunt's newsletters for writers:
angelahunt.substack.com

WRITING LESSONS FROM THE FRONT

To all the teachers who ever scribbled my pages with a red pen: thank you.

INTRODUCTION

Welcome to the writers' workshop in a book!

I began writing these booklet lessons when I realized that I no longer had the energy or the desire to travel to a dozen writers' conferences every year. I had begun a second career that required my attention, I had a darling granddaughter, and I was continuing to write as much as ever. So why not write what I taught?

So I wrote the first *Writing Lessons from the Front* booklets as I taught them, and they've been generally well received. When I finished the tenth book, I realized that a compilation might be in order for people who don't want to turn their libraries upside down in search of a thin little volume with helpful information.

So here it is, the first ten writing lessons in one volume. You will certainly find some repetition within these pages if you read from cover to cover, but I hope you'll feel as I do and agree that repetition is often good reinforcement. In any case, I have tried to keep the repeated material brief so you can move on to a new concept.

If you learn better from video than the printed page, check out my video writing course. You'll find a link on my website. It contains all the material in this book and more because it was taped during an actual writing workshop.

Enjoy these lessons. And if after reading these pages you have questions or suggestions for future booklets, feel free to drop me a note through the contact page at www.angelahuntbooks.com.

Wishing you success,

Angela Hunt

The Plot Skeleton

The head:
one obvious need
one hidden need
admirable/sympathetic
qualities

The neck: inciting incident

The inciting incident leads
to the end of the spine, the
goal. The spine connects all
the major events of your
story.

The ribs: the complications
They curve and swing from
positive to negative events

The last complication leads to the bleakest
moment. No more hope for your character.

After the bleakest moment,
your protag needs HELP.
Someone gives
him a push in the right
direction.

After considering what
the helper said/did,
Your protag learns a
lessonand makes a
decision

Which leads to his resolution-
he either meets
his goal or doesn't,
and he lives happily ever
after OR he's sadder, but wiser.

Chapter One

THE PLOT SKELETON

W HEN WE WERE IN SCHOOL, OUR ENGLISH TEACHERS GAVE US explicit details about how to write a five-paragraph theme: introduction, thesis sentence, point one, point two, point three, and conclusion. But when it came to writing creative fiction, odds are that your teacher said, "Just tell me a story."

No wonder so many storytellers falter when it comes to creating their own stories! We move from the ordered world of nonfiction into a world that can appear to be a whirling ebb and flow of ideas. To the uninitiated, it can feel like a riptide and it's hard to make any headway.

But creative fiction does have a structure, and it's been around for ages. From Joseph Campbell's study of the hero's journey to Syd Field's exploration of screenwriting structure, others have found and analyzed plot structure with sometimes confusing terms.

A few years ago, I was hired to teach writing to homeschooled students from third through twelfth grades. I wanted to teach them to plot, so I searched for a method that was easy to understand and yet completely sound. After studying several plotting techniques and boiling them down to their basic elements, I developed what I call the plot skeleton. It combines the spontaneity of "seat of the pants" writing with the discipline of an outline. It requires a writer to know where he's going, but it leaves room for the joy of discovery on the journey.

Best of all, the method is visual. You don't have to have a lick of artistic ability, but if you can draw a round head, some ribs, and some skinny leg bones, you can draw a skeleton that will guide you through the plotting process.

A Bare Bones Outline

Imagine, if you will, that you and I are sitting in a room with one hundred other writers. If you were to ask each person to describe their plotting process, you'd probably get a hundred different answers. Writers' methods vary according to their personalities and we are all different. Mentally. Emotionally. Physically.

If, however, those one hundred writers were to pass behind an x-ray machine, you'd discover that except for slight gender differences we all possess remarkably similar skeletons. Unless someone has been unfortunate enough to experience some kind of deformity, beneath our disguising skin, hair, and clothing, our skeletons would be nearly indistinguishable.

In the same way, though writers vary in their methods, good stories are composed of remarkably similar skeletons. Stories with "good bones" can be found in picture books and movies, plays and films. The only difference in most stories is length, and length is usually determined by the breadth of the work—how many subplots are involved, and how many complications the protagonist must face.

Many fine writers carefully outline their plots before they begin the first chapter while others describe themselves as "seat of the pants" plotters. But when the story is finished, a seat-of-the-pants novel will usually contain the same elements as a carefully plotted book. Why? Because whether you plan from the beginning or work through intuition, novels need structure to support the story.

When I sit down to plan a new book, the first thing I do is sketch my smiling little skeleton.

To illustrate the plot skeleton in this article, I'm going to refer frequently to *The Wizard of Oz, The Sound of Music,* and a lovely foreign film you may have never seen, *Mostly Martha.*

One more thing: my lessons are never intended to be a set of rules that must never be broken. What I want to offer are guides to the art of writing. Take what you learn here, visualize it, practice it, and then use it in your own way to create your story.

The Skull

The skull represents the main character, the protagonist. A lot of beginning novelists have a hard time deciding who the main character is, so settle that question right away. Even in an ensemble cast, one character should be more predominant than the others. Your reader wants to place himself into your story world, and it's helpful if you can give him a sympathetic character with whom he or she can relate. Ask yourself, "Whose story is this?" That is your protagonist.

At the very beginning of your story, this main character should be dealing with two situations, which I represent in the skeleton by two yawning eye sockets: one obvious problem, one hidden need.

Here's a tip: hidden needs, which usually involve basic human emotions, are usually resolved or met by the end of the story. They are at the center of the protagonist's "inner journey," or character change, while the "outer journey" is concerned with the main events of the plot. Hidden needs often arise from wounds in a character's past.

Consider *The Wizard of Oz.* At the beginning of the film, Dorothy needs to save her dog from Miss Gulch, who has arrived at the farm to take Toto because he bit Miss Gulch's scrawny leg—a straightforward and obvious problem. Dorothy's *hidden* need is depicted but not directly emphasized when she stands by the pigpen and sings "Somewhere Over the Rainbow." Do children live with Uncle Henry and Aunt Em if all is fine with Mom and Dad? No. Though we are not told what happened to Dorothy's parents, it's clear that something has splintered her family and Dorothy's unhappy about the result. Her hidden need, the object of her inner journey, is to accept her new home.

The Sound of Music opens with young Maria dancing and singing in a mountain meadow. As we watch, we learn that this free spirited woman loves music and life, and that she has voluntarily entered a convent—to serve God and others, we may safely assume. But the girl, dear as she is, is simply not fitting in. The other nuns love her, but she distracts them from their prayers and she can't seem to keep her lively spirit from showing up at times when she should be quiet and contemplative. The nuns sing, "How Do you Solve A Problem Like Maria?" Like the song says, molding Maria to convent life is like holding a moonbeam in your hand—impossible. A fairly obvious problem.

Maria's hidden need is the very urge that brought her to the convent. She has a need to love God and serve others, and that's what she's trying—not very successfully—to do at the convent.

Mostly Martha opens with the title character lying on her therapist's couch and talking about all that is required to cook the perfect pigeon. Since she's in a therapist's office, we assume she has a problem, and the therapist addresses this directly: "Martha, why are you here?"

"Because," she answers, "my boss will fire me if I don't go to therapy."

Ah—her obvious problem involves her work and her boss. Immediately we also know that Martha is high-strung. She wears her hair tightly wound into a bun and is precise and politely controlling in her kitchen. This woman lives for food, but though she assures us in a voiceover that all a cook needs for a perfectly lovely dinner is "fish and sauce," we see her venture downstairs to ask her new neighbor if he'd like to join her for dinner. He can't, but we clearly see that Martha needs company. She needs people in her life. Like all of us, she needs love and companionship.

So—as you consider the story you're writing, have you settled on one protagonist? There will be other characters, of course, but have you found the one character who will change the most? The person the reader can "inhabit" for the length of the story? This should probably be the character who undergoes the greatest change over the course of your story.

Now, have you opened *in medias res*, or in the middle of the action? You don't have to open your story with a bomb blast or a kidnapping, but you should open in the middle of an interesting problem—the protagonist is rushing to meet someone and has a flat tire, or she's trying to cook the perfect dinner and burns the entrée. Let us see this character up to his neck in ordinary life, and let us see how he handles stress. Let us hear what his neighbors think of him. Let us watch him grapple with an interesting problem, and then, through subtext, action, and reaction, let us see the hidden need in his life. Don't explain it, just reveal it by letting us observe him in his ordinary world.

Before we leave this development of the protagonist—and you may need up to 20 or 25 percent of the book to paint a complete picture—add a little smile to that face on your skeleton. Let it remind you that the reader needs to see something admirable in your protagonist.

Maybe she keeps her chin up when she loses her job; maybe he can remain calm when everyone else panics. Maybe she's a single mother who gives up dinner with a handsome man in order to help her son with his homework. Maybe he's a judge who refuses a bribe offered by a Mafia messenger . . . at great personal risk.

We admire Dorothy because she's loyal to her dog, she's plucky, and she's brave enough to run away from home, then compassionate enough to return when she realizes that Auntie Em might worry about her.

We admire Maria from the convent because she is a free spirit, because the nuns love her, and because she's so *good*. She's pretty, and she sings, so what's not to love?

We admire Martha the chef because she's a true artist, and exceptionally good at her job. We nearly always admire those who have reached the top of their craft because we know it takes skill and hard work to achieve that kind of success. So we admire

Martha for knowing how to cook a pigeon . . . and then we sympathize with her when she can't find someone to share her elegant dinner.

Even if your protagonist is what would traditionally be considered a bad guy, let us see *something* in him that's admirable. *The Godfather's* Don Corleone was the godfather of a major crime syndicate, but the Don and his family had a set of ethics. Yes, they killed people, but they drew the line at selling drugs because they didn't want to harm children.

Though he wasn't the protagonist of the *Silence of the Lambs*, Hannibal Lecter was a sadistic serial killer and cannibal, yet he was so clever and intelligent that some part of us couldn't help but admire how he managed to outsmart the slimy prison warden. And we certainly rooted for Clarice, the wounded F.B.I. trainee who was trying to find a serial murderer.

We want to admire the protagonist; we yearn to feel sympathy and understanding for him. Because once we develop a solid affinity for him, we'll stick around when the real action begins.

Take a good look at your protagonist—from what you've written thus far, will the reader find him admirable? Can you make him really, really good at what he does? Can you give him a vulnerability, a real soft spot for his child, his dog, his wife? Can you take a moment to show us that he has strong character and a sense of morals? Can you display his sense of humor? We always admire people who can keep smiling in the midst of turmoil.

And the head bone's connected to the neck bone . . .

Usually the first few chapters of a novel are involved with the business of establishing the protagonist in a specific time and place, his world, his needs, and his personality. The story doesn't kick into gear, though, until you move from the skull to the spine, a connection known as the *inciting incident*.

We want to begin our story in the middle of the action, but this is not the same as the Big Incident. Save the big event for a few chapters later, after you've given us some time to know and understand your character's personality and his needs.

When I am teaching in front of a large group, I often engage a kindly conspirator to help me illustrate a point. As I talk about the skull of the plot skeleton, my conspirator will walk toward me and hand me a folded slip of paper. I open it, read it silently, then look out at the crowd and, with a woeful expression, tell them that Billy (or Jimmy or Paul or Elizabeth) has died.

The members of the audience give me sympathetic looks, but not until I say, "Excuse me—I meant Billy *Graham*" (or Jimmy Carter or Paul McCartney or Queen Elizabeth) do their faces register real shock and dismay.

The final effect depends upon what sort of crowd it is, but the difference in their reactions is remarkable. Why? Because they have memories of and feelings about Billy Graham or Paul McCartney or Queen Elizabeth. They don't have to be personally acquainted with Billy or Paul or the queen, but because they've heard about those people for years, there is a strong connection. And that's the sort of bond we want to develop in the first part of our novel. We want the reader to admire the protagonist, feel sympathy for him, like him, laugh with him, and root for him. We strive to build connection *before* the big story event takes place so the reader will truly care when the inciting incident occurs.

In the first 20 percent of *The Wizard of Oz* we learned that Dorothy loves Toto passionately. In the first 20 percent of *Mostly Martha* we learn that Martha is a perfectionist chef. Yes, start in the middle of something active, but hold off on the big event for a while. Let us get to know your character first . . . because we won't gasp about their dilemma until we have thoroughly identified with them.

In a picture book, the inciting incident is often signaled by two words: "One day . . ." Those two words are a natural way to move from setting the stage to the action. As you plot your novel, ask yourself, "One day, what happens to move my main character into the action of the story?" Your answer will be your inciting incident, the key that turns your story engine.

After Dorothy runs away, if she'd made it home to Uncle Henry and Aunt Em without incident there would have been no story. But the inciting incident occurs: the tornado picks up Dorothy and drops her, along with her house, in the land of Oz.

Maria the postulant would have kept singing and not fitting in if not for the day Reverend Mother called her into her office and explained that the Von Trapp family needed a governess—and that Maria would be the perfect candidate.

A ringing telephone signals the inciting incident in *Mostly Martha*. When Martha takes the call, she learns that her sister, who was a single mother to an eight-year-old girl, has been killed in an auto accident.

Often—but not always—your protagonist doesn't want to go where the inciting incident pushes her. Obviously, Martha doesn't want to hear that her sister is dead, and she certainly doesn't want to be a mother. She takes Lina, her niece, and offers to cook for her (her way of showing love), but her effort is neither welcomed nor appreciated. Lina wants her mother, not gourmet food.

Maria the postulant is surprised to hear that the Reverend Mother wants to send her away from the convent, but she is guided by her faith in God and her obedience to her authority. So off she goes.

And Dorothy, of course, did not want to get picked up by a tornado, but she was helpless before the strong winds of Story. Like all protagonists, she found herself smack dab in the middle of the Story World, a place vastly different from the world she'd known before.

What is the inciting incident that pulls your protagonist out of his ordinary world and sets him on a different path? Is he set in motion by a letter or a summons?

I once heard a writer say that most stories commence when someone either comes to town or leaves town. That's not far from the truth—maybe your protagonist enters a special story world when someone comes to town and enters *his* world, thereby changing it.

Take a moment to jot down the situation that moves your

protagonist from status quo to something new. Is it unique? Can you make it better?

Even if your protagonist has actively pursued a change, he or she may have moments of doubt as the entrance to the special world looms ahead. When your character retreats or doubts or refuses to leave the ordinary world, another character should step in to provide encouragement, advice, information, or a special tool. This will help your main character overcome those last-minute doubts and enable her to establish—

The End of the Spine: the Goal

At some point after the inciting incident, your character will establish and state a goal. Shortly after stepping out of her transplanted house, Dorothy looks around Oz and wails, "I want to go back to Kansas!" She's been transported over the rainbow, but she prefers the tried and true to the unfamiliar and strange. In order to go home, she'll have to visit the wizard in the Emerald City. As she tries to meet an ever-shifting set of subordinate goals (follow the yellow brick road, overcome the poppies, get in to see the wizard, bring back a broomstick), her main goal keeps viewers glued to the screen.

This overriding concern—will she or won't she make it home?—is sometimes called "the dramatic question." The dramatic question in every murder mystery is *who committed the crime?* The dramatic question in nearly every thriller is *who will win the inevitable showdown between the hero and the villain?* Along the way readers will worry about the sub goals (Will the villain kill his hostage? Will the hero figure out the clues?), but the dramatic question keeps them reading until the last page.

Maria's goal is simple: if God wants her to be a governess, she'll be the best governess she can be. But can she do that in Captain Von Trapp's unusual household?

Martha finds herself trying to care for a grieving eight-year-old who doesn't want another mother. So Martha promises to track down the girl's father, who lives in Italy. She knows only that his name is Giuseppe.

Make sure that your protagonist has an *observable* goal, one that would be filmable if you were making a movie. If her goal is simply to be a better person, how can that be measured? Instead, let your self-centered debutante decide to raise a million dollars for breast cancer research because it will help her get into Harvard, and then let us see how she becomes a more caring person on her quest to reach that goal.

Once your protagonist enters the special world, what goal does he set? Are there smaller tasks he must achieve in order to reach the ultimate goal? How will he measure his forward progress?

And ask yourself this—what happens if your character doesn't achieve his goal? If your answer is "life just returns to normal," you probably need to increase the risks your protagonist is taking. As he strives to reach his goal, he will need to mortgage the farm, burn a bridge, or walk away from a relationship. This undertaking can't be light or trivial; in order for it to mean a lot to the reader, it must mean a lot to the character.

After all, on her journey home Dorothy nearly loses Toto and her life to the witch. What is your character prepared to lose?

The Ribcage

Even my youngest students understand that a protagonist who accomplishes everything he attempts is a colorless character. As another friend of mine is fond of pointing out, when we tackle the mountain of life, it's the bumps we climb on!

If you're diagramming, sketch at least three curving ribs over your spine. These represent the *complications* that must arise to prevent your protagonist from reaching his goal.

Why at least three ribs? Because even in the shortest of stories—in a picture book, for instance—three complications works better than two or four. I don't know why three gives us such a feeling of completion, but it does.

While a very short story might have only three complications, a movie or novel may have hundreds. Complications can range from the mundane—John can't find a pencil to write down Sarah's number —to life-shattering. As you write down possible complications that could stand between your character and his ultimate goal, place the more serious problems at the bottom of the list.

The *stakes*—what your protagonist is risking—should increase in significance as the story progresses. In *Mostly Martha*, the complications center on this uptight woman's ability to care for a child. Lina hates her babysitter, so Martha has to take Lina to work with her. But the late hours take their toll, and Lina is habitually late for school. To pour salt in the wound, Lina keeps refusing to eat anything Martha cooks for her.

I asked you to make the ribs curve because any character that runs into complication after complication without any breathing space is going to be a weary character . . . and you'll weary your reader with this frenetic pace. One of the keys to good pacing is to alternate your plot complications with rewards. Like a pendulum that swings on an arc, let your character relax, if only briefly, between disasters.

Along the spiraling yellow brick road, Dorothy soon reaches an intersection (a complication). Fortunately, a friendly scarecrow is willing to help (a reward). They haven't gone far before Dorothy becomes hungry (a complication). The scarecrow spots an apple orchard ahead (a reward). These apple trees, however, resent being picked (a complication), but the clever scarecrow taunts them until they begin to throw fruit at the hungry travelers (a reward).

See how it works? Every negative complication is followed by a positive reward that matches the seriousness of the complication. Let's fast forward to the scene where the balloon takes off without Dorothy. This is a *severe* complication and it leads to *the bleakest moment*. Whether your story has had three or three hundred complications, the bleakest moment is the final rib in the ribcage, leading to the moment when your protagonist loses all hope.

In *The Sound of Music*, the complications are broader and slower-

paced than in *The Wizard of Oz* which is, after all, a children's story.
Who is the first person or group of people who stand between Maria
and her goal of being the best governess she can be? That's right—
the children themselves. They don't want a governess, and they
pretty much tell her so when they are first introduced to her. The
boys put a pinecone in her chair and a frog in her bed; they talk
about how they got rid of their other governesses in no time flat.
That's a complication.

But when a storm ensues, they run to Maria for comfort, and she
allows them to snuggle with her while she sings them a song to make
them forget their fears. And in no time at all, Maria has become one
of their favorite things.

Who is the next person or persons who stand in the way of Maria's
goal? The captain himself, of course. He has been (rather conveniently)
away while Maria dealt with the complication of the children, but the
highly disciplined widower arrives back home to find his children
climbing trees in clothing made from curtains. He's horrified, and he
blinks in astonishment after he announces that he will summon Maria by
a certain whistle and she tells him that she doesn't *do* whistles, thank you
very much. But he watches her even as they butt heads, and because she
is warm and loving and truly cares for his children, she wins him over.

There's a third complication in Maria's story, and it does lead to a
bleak moment. Who's the third person or persons who stand in
Maria's way of being the best governess she can be? Most people
immediately assume it's the Baroness, but it's not. Let me remind
you of the pertinent scene:

The adults are all inside at the fancy dress ball to honor the
Baroness, while Maria and the children are out on the patio. She's
trying to teach them an Austrian folk dance, but Hans or Franz or
whatever the oldest boy's name is can't seem to get the hang of it.

Suddenly Captain Von Trapp steps out onto the patio. With great
dignity he says, "Allow me," and he takes Maria into his arms and
they do the folk dance perfectly. When it's over, the captain returns
to the ball and a flushed Maria turns to face the children.

Enter the Baroness. She sashays over to Maria and, ignoring the children, says, "You blushed in his arms just now," and Maria claps her hands to her burning face, then turns and runs . . . all the way back to the convent.

Let me ask again: who is the person who stands in the way of Maria's goal of being the best governess she can be? It's not the Baroness, though that lady did point out something crucial. The complication lies in Maria's own traitorous heart. She's in love with the captain, and how can a nun-in-training be a good governess if she's secretly in love with her employer?

She can't. And because Maria can't see any way out of her situation, she runs back to the convent, where she can tend to her broken heart in private. That is her bleakest moment.

So—what is the bleakest story in your existing plot? What has your character risked—and lost? A scholarship? The love of his life? His reputation? His freedom?

If the situation he's facing isn't the worst complication he could face, or if there's an obvious way out of the problem, you need to rethink your plot. He needs to be at the end of his rope, and he should feel the pain of defeat. Your hero needs to be tested, as it were, through the fire in order to come out refined and strong.

Is your bleakest moment bleak enough? Has your protagonist truly found himself without hope?

The Thighbone: Send in the Cavalry

At the bleakest moment, your character needs *help*, but be careful how you deliver it. The ancient Greek playwrights had actors representing the Greek gods literally descend from a structure above in order to untangle their complicated plots and set things to rights. This sort of resolution is frowned upon in modern literature. Called *deus ex machina* (literally *god from the machine*), this device employs some unexpected and improbable incident to bring victory or success. If you find yourself whipping up a coincidence or a miracle after the bleakest moment, chances are you've employed deus ex machina. Back up and try again, please.

Avoid using deus ex machina by sending help, represented on the plot skeleton by the thigh bone. Your character obviously needs help; if he could solve the problem alone, he would have done it long before the bleakest moment. Having him conveniently remember something or stumble across a hidden resource smacks of coincidence and will leave your reader feeling resentful and cheated.

So send in the cavalry, but remember that *they can't solve the protagonist's problem.* They can give her a push in the right direction, they can nudge, they can remind, they can inspire. But they shouldn't wave a magic wand and make everything all right.

For Maria the nun-in-training, the Reverend Mother supplies the help she needs by reminding Maria that she shouldn't run from her problems, but find the courage to face them. And that she must "climb every mountain" until she finds her dream.

For Dorothy, help comes in the form of Glenda the Good Witch, who reveals a secret—the ruby slippers have the power to carry her back to Kansas. All Dorothy has to do is say "There's no place like home"—with feeling, mind you—and she'll be back on the farm with Uncle Henry and Auntie Em. Dorothy's problem isn't resolved, however, until she applies this information internally. At the beginning of the story, she wanted to be anywhere *but* on the farm. Now she has to affirm that the farm is where she wants to be. Her hidden need—to find a place to call home--has been met.

In *Mostly Martha*, the bleakest moment arrives with Lina's father, Giuseppe. He is a good man, and Lina seems to accept him. But after waving goodbye, Martha goes home to an empty apartment and realizes that she is not happy with her former childless life. She goes to Marlo, the Italian chef she has also begun to love, and asks for his help.

Who arrives to help your protagonist? To whom does she run for help? Does this person offer advice and a helping hand? Remember that the helper isn't meant to solve the problem, but to encourage and strengthen the protagonist until she realizes what she must do in order to reach her goal.

The Kneecap and Leg bone: A Lesson Leads to a Decision

Martha realizes that her old life was empty—she needs Lina, and she needs Marlo. So she and Marlo drive from Germany to Italy to fetch Lina and bring her home.

Draw a round kneecap and a shin bone—they represent the lesson learned and a decision to act. Both are important to story structure.

You may be hard pressed to cite the lesson you learned from the last novel you read, but your protagonist needs to learn something. This lesson is the *epiphany*, a sudden insight that speaks volumes to your character and brings them to the conclusion of their inner journey.

James Joyce popularized the word *epiphany*, literally *the manifestation of a divine being*. (Churches celebrate the festival of Epiphany on January sixth to commemorate the meeting of the Magi and the Christ child.) After receiving help from an outside source, your character should see something—a person, a situation, or an object—in a new light.

When the scarecrow asks why Glenda waited so long to explain the power of the ruby slippers, the good witch smiles and says, "Because she wouldn't have believed me. She had to learn it for herself."

The scarecrow then asks, "What'd you learn, Dorothy?"

Without hesitation, Dorothy announces that she's learned a lesson: "The next time I go looking for my heart's desire, I won't look any farther than my own back yard."

She has learned to appreciate her home, so even though she is surrounded by loving friends and a beautiful emerald city, Dorothy chooses to return to colorless Kansas. She hugs her friends once more, then grips Toto, clicks her heels, and *acts* upon what she's learned: home is where your loved ones are. Her hidden need, depicted at the beginning of the story, has been met.

Back in Austria, young Maria the postulant makes the decision to return to the Von Trapp family mansion in order to fulfill her promise to be a governess. The children are very happy to see her, and she tells the captain that she will remain as governess until he marries, then she'll leave.

And the captain says, "But I'm not marrying the Baroness . . . how could I, when I'm in love with someone else?"

And Maria learns that the captain loves her, and suddenly the family is planning a wedding.

The Sound of Music could have ended perfectly well at the wedding scene, but the film includes a few more scenes to explain how the Von Trapp family came to America to escape the Nazis. But the film is not a story about Nazis, it's a love story about the romance between a free-spirited postulant and a starched Navy captain. The movie is about love, not war, and at the end of the film we see that Maria's hidden need—to love and serve God and others—has been met many times over.

What does your protagonist learn in the course of his trial? What has he realized about his life, his past, or his future? Does he appreciate something or someone he used to take for granted? Write down what your character has learned, then show us how he can put this knowledge into action.

Armed with this new realization or understanding, what does your protagonist do that he could not do before? Does he go up against the villain with new strength or courage? Does he have a quality or a weapon he has suddenly begun to value? Does she humble herself for the first time, or confess something she would never have confessed before? What can your protagonist do to show the reader that he or she has truly experienced a deep and personal shift in attitude?

The Foot: The Resolution

Every story needs the fairy-tale equivalent of "and they lived happily ever after" as the protagonist leaves the story world and returns to his ordinary world a changed person. Not every story ends happily, of course, though happy endings are undoubtedly the most popular. Some protagonists are sadder and wiser after the course of their adventure. But even if a protagonist does not get what he worked for, a novel should leave the reader with hope.

The resolution to *Mostly Martha* is portrayed during the closing of the film. As the credits roll, we see Marlo and Martha meeting Lina in Italy, we see Martha in a wedding gown (with her hair down!) and Marlo in a tuxedo, we see a wedding feast with Giuseppe, his family, and Martha's German friends, we see Martha and Marlo and Lina exploring an abandoned restaurant—clearly, they are going to settle in Italy so Lina can be a part of both families. In the delightful final scene, we again see Martha with her therapist, but this time he has cooked for *her* and she is counseling him.

Many movies end with a simple visual image—we see a couple walking away hand-in-hand, a mother cradling her long-lost son. That's all we need to realize that our main character has struggled, learned, and come away a better (or wiser) person. As a writer, you'll have to use words instead of images, but you can paint the same sort of reassuring picture without resorting to "and they lived happily ever after."

Your story should end with a changed protagonist—he or she has gone through a profound experience and has changed as a result, hopefully for the better. Your protagonist has completed an outer journey (experienced the major plot events) and an inner journey that addressed some hurt from the past and resulted in a changed character. When he reenters his ordinary world, he has a new understanding or circumstance to share with others.

What scenes can you depict that show us that your character has changed permanently? Is a wedding appropriate? A change of career? A change of scenery? Come up with a simple scene or two that lets the reader know that life is going to be different for your protagonist from this point on.

. . .

Does Every Character Need a Skeleton?

Yes and no. I usually sketch out brief plot skeletons for all the
major characters if only to remind myself that they need goals and a
reason for being in the story. If your secondary characters are only
hanging around to interact with the protagonist at appropriate
times, they'll be as thin as an insincere smile. You don't have to
create their plot skeletons all the way down to the thighbone, but
they should have histories and goals.

Remember the Scarecrow, the Tin Man, and the Cowardly Lion?
These secondary characters in *The Wizard of Oz* had histories (far
more developed in the book than in the film), and they spent a lot of
time pursuing personal goals while at Dorothy's side. We cheered for
them when they received something better than a brain, a heart, and
courage. They received the recognition that they had already proved
themselves intelligent, loving, and brave friends to our heroine from
Kansas.

So give your secondary characters a full life, and use the plot
skeleton to pinpoint their highlights. Give them goals, and weave
their pursuits along with the protagonist's. You never know what
unexpected developments might occur when the two storylines
intersect.

Is That All There is to It?

Depends. You have probably heard that some stories are more
plot-driven or character-driven, and that's true. Let's leave the
skeleton for a moment and focus on a circle. Let's say that the right
side of the circle represents the plot action while the left side of the
circle represents character growth.

In some action movies—the James Bond franchise comes to mind—
nearly all the story is contained on the right side of the circle. James

changes very little as a person, and we learn very little about him. (I've been pleased to see that we are beginning to learn about James in the more recent Bond films—maybe we'll have some real character development in the future!)

James is focused on saving the world from evil henchmen, and when that's done, he seems to care only about the beautiful woman he met in the course of his adventure.

On the other hand, in other stories the emphasis is on the character side of the circle. In my book *The Fine Art of Insincerity*, three sisters gather together over Labor Day weekend to clean out their late grandmother's beach house. That's about all the action there is.

But while the sisters are together, the oldest woman learns that her husband has been unfaithful and that her youngest sister was planning to commit suicide on the drive home—earth-shattering revelations that rock her world. The sisters come together to confront, accuse, confess, and reconcile all the traumatic events of their shared past.

A character driven story still needs a plot—you need something to get the characters together and move them around—but most of the emotion is invested in what the characters are feeling and how they're reacting to one another. They're not out to save the world, find romance, or win a prize; they are out to restore faded relationships or establish new ones.

An acquaintance once told me that character-driven stories always win the Oscar for Best Picture at the Academy Awards. *Driving Miss Daisy* and *Steel Magnolias* are prime examples of character stories. They can make me cry just by talking about them.

Let's look first at *Driving Miss Daisy*. Daisy Werthan is the protagonist, and she has an obvious problem at the opening of the story—she needs a driver, because she's aging and her son insists that she's no longer safe behind the wheel. Ms. Daisy has a hidden need, too, one that no one sees: she is a prejudiced product of her generation.

So Daisy, grumbling the entire time, soon receives Hoke, a black chauffeur. A great distance exists between Daisy and her driver, illustrated at mealtimes: Daisy eats alone in the dining room, while Hoke eats in the kitchen with Idella the cook. The kitchen is filled with laughter and warmth; Daisy remains alone in the chilly silence.

After a while, Daisy asks Hoke to drive her to Alabama. He does, but on the long journey, he asks permission to stop the car so he can "make water." He is clearly uncomfortable to have to ask, and Daisy is horrified at the request and refuses to allow him to stop. But Hoke, driven by physical necessity, finally stops, and we realize that Daisy could not even admit that Hoke was a man, with a man's need to relieve himself.

Later, Daisy's synagogue is bombed, and she is terribly shaken that anyone could be so evil and prejudiced. How could such things happen? She cannot see that in her own way, she is as prejudiced as those who hate Jews.

When Martin Luther King Jr. comes to town for a dinner, Daisy plans to give her extra ticket to her son Booley, but he has to back out at the last moment. So Daisy sits next to an empty chair at the banquet, a seat that could and should have gone to Hoke, but Daisy can't even imagine the idea of a black driver sitting next to her at such an important banquet. Hoke has to listen to Dr. King's speech on a car radio in the parking lot.

But in Daisy's bleakest moment, when her dementia worsens and she wakes up one morning thinking that she's a schoolteacher once again, it's Hoke who calms her and cares for her and calls her son.

And at the end of the film, when Daisy is in a nursing home, it's Hoke who comes to visit her. She looks at him, smiles, and says, with deep feeling, "You're my best friend."

And he is.

Daisy has come a long way in that character arc, and that's where the true heart of the story lies. *Driving Miss Daisy* isn't about a woman's need for a driver. It's about the friendship that develops between a white Jewish woman and a black man.

In *Steel Magnolias*, M'Lynn is the protagonist, even though she's surrounded by a stellar supporting cast who play colorful strong characters. M'Lynn's obvious problem is that her daughter's getting married and everything's hectic, but goal soon becomes obvious: Shelby, her daughter, has severe diabetes, and M'Lynn is determined to nag, scold, remind, and do anything she has to do in order to protect her daughter's life and health.

But Shelby cares more about living than being protected, and though she and her mother are constantly butting heads, Shelby prevails. She marries her sweetheart, has a baby, survives a kidney transplant, and then, tragically, her body gives out and she dies.

M'Lynn doesn't achieve her goal, and she is devastated. But through the care and support of her friends, she learns that life goes on. She has Shelby's son to live for, and the future beckons even though she will always grieve for the daughter she lost.

Yes, there's a plot—M'Lynn is always trying to protect Shelby. But the true heart of the story is about how women support and care for one another.

How can you tell if a story is more character- or plot driven? Try to describe the story to a friend. If you say, "This is about a boy and his dog as they try to win an Alaskan race," then clearly it's plot-driven. But if you find yourself saying, "This is about a boy and how he becomes a man through loving and caring for his sled dog," then you're apt to be describing a character story.

Stories should have both plot and character arcs, and they may be evenly balanced. Events move the story along and characters grow and change as the story progresses. But the balance between plot and character can shift from one side to the other without changing the quality of the story. One emphasis is not better than the other because the balance will depend upon the sort of story you want to tell.

Write what is best-suited for the story you have in mind. You will tell it unlike anyone else.

Brandon takes a Bath

While I would love to take one of my novel manuscripts and point out exactly how the bones of the plot skeleton fit into the story, I can't squeeze all those words into this little book. So to illustrate how simple plotting by skeleton is, let me present the script to one of my picture books. Picture books are spare by design, with a limited number of words, and often some of the plot elements are implied. But I think it should be easy to see how it all comes together in even a simple little story like this one.

I've put my plot comments in brackets and bold type.

The opening: the protagonist's (Brandon's) ordinary world:

Yesterday I spent the day at my cousins' house. Aunt Molly, Uncle George, and my cousins Sam and Tricia are calm, quiet people, but Brandon is something else.

Brandon played outside in the mud and wrote on himself with colored markers. At dinner, he put spaghetti on his head. It was a messy, dirty day. [**Obvious need: a bath. Hidden need: like all little kids, Brandon needs to know he's loved.**]

After supper Aunt Molly asked, "Brandon, are you ready to take a bath?" [**The inciting incident: Mom's invitation.**]
Brandon shook his head. "No," he said. "I'm not ready to take a bath." [**Brandon's goal: avoid the bath! Bathtime signals an end to the day, an end to his fun.**]

[**We move into the Story World: the bathroom.**]
"But Brandon," Uncle George said, "if you take a bath you will be clean and sweet-smelling." [**He's urging Brandon toward the tub.**]
Brandon made fish faces at Tricia. "I'm not ready to take a bath."

[**Brandon counters by doing something else. This pattern will be repeated many times.**]

"Brandon," Aunt Molly said, "I'm giving the bath water a squirt of bubbling super soap. You can soak in mountains of bubbles."

Brandon twirled on his toes and said, "I'm not ready to take a bath."

"Brandon," Sam said, "I'm putting my toy boat in the tub. You can sail it."

Brandon stood on his head and said, "I'm not ready to take a bath."

"Brandon," Tricia said, "I'm putting toy dishes in the tub. You can pretend to pour milk and coffee."

Brandon somersaulted across the floor. "I'm not ready to take a bath."

"Brandon," Aunt Molly called, "I'm putting your beach bucket and shovel in the tub. You can scoop up bubbles and put them in the bucket."

Brandon marched like a soldier and said, "I'm-not-rea-dy-to-take-a-bath."

"Brandon," called Uncle George, "I'm blowing up your swimming ring seahorse for the tub."

Brandon started pulling the laces out of his dad's sneakers. "I'm not ready to take a bath."

. . .

"Brandon," Sam said, "I'm putting Howard in the water. You can swim with your pet turtle."

Brandon found the day-old lollipop he'd stuck under the table. "I'm not ready to take a bath."

"Brandon," I said, holding up a bottle from the kitchen, "I'm squirting green drops in your bath water. You can play in colored bubbles!"

Brandon hopped like a rabbit and squeaked. "I'm not ready to take a bath."

Uncle George sighed and turned to Aunt Molly. "I suppose we could skip bathtime and move straight to bedtime. Because Brandon simply doesn't want to take a bath." **[The opposition closes in, leading to Brandon's bleakest moment—though, admittedly, in this children's story it's not terribly bleak.]**

"*Now* I do," Brandon shouted. "But there's no room for me in the tub!" **[Cornered, Brandon takes the most favorable option.]**

"No problem," said Uncle George. "We'll make room."

Uncle George took out the seahorse.

Aunt Molly took out the bucket and shovel.

Sam took out the turtle and the boat.

Tricia took out the toy dishes.

But I *couldn't* take the green drops out of the water. **[The unseen narrator acts as helper. She has inadvertently provided Brandon with a means of escape.]**

Brandon took off his dirty clothes and climbed in the tub. He splashed and played, and played and splashed. Finally he called, "I'm ready to get out!"

· · ·

"Oh no!" Aunt Molly said, peeking in at him. "He's green!"

"Brandon," said Uncle George, "Wouldn't you like to take a nice, clean bath?"

Brandon shook his green hair and climbed out of the tub. "Not now. I'm not ready to take a bath!" **[Resolution: Brandon runs out of the bathroom, heading back to his ordinary world of play and fun with two easy-going parents and siblings.]**

Learning to Spot the Bones

Now that you've learned what the elements of plot structure are, be alert for them. Because screenplays are so tightly-formatted due to time constraints, the inciting incident usually falls somewhere around 20-25 minutes into the movie. My husband is accustomed to me looking at my watch and saying, "Something big is about to happen right . . . now."

So as you watch movies and read books, take notes and see if you can pinpoint the moments when the character establishes a goal, faces a new complication, and experiences a bleakest moment. Who comes to help him? What decision does he make after that? What does he learn about himself? How does he change over the course of the story? And what can he do at the end of the story that he could not do at the beginning? That action or attitude is evidence that his hidden need—his wound from the past—is healing.

Learning how to identify the bones of plot structure will help you plot your own stories more easily. And once you have sketched out the bones of your own story, you don't have to pull out your hair over writing a synopsis—just turn your plot skeleton into brief paragraphs and you're done. You have a beginning, a middle, and an end. You have everything you need to put into a proposal for a novel or to start crafting that screenplay. Or, if you're writing something shorter, you have everything you need to start working.

Now you're ready to begin writing scenes. Tape your synopsis to your desk, take a deep breath, and plunge ahead. Don't forget your plot skeleton—keep it in view and refer to it often.

Whenever I have found myself bogged down in a story and unsure of where to turn next, it's invariably because I've gone down a rabbit trail or somehow become unfocused. Whenever that happens, I pull out my plot skeleton and remind myself of what it is my characters are working toward. What is their hidden need, and how are they changing so that it will be met? What is their goal, and how do their current activities either push them toward their goal or distract them from it?

With a little reminder from my scrawny plot skeleton, I am back on my way within minutes.

Now it's your turn. Go write something wonderful.

PLOT EXERCISES

1. DRAW THE PLOT SKELETON ON A BLANK SHEET OF PAPER—IT doesn't have to be a work of art; it simply has to have the necessary bones. Now watch your favorite movie and identify the bones as they appear. What was the main character's obvious problem in the beginning? What was his hidden need (that was resolved at the end?) What was the inciting incident? What was his goal? What were the complications? What was his bleakest moment? What lesson did he learn, and what decision did he make as a result? Finally, how was his life changed because of everything that happened to him?

2. Now sketch out the plot skeleton for a short story—you will need at least three complications, but no more. All the other bones should be there. How is this different from the movie you sketched out earlier?

3. Sometimes we get so caught up in a story that we have trouble seeing the "bones" the first time—when I first watched *Lars and the Real Girl*, I thought Lars's goal was to have a relationship with Bianca, the doll . . . then I realized I had it all wrong. He wanted the relationship with the new girl at work. If you have trouble sorting out the bones, watch the movie again, looking for the protagonist's clear goal. He may not accept it at the end—a man seeking revenge,

for instance, may decide not to take it—but clarify this question: what is the main character striving to accomplish?

4. Watch *Lars and the Real Girl* and sketch out the bones. Then compare your analysis with mine, but no peeking beforehand!

Obvious Problem: Lars is being pressured by his sister in law to have breakfast with her and his brother. Lars refuses. (A simple matter, but it's something he just can't do.)

Hidden need: Lars is deeply, painfully shy and cut off from people—even those he loves/ Why? This will be answered in the backstory—which is in the BACK of the story, not up front. His hidden need is emotional and physical connection.

Admirable qualities: so many! He's cute. He's lonely (makes us sympathize with him because we've all been lonely). He's concerned for his SIL, and gives her a blanket because it's cold and she's pregnant. He goes to church. He's a good man, despite his social awkwardness.

Inciting incident: two things happen, and the first leads to the second. First, he meets the new girl at work, and she's cute. This leads to the BIG CHANGE, which is when Bianca arrives via the UPS truck.

Lars establishes a goal: He wants a relationship with Margo, but he simply can't—he's not ready. So he will have a relationship with Bianca, a doll, because he can't have a relationship with a real girl. This relationship is innocent, it's like a first crush, because this is all new territory for Lars.

First complication: His brother and sister in law don't know what to do about Lars' new friend. They decide he's crazy. SWING from negative to positive: they take him to the doctor/shrink, who wisely explains that Lars has a delusion, and he will have it until he doesn't need it any more.

Second complication: Can Bianca go to church? The church folks have a meeting and are inclined NOT to allow Bianca until someone asks, "What would Jesus do?" Then Bianca is not only invited to church, she is given flowers and warmly welcomed.

Third complication: While the doctor treats Bianca for her "sickness," she is also treating Lars. She learns (and we learn along with her) that Lars is worried about his SIL's baby. Women die in childbirth—his mother did. He never knew her, and probably suffers from guilt. But he is attached to the blanket she made for him—it symbolizes her love, something he needs. (Note the presence of the blanket throughout the film—where it appears and where it doesn't.) In these treatments, Lars exposes a problem, and the doctor talks him through it. We also learn that Lars cannot stand the human touch.

Fourth complication: the office Christmas party. Lars goes with Bianca, and a situation that could have been filled with taunting and jibes turns into a supportive affair. Oh, the guys make rude and suggestive comments, but Lars ignores them all.

Meanwhile, at the office, another **complication**: Margo, the new cute girl, begins to date someone in the office. Since she is the real object of Lars' interest, he becomes even more attached to Bianca. Bianca is voted onto the school board, she gets a new hairdo, she reads to the children at the hospital . . .

Complication: Margo breaks up with her boyfriend from work. She invites Lars to go bowling, but Lars has learned some lessons about growing up, and a "man never cheats on his woman." So Margo and Lars go bowling as FRIENDS, and that night—he takes off his glove to shake her hand.

Note: Consider the aspect of *seasons*—in what season does the movie begin? How is this significant? What about when Margo/Lars are talking and he says, "Winter's not over until Easter." (Resurrection theme.)

Now that Margo is available, Lars and Bianca begin to fight. And after Margo and Lars make progress, Bianca begins to weaken. Finally, Lars announces that she's dying.

The bleakest moment: Bianca dies. Lars has no hope of a relationship with her, he suffers the loss of his first love.

What is the symbolism involved in the scene at the lake? We are born in water (childbirth again, and baptism); Bianca "dies" in it. Lars is the one raised to walk in a new life. Why did the filmmaker choose to have us see this through Gus's perspective, from a distance?

Helper: the entire town helps Lars through his grief. At the funeral, when the pastor talks about Bianca's courage, he's really talking about *Lars*'s courage. Consider the subtlety of when the minister says, "When I was a child, I thought as a child . . ." and we are left to fill in "but when I became a man, I put away childish things."

Lesson Learned: Lars realizes it's time to put his doll/delusion away. You could say that Lars does this subconsciously when Bianca begins to die.

Decision Made: When Margo approaches at the graveside, Lars decides to ask her to go on a walk with him.

Resolution: And we see him doing something he could not have done at the beginning of the movie.

In the "hero's journey," the protagonist comes back bearing a gift for the people of the "ordinary world." What is Lars' gift to the town? They have all grown closer, learned compassion, and worked together to help one of their own.

How did you do? The more you practice plot analysis, the better you will get at plotting. it's easy to spot the bones with a little practice!

Chapter Two

CREATING EXTRAORDINARY CHARACTERS

IN LIGHT OF ALL THE BOOKS I'VE WRITTEN, PEOPLE ARE ALWAYS asking me to name a favorite. I tell them—truthfully—that I don't have a favorite because I see all my books as children that I've conceived and birthed, and parents shouldn't pick favorites.

If I'm feeling particularly forthcoming, I tell them—truthfully—that my favorite book is always the one I've just gotten off my desk.

But then I confess something else: I may not have a favorite book, but I do have a favorite character: Sema, the gorilla in *Unspoken*. I love her because she's unique, but most of all I like her because she is loving, protective, funny, sweet, and adorable.

What's not to love?

If you think over the books and movies that have remained with you long after you have turned the last page or left the theater, I'm sure that story's characters made a distinct impression on you. Scarlett O'Hara, Anne Shirley, Pippi Longstocking, James Bond, Sherlock Holmes, Katniss Everdeen . . . we remember these films and books because we fell in love with the *characters*.

What Makes a Character Memorable?

A character becomes memorable because the author creates him with a boatload of admirable qualities and at least one deep wound.

If you've read *The Plot Skeleton*, the first book in this series of lessons, you know how important it is to spend the first 20 or so percent of your novel developing the protagonist in his *ordinary world*. We meet Scarlett O'Hara in her ordinary world of barbecues and beaus, party dresses and rigid manners. She has half a dozen men on a string and her biggest worry is that Ashley Wilkes, the one man who refuses to remain in her circle of admirers, might marry someone else.

Margaret Mitchell spends eighty-eight pages (12 percent of the story) developing Scarlett's Southern home and heritage, and then war breaks out. The inciting incident sweeps Scarlett away from Tara, the family plantation, and into war-time Atlanta.

The "wound" that Scarlett carries is Ashley's indifference to her declaration of love, but that hurt will pale in comparison to the wounds she suffers in the war: she loses her husband, then her beloved mother and father. Still nursing the superficial hurt Ashley inflicted, she turns a blind eye to the one man who truly loves her, and then she loses him, the daughter she adored, and Melanie Wilkes, the only true friend Scarlett has ever had. With Melanie dead, Scarlett is finally free to love Ashley, but within minutes of realizing this, she sees how foolish she has been. Scarlett has cherished and protected a wound that didn't deserve more than five minutes of her time and energy.

We remember Scarlett because she was a rascal—strong, conniving, loyal (to her own pursuits), bold, brave, charming, creative, and an iconoclast. She was obstinately self-centered and totally focused on her own wants and needs, yet we admired her. Why? Because she was good at what she did. She had the "smallest waist in three counties," she charmed more men than any other woman at the barbecue, and, after the war, she ran a business in Atlanta while most women remained in the home and upheld the social codes of the south. Scarlett did whatever was necessary to survive, and while we may not agree with her decisions, we cannot help but admire the pluck and courage that drove her to meet every challenge head-on.

And who can forget Anne Shirley? Anne is an orphan—many child protagonists bear the wound of the tragic loss of one or both parents—but she goes to live with Marilla and Matthew Cuthbert in the house with the green gables. She is outspoken and brave and loving and imaginative and daring, quick-tempered and delightful. She has flaming red hair, she speaks like a poet, and she loves life with a passion.

And we cannot forget her.

Katniss Everdeen is only fifteen when we first meet her, but from page one of *The Hunger Games* we see that she is brave and resourceful. The family's father has died and the mother still too grief-stricken to rise to the task of caring for her two daughters, so Katniss has risen to the challenge. Every day she risks her life by entering forbidden territory to hunt squirrels, rabbits, or deer with her bow and arrow. She is self-less; she trades with the government official by agreeing to put her name into the national lottery additional times, thus increasing the risk to her own life. Despite all this, she is self-deprecating, humble, and loving, watching over her little sister, Primrose, like a devoted mother hen.

When I started reading *The Hunger Games*, I cried on page twenty-four . . . and the writer part of my brain marveled that the author, Suzanne Collins, had made me care so much so quickly. How'd she do it? She created a wonderful character with admirable qualities, then let me see those qualities right up front.

So before you do anything else in creating a character, jot down a list of three or four qualities that you admire in a person. Compassion? Fairness? Unfailing cheerfulness? Brilliance in a specific field? Skill at a certain task? An unusual talent?

Choose the qualities you admire, then prepare to inject them into your protagonist.

Instilling Admirable Qualities

How can you make your protagonist admirable? First, get rid of any notion that your character is going to be ordinary. People don't want to read about ordinary people because we're surrounded by ordinary people every day. We want to read about *extraordinary* people because we read to escape the commonplace.

One of my favorite movies about a writer is *American Dreamer*, starring JoBeth Williams. On the surface, this movie seems to break the "no ordinary people" rule because it's about an ordinary housewife and mother with two little boys and a patronizing husband. But Cathy Palmer has a hidden talent for writing, and when she enters a contest to honor a series of spy novels featuring super-spy Rebecca Ryan, Cathy actually wins . . . and the prize is a trip for two to Paris. Maybe she's not so ordinary after all.

With the help of her little boys (who read the chapter she entered in the contest and loved it), Cathy plans a celebratory dinner to surprise her husband. But instead of celebrating with her, her husband practically pats her on the head and says, "good girl," then he tells her that they simply can't go to Paris. No way.

He is walking up to the house the next day with his golfing buddies, telling them that you've got to know how to keep a woman in her place, but Cathy meets him at the door with suitcases in hand. She worked hard on her entry for that contest, she won, and, by golly, she's going to Paris with or without him. And she does.

In Paris, she savors a bottle of wine in the moonlight from the window in her hotel room, and on her way to the awards banquet the next day she asks the driver to stop so she can take photos of famous landmarks—the Eiffel Tower, Notre Dame Cathedral, etc. When he doesn't give her nearly enough time to even compose her shots, she offers to walk to her awards banquet—after all, it's right around the corner.

But while crossing the street, Cathy is hit by a car. She wakes in a Paris hospital with a peculiar form of amnesia—she believes she is super-spy Rebecca Ryan. And for most of the rest of the movie, she lives fully in her assumed identity, speaking foreign languages, running up bills like a millionaire, flirting outrageously, sprinting through crowds, beating back attackers, and inadvertently foiling a *real* murder plot. Our "ordinary housewife" has turned out to be anything but.

Yet perhaps all the writer did was reveal qualities that had been buried inside Cathy all along. Even before the inciting incident involving the bump on the head, we saw that she was a loving mother, a creative writer, a devoted reader, a faithful wife, a good cook, a thoughtful spouse, and a risk-taker. And when we see her stand up to her condescending, self-centered husband, we see a glimmer of Rebecca Ryan's courageous persona.

Maybe Cathy is more like Rebecca Ryan than she realized.

As you are creating the protagonist for your story, ask yourself:

*What can your character do better than anyone else?

*What makes your character *look* different from everyone else?

*What positive character qualities does your character possess? How can you demonstrate those without having someone tell us about them?

*What negative character qualities does your character possess? (No one is perfect.) How can you hint at those without making us dislike this character?

*Is your character really, really good at his job?

*Can you give your character a good sense of humor?

*Can you put your character into a situation where we feel sorry for him? How can he react to this situation in a positive way? We like people who can handle tough times and keep going. We like characters with self-deprecating humor. We *don't* like characters who whine and complain.

*What is the wound your character received in his past? How has this resulted in a hidden need or character flaw?

Perhaps his first wife died from cancer, and he has always blamed God for not healing her. This has left him completely without faith and cynical in all matters religious. Or perhaps his first wife walked out on him, leaving him distrustful of all women and unwilling to love again.

Remember this: hurt people . . . hurt people, so whenever anyone gets too close to your character's wound, he or she is likely to lash out.

Now that you've done a good job of fleshing out your protagonist, go through the same steps for your antagonist and any other major characters in your story.

Now That You've Sketched Out A Few Things . . .

Let me confess that I use a shortcut in characterization. It's easy, painless, and I shamelessly recommend this method to all my students.

But before I let you in on the secret, let me tell you what others do.

I have a dear friend who completely immerses herself into her character's personality and journals in that character's voice for weeks. She has a different blank book for each protagonist (she buys a style her character would like), and for her it's like a complete baptism into that character's mind, heart, and voice. That method works for her.

It would drive me crazy because I don't have time for that kind of immersion. I generally take only a week or two, tops, to outline a plot, flesh out my characters, and do any research that needs to be done before beginning a book. I research well enough to get the big picture, and I leave the smaller details until after the first draft. At that point I know what details I'll need to flesh out the scenes, so I don't waste time studying arcane bits of information that I'll never use.

I'm sure you've seen books on characterization that give several blank pages and ask you to jot down everything about a character, including his favorite food, his recurring nightmare, and the names of all his past girlfriends. (I'm exaggerating. A little.)

I am averse to doing work that I don't *have* to do. So I want to know the basics, a little backstory, and enough facts about the broad topic to establish credibility. Why am I so brief? It's not because I'm lazy, it's because I love learning new things. It would be easy for me to get lost in doing research and designing a character; I could spend weeks investigating my settings, photographing the architecture, and interviewing people about the local history.

But all that work would probably end up on the cutting room floor, especially in this age. Ours is a video generation; we expect stories—whether they're in a book or on film—to unwind at a brisk pace. We have no patience with irrelevant backstory, paragraphs of detailed description, or long-winded dialogue. We want the story presented in a simple, elegant, and spare fashion.

So when it came to fashioning characters, I needed a method that would enable me to create real, breathing, fully-fleshed story people in a very short time.

I have the process down to about sixty seconds.

The tool you use for this simple characterization is the Myers-Briggs Personality Indicator.

How It Works

I don't want to spend a lot of time talking about personality theory, but let me say that people are wired differently from the moment they are born. We all have a personality that is affected to some degree by the way we are nurtured, but we also have an inborn character that remains basically the same throughout our lives. We can adjust to our environment and we may mellow with age, but all people tend to fall into one of sixteen different personality camps.

Because I'm fascinated with the idea of human personalities, I've taken all kinds of tests and questionnaires and surveys. I've been diagnosed as everything from a Lion to a chlor-mel. But nothing rang true for me until I took one of the personality tests tied to the Myers-Briggs Type Indicator.

If you've never taken a Myers-Briggs test, you can Google one online. Or you can find a free quiz at this link, under the heading "Jung Typology Test:"

http://www.humanmetrics.com/cgi-win/jtypes2.asp

Take the test, or one like it, and your answer will be a group of four letters. I am an INTJ; my husband is an ESFP (clear evidence that opposites attract).

Then you can use an Internet search engine to search for your letter combination: ISTJ, ISFJ, INFJ, INTJ, ISTP, ISFP, INFP, INTP, ESTP, ESFP, ENFP, ENTP, ESTJ, ESFJ, ENFJ, or ENTJ. Several pages will come up, and on those pages you will be able to read all about yourself—your style of communication, your parenting style, what you were like as a child, how you behave as a spouse, how you dress, what sort of home you prefer, the arrangement of your desk, your favorite car, etc. The report may not describe you 100 percent correctly, but it will be pretty close. I'm always amazed at how accurate these results can be.

"All right," you may be thinking, "this is all very interesting, but how does this apply to my writing? How am I supposed to create a fictional character from all this information?"

Easy. Each of the four letters in your label corresponds to a key question. All you have to do is think of a character in your novel, and then answer the four questions with your character in mind.

For the purpose of illustration, let's say that Jesus is a character in your novel. I know he was God incarnate, but he was also fully human, so he had a personality . . . and I think Scripture gives us enough information to help us figure out what type he is. We will also analyze the character of computer expert Penelope Garcia, part of the ensemble cast on the TV show *Criminal Minds*.

1. The first question to ask deals with the first category Myers-Briggs addresses: **Extravert or Introvert?** And the best way to phrase this question is to ask, "Does this character recharge his batteries by going to a party or by going off by himself?" If that doesn't work for you, try "At a party, does this character speak to everyone, including strangers, or does he spend most of his time with a few friends he knows well?"

Jesus traveled from town to town speaking to anyone who would listen, but over and over the writers of the gospels told us that when he was tired, he withdrew. And as we look at his disciples, we see that he had seventy who followed him, then he had the twelve, then he had an inner circle of three: Peter, James, and John. I can imagine that Jesus was like many people I know—they are perfectly at ease speaking before hundreds of people, but when they come off that platform, they retire into the circle of their friends. At a party, they stick with the people they know, because while mingling with strangers is possible for them, it's also exhausting.

I would vote for Introvert in Jesus' case. He spent his days among the people, but he withdrew from them in order to recharge and rest. The people drained him, but people energize an extravert.

Penelope Garcia, on the other hand, is probably an extravert. She spends most of her day in a small room surrounded by computer screens, but being with people energizes her and she's not at all intimidated by strangers. She wears clothing designed to call attention to herself and often dyes her hair bright red—she's not exactly shy. But even if she were, Penelope is a clear extravert. She loves being around people and is energized by them.

2. The second question to ask yourself about your character is "Intuitor or Sensor?" If you're not familiar with the way Myers-Briggs uses those terms, ask yourself this: "Does this person take in information through their senses (seeing, hearing, tasting, touching, smelling), and stop there, or do they take in information and then draw on interior feelings to imagine or dream of something else?" Sensors are described as sensible, down-to-earth, and they place a high value on experience and realism. Intuitors, on the other hand, may be described as having their heads in the clouds, lost in fantasy, or imaginative. They prefer fiction over facts, they make decisions based on hunches while the Sensor relies on his experience.

It's a little tricky to evaluate a Jesus character when you realize that he was omniscient and knew everything, but did he base his decisions on his senses or his gut? I'd give the edge to N for Intuitor. Christ saw people not only as they were (sensory information), but as they could and would be. He called Peter a rock when Peter was still trying to find his footing in his faith, and upon meeting Nathaniel Jesus proclaimed, "Now here is a genuine son of Israel—a man of complete integrity" (John 1:47). He could not have realized that through sensory details alone.

Penelope Garcia, however, appears to be a sensor. She lives in a world of hard facts and rarely do we see her going beyond the facts she has collected to imagine how the pieces fit together—that's usually the job of others on her FBI team. She gathers the facts and background information; the profilers put the pieces together. So Penelope gets an S.

3. The third question to ask yourself with your character in mind is "thinker or feeler?" Now these are not absolute—of course feelers think and thinkers feel. I'm a thinker, but I cry easily and often, so that's no barometer. Both groups experience deep emotions and both groups can make decisions based on logic.

But T or F indicates which is the primary emphasis. A man may speak to a group and afterward the Thinkers will say, "His speech was very good—well organized and informative." The Feelers in the audience will say, "I loved his speech! He was so warm and compassionate in his presentation!"

Both groups are telling the truth, but Thinkers and Feelers respond to the same presentation in different ways.

Which was Jesus? Again, this could be tricky, but though Jesus had all knowledge as God, what does Scripture tell us? Over and over, the writers of the gospels go out of their way to write that this all-knowing man was "moved with compassion." It's almost as if they are taking pains to point out how deeply he felt. So I'd give the nod to the F.

Penelope Garcia is brilliant—she even answers the phone with quips like, "Fountain of wisdom, at your service." But despite the fact that she is intelligent, Penelope is primarily a feeler. She can't handle brutal crime scene photos, and she refuses to think about or discuss the details of some particularly heinous crimes. She feels deeply, as do others on the team, but feeling is Penelope's dominant function.

4. The last question to ask yourself regarding your character is "judger or perceiver?" Or, to put it in my personal shorthand, "if you

looked at this person's desk, would you see that he's a filer or a piler?"

One day I was in my husband's office while he stepped out. I looked at his cluttered desk and thought I'd help him out by clearing off the dozens of tiny piles of papers and cards and envelopes on his blotter—and then I realized that I couldn't. He knew what was in his piles and I didn't, nor did I know where they were supposed to go.

My desk, on the other hand, does have a few piles, but they're temporary. When I'm done with a project, all those books and papers get neatly filed away where they belong. (I think my blood pressure actually goes up when my desk is messy. I just can't stand it.)

So . . . is your character a planner? Does she create to-do lists? Does she plan her recreation time? Does she sometimes create a list just for the pleasure of scratching something off it? Or is she more spontaneous, a fly-by-the-seat-of-her-pants kind of gal? Is she the sort who would call at a moment's notice and invite you out for coffee . . . or to drive across the state? The first group is made up of judgers; the more spontaneous group is composed of perceivers.

So, what was our Jesus character? He lived before day-timers and smart phone calendars, but when he fed five thousand men plus women and children, he had the people sit down in groups of fifty, then he ordered a proper distribution and collection of the leftovers.

I'm thinking that Jesus was a J, or Judger. He appreciated organization.

So does Penelope Garcia. Yes, despite the fact that she often looks like she encountered a spontaneous whirlwind in her closet, she is very organized, her outlandish outfits have carefully been coordinated, and she undoubtedly has a checklist for every element in her day.

After you've answered the four questions for your character, put them together. Jesus would be INFJ.

A brief synopsis of INFJ personalities would reveal that these folks are people whose faith can move mountains. They are happiest when they see their insights helping other people. Many INFJs work so apparently comfortably with others that their associates do not realize they prefer introversion. Because of their clear goals, skill at working with people, and willingness to work hard and long, they may be put in executive positions. They often prefer, however, to work behind the scenes.

Penelope Garcia, on the other hand, would be an ESFJ. A synopsis of her personality type reveals that ESFJs love people. They shine at social occasions; they love celebrations in beautiful surroundings with excellent food and drink and warm fellowship. Happiest when they are doing something nice for someone, they are usually able to say whatever is needed to make everyone feel comfortable. They are likely to choose work that lets them interact with others, and they are most effective when they are given plenty of encouragement and approval.

You have asked yourself those four questions about a character you are trying to develop, so you should have the four letters that make up his personality type. Google those letters. You'll find several reports, so read a few and see how that information fits with what you need your character to be.

Sometimes you may find that the personality report you get doesn't quite fit the character you have in mind. It may be close, but there's just something a little off. If that's the case, then change one letter—try an S instead of an N. Or try a T instead of an F. Or a J instead of a P.

Read the resulting report from that combination and see if it is a better fit for your character. It's very likely that by trying a different combination of letters, you will find the perfect character sketch online.

How Character Types Play Out in Story

Not only will knowing the Myers-Brigg type help you do a quick sketch of your protagonist and other characters, it can also help you with plot development. How?

First, we know that opposites attract. So if you have an INTJ protagonist, give her an ESFP spouse. Their strengths and weaknesses will compliment each other, but you will have a fertile field available for conflict. He, a feeler, won't react to grief in the same way she will because she's a thinker. She will be neat and orderly and he will never remember to put away his socks. He will want her to drop everything and go away for a romantic weekend, but she will resist because she had planned to clean the oven on Saturday afternoon. Worse yet, she will know she's being inflexible, but he should have known her well enough to know she wouldn't want to change her plans at the last minute, and why doesn't he ever exhibit the common courtesy of giving her time to adjust her schedule?

See how it works? Playing character types against one another is natural, simple, and it rings true.

Character type can also influence your character's backstory. Most "feelers" are female, as you might expect, so what happens to the INFP boy? He is sensitive when he's growing up, he abhors violence and roughhousing, and the other kids make fun of him when he cries. So he learns to cover up that tender interior with attitude and a swagger. Now, years later, he finds it hard to dump the old façade to let his wife really understand what's going on in his head and heart . . .

I would do a complete character sketch on each of the major characters in my novel. You don't have to do one on the guard or the doorman, but if any character is going to significantly interact with your protagonist, I'd take the time to flesh him out. You may not use all the information you jot down, but you'll have it if you need it.

Personality Type is a Tool

Now that you have your character's personality type, use it for the tool that it is, but don't let it overtake your story. I always read through the personality description and file it away, pulling it out only when I want to double-check something.

Don't let the personality type dominate your story or your story telling. Think of it as the framework upon which your house is built, and remember that a house is far more than its frame. Go ahead and give your character talents, skills, abilities, quirks, and flaws. Just make sure they fit his "personality frame."

For example, I'm an INTJ and I've been an INTJ on every type test I've ever taken. Otto Kroeger and Janet Thuesen, authors of *Type Talk*, say that other likely INTJs include Thomas Edison (inventive genius), Richard Nixon (political genius), and Katharine Hepburn (dramatic genius). The website www.celebritytypes.com lists Karl Marx, Isaac Newton, Mark Zuckerberg, John Adams, Martin Luther, and Jane Austin as likely INTJs. All these people were marked by confident independence, a key trait of an INTJ, yet they are completely different.

So use the Myers-Briggs to help you define and refine your character, establish his career (unless you want him to be miserable in his work), and determine his parenting style. After that, take him wherever you need him to go, and use his personality type to establish the way he reacts to life.

But don't be a slave to the personality report. It's a tool, not a master plan for your story.

For Further Reading

The more you read about personality types, the better you will become at understanding what type you need for each character. I've been studying it for so long that I can usually guess a person's type after spending a few hours with them.

Whenever I take a collaboration assignment, I often ask my client to take a quick Myers-Briggs test to help me understand them better. Not only does it help me write their story with more insight, but it helps me understand the best way to approach my client when I'm discussing how the book needs to be written or edited.

If you'd like to have information at your fingertips instead of on the web, you may find the following books helpful.

Please Understand Me: Character & Temperament Types, by David Kiersey and Marilyn Bates.

One of a Kind: Making the Most of Your Child's Uniqueness, by LaVonne Neff.

Type Talk: The 16 Personality Types that Determine how We live, Love, and Work, by Otto Kroeger and Janet M. Thuesen

The Art of SpeedReading People: Harness the Power of Personality Type and Create What You Want in Business and in Life, by Paul D. Tieger and Barbara Barron-Tieger

What Type Am I? Discover Who You Really Are, by Renee Baron.

A quick search of "Myers-Briggs type indicator" on Amazon.com will bring up dozens of titles with dozens of different applications.

Most books about personality type seem to be found in the business section of the bookstore, probably since most of these titles focus on how to develop and maintain business relationships. But the Myers-Briggs personality indicator can be a valuable tool for writers, as well.

After you have found a personality type that fits the character you have in mind, copy or print the information and store it in your working notebook or computer program. You will want to frequently check back and reread the personality report to make sure your character is still ringing true.

"But," you may be muttering, "sometimes people change. They do things that might not fit with their type."

You're right about that—to a point. Because what people *do* and what they *are* are two completely different things. More on this later.

Characters at a Glance—the Notecard

As you are writing, at some point you will need to remind yourself of something about your character—how does he feel about family? What color were his eyes? What year did he graduate from college?

In order to answer these questions quickly, you need to keep all that information at hand. Writers have different methods for keeping this info handy, and I can recommend two: 4 x 6 note cards, or within a computer program.

When I first started writing novels back around 1985, I used notecards. The 4x6 cards gave me lots of room to write, and I could keep them in a rubber-banded stack on my desk. Plus, I could color code them if I wanted—pink for girls, blue for boys, green for plot notes, blue for historical notes. Simple.

Within a few months, I developed a system for what went on that notecard as I began to develop characters and plan my novels. I made sure to make a brief note on the front of each card for these things:

1. Character's full name, followed by his personality type.
2. Date of birth, including the year. Not for astrological reasons, but because birthdays can color our lives. I'm a December baby, and during our first year of marriage my husband made the mistake of bringing me a birthday cake with poinsettias on it.

If your character was born on the fourth of July, he's going to have strong feelings about that holiday.

1. Character's physical appearance: hair color? Eye color? Short, tall, or medium? Thin, heavy, or average? I am not one for giving much description, and I only mention something unusual—such as a jagged scar across a character's forehead—unless that is going to be significant to the story. If you call attention to it, it had better mean something.
2. Character's dominant personality characteristic—what do people first notice about him? His awkwardness? His quick smile? His tendency to brag?
3. The character's goal. Some characters may keep this secret, but everyone in your story should want something

badly. Every major character should have their own script and personal goals that will, at some point, bring them into conflict with the world and/or with your protagonist.

4. The character's secret: this may not be revealed in the story, but when you get stuck, just have someone slip and spill the beans. Delicious.

5. The character's favorite possession: a toy teddy bear from childhood? A photo album? A Bible? A faded corsage? Whatever it is will speak volumes about your character and may be just the thing to reveal if you need a poignant moment.

6. The character's self-image: we do not always see ourselves as the world sees us. Does this character see himself as a Lothario? As a successful businessman? Is she sixty and yet still thinks of herself as a kittenish bombshell? The greater the gap between the character's self-image and reality, the more potential for conflict . . . and fiction *requires* conflict.

7. Fill the rest of the remaining space on the front of the card by jotting down terms from the character's Myers-Briggs type: Practical, generous, imaginative, orderly—whatever the specific report said.

Now that you've filled out the card front with quick-glance facts, use the back of the note card to write down and any personal historical details you might need in the course of the story. Where and when was the character born? When and where did he attend high school? Graduation year? College, when and where?

When and where did he meet his wife? When did they marry? How old were they? When were the children born?

Creating a brief record of these things at the beginning will save you some frustration later. Let's say you're working hard, the writing is flowing, and suddenly your character leads you via flashback to a day when he was a senior in high school. His best girl is beside him in the front seat, he's wearing comfortable Levis, and something is playing on the radio . . .

What's playing? If you know the year he graduated high school (from your notecard), all you have to do is do a quick Google for top ten popular songs in that year. Presto! You'll have your answer in a flash and can immediately drop back into the flow of writing. If you hadn't figured that out beforehand, you'll have to stop and write up a mini-timeline to figure out the when and where . . . trust me, it's easier to do this while you're still developing characters and plot.

I mentioned that I used to use notecards for this sort of thing—I now keep it all on computer, in the same file I use for writing the manuscript.

I used to write with several computer programs open—Excel to keep track of my timeline, Ask Sam to keep track of all my research and notes, and Word to write in. Plus I had notecards on my desk and other information in a notebook.

All that changed a few years ago when I discovered Scrivener. Since then I've discovered that my Scrivener file—just one file for each writing project—can handle all my research, my notes, my manuscript, character sketches *and* character photos, and lots more. Plus, with the click of a single icon I can have the program read my manuscript back to me, allowing me to hear all my repetitions, clunkers, and omitted words.

I didn't intend to include a commercial for Scrivener in this lesson, but I highly recommend it. I use it for every writing project these days, fiction and nonfiction, and only use Word at the last possible moment, when I convert my Scrivener file to a Word file so my editor can read it.

If you're interested in Scrivener, at the time of this writing it can be found at www.literatureandlatte.com, and you can download a PC or Mac version for a free 30-day trial. Enjoy!

Revealing character

Once you've outlined your plot skeleton and done character sketches for all your major characters, you're ready to begin writing. And your first task is to create an opening that will reveal the character is his ordinary world, dealing with an interesting and obvious problem, while showing us his hidden need. Oh, and you also ought to demonstrate his admirable qualities so that we care enough about the protagonist that we're willing to spend nonrefundable hours of our finite lifespan with that character.

No small task, is it?

But you can reveal character in several ways:

- through action
- through the character's thoughts (interior monologue)
- through dialogue
- through the eyes of other characters
- through setting

Revealing Character Through Action

We discussed the plot issues in book one, *The Plot Skeleton,* so let's focus on the issues of characterization at the beginning of your story. How do you reveal character through actions that don't feel obvious to the reader?

The good news is that plot and characterization work together. At the beginning you are striving to show your protagonist dealing with an obvious problem that can be anything from running late and trying to catch a plane to steadying your pounding heart so that your trembling hands won't jostle the sniper rifle you've aimed at Hitler.

While you write about trying to find a missing shoe or sipping coffee in the snow or chasing the dog who has your boarding pass, you reveal character.

If your protagonist is searching for the missing shoe, how does she try to cajole the toddler who probably hid it? Does she curse at him or turn the search into a game? Whatever she does, we're seeing her character.

If your sniper is sitting on a rooftop in Berlin during a blizzard, if he's sipping lukewarm coffee and has only his thoughts for company, use point of view to tell us what he's thinking. Is he contemplating the end of the war with Hitler's demise? Or is he wondering if he will ever again return to the soft bed and warm wife he left in the early morning hours?

One of my favorite character-revealing openings comes from the movie *Lars and the Real Girl.* The film opens with a wintery shot of what looks like a typical Minnesota farmhouse—two-story white building with a porch, detached garage in back, snow dusting the driveway. The camera turns to the window in the detached garage, then we see Lars, a twenty-something year old man who's wearing a knitted blue scarf around his neck. He is simply standing there, watching the world go by, and then we see the back door open at the big house. A young, pregnant woman comes out, wearing only a short dress and a sweater.

Immediately, Lars ducks out of the window and hides against the wall so the young woman can't see him. Why? Is he afraid of her? We realize that's not the case when she knocks and he comes to the door slowly, but willingly. But he doesn't open the door.

She invites him up to the house for breakfast, and Lars smiles and says he can't come because he has to go to church.

"Then come after church," she says. "Okay?"

The young woman begs, and we realize that she is Lars's sister-in-law, and clearly pregnant. And even while Lars shakes his head and refuses her invitation, he opens the door and takes the knitted scarf from around his neck and gives it to the woman because she's not wearing a coat. He tells her he doesn't want her baby to get sick.

Intent on persuading him to accept her invitation, she continues to beg, then Lars says okay.

"Okay?" she repeats, disbelieving.

Lars nods and steps back into the house, clearly relieved to be ending the conversation. But before he goes, he points to the knitted scarf, smiles, and tells her to "put the whole thing on" because "it's so cold."

So the young woman smiles and goes back to the main house

while Lars returns to his garage apartment, slamming the door on the outside world.

The young man has an obvious problem—he's painfully, awkwardly shy. But our hearts break for him because he cares about the young woman, he sacrifices the scarf around his own neck (after all, he wasn't wearing a coat, either), and he cares for her unborn baby. Lars is a churchgoer, a nice guy, and a gentleman, so we fall a little in love with him as we silently urge him to accept her invitation.

But he can't. Because something in his past has made him so shy around people that he would rather remain in his garage apartment than engage with his brother and sister-in-law, the two people who should be closer than anyone else in the world. His hidden need is to overcome that wound in his past so he can be at ease around people, live a full life, and find someone to love.

In the next scene we see Lars at church, where he's helpful to little children and old ladies. One of the older women urges him not to wait too long before finding someone to settle down with, then she gives him a flower and urges him to give it to "someone nice."

Just then a girl his own age walks up and shyly says, "Hello, Lars," and Lars instinctively throws the flower as far away as he can.

This kind, generous young man has a problem, and both his goodness and his problem are demonstrated through his actions.

Revealing Character through Interior Monologue

In James Collins's novel, *Beginner's Greek*, the protagonist studies a young woman who sits next to him on a plane:

> The young woman sat down. As well as he could, while pretending to idly look around the cabin, Peter studied her. She appeared to be about Peter's age, and she had long reddish blond hair that fell over her shoulders. She wore a thin, white cardigan and blue jeans. What Peter first noticed in her profile was the soft bow of her jaw and how the line turned back at her rounded chin. It reminded Peter of an

ideal curve that might be displayed in an old painting manual. His eye traveled back along the jaw, returning to the girl's ear. It was a small ear, beige in color, that appeared almost edible, like a biscuit.

Nice description, isn't it? We get a fairly good picture of an attractive young girl, but in that paragraph we are getting a far better picture of Peter, the character who is thinking about the girl. (By the way, notice that there are no italics to indicate thought, nor are there any thought attributions like "he mused." Those are not needed when you're using point of view skillfully. Using third person, James Collins has taken us inside Peter's head, so we know we are reading Peter's thoughts. Using italics to indicate thought and switching to first person is an outmoded technique that's simply not necessary. Why switch POV and use a fancy font when you can simply write it out?)

From the paragraph above, we learn a great deal about Peter. What is his education level? Clearly, he's been to college, probably an Ivy League school that offered a classical education. He was more likely to have studied Humanities than engineering. He knows about art. But most notably, he's attracted to this young woman . . . so attracted that he would like to eat her up.

At another point, Peter visits an office and meets a secretary.

Peter entered and the woman quickly rose to greet him. She was full-figured and in her fifties, with brassy red hair, black eyebrows, and one discolored front tooth. She made every utterance with great enthusiasm.

Notice that the author doesn't give us a string of details. We don't know what she's wearing, nor do we hear any of the exact words she says. Instead, the author chooses the details most likely to give us pertinent information. We read that the woman's red hair is "brassy," so we infer that it came from a cheap home dye job. We read that she's "full-figured" instead of being "svelte," and she has black eyebrows—which do not match the brassy red hair. But the most telling detail of all is the discolored front tooth. With that one element, the author—and Peter, as the point of view character— reveals that this woman most likely did not go to college and this is the best job she can get. She can't afford to get the tooth fixed, and she is not relaxed on the job, so she's making every utterance "with great enthusiasm."

I don't know about you, but I feel sorry for the woman. I'm also a little annoyed with Peter for pointing out her flaws.

Revealing Character Through Dialogue

The following is from the first scene of my novel, *The Offering*. I have omitted some of the narrative bits.

Marilee and I were trying to decide whether we should braid her hair or wear it in pigtails when Gideon thrust his head into the room. Spotting me behind our daughter, he gave me a look of frustrated disbelief. "Don't you have an important appointment this morning?"

Shock flew through me as I lowered the silky brown strands in my hands. Of course, this was Monday. At nine I had a tremendously important interview with the Pinellas County school system.

How could I have let time slip away from me on such an important day? Good thing I had a helpful husband.

"Gideon!" I yelled toward the now-empty doorway. "Can you call Mama Isa and tell her I'll be late this morning?"

"Just get going," he yelled, exasperation in his voice. "Your coffee's in the kitchen."

I squeezed Marilee's shoulders. "I'm sorry, sweet girl, but this morning we have to go with something quick."

"Okay. Can I wear it like Princess Leia tomorrow?"

I frowned, trying to place the name. "How does Princess Leia wear her hair?"

"You know." Marilee held her hands out from her ears and spun her index fingers in circles. "She has honey buns on her ears."

I laughed, placing the image—she was talking about the princess in *Star Wars.* "Sure, if you want to have honey buns over your ears, that's what we'll do. We aim to please."

I pulled the long hair from the top of her head into a ponytail, looped an elastic band over it, and tied a bow around the band. Then I kissed the top of her head and took a moment to breathe in the sweet scent of her strawberry shampoo. "Love you," I murmured.

She grinned. "Love you, too."

Twenty minutes later I stood in my closet, wrapped in a towel and dripping on the carpet. What to wear? I had a nice blue skirt, but the waistband had lost its button and I had no idea where I'd put it. The black pantsuit looked expensive and professional, but sand caked my black sandals because I wore them to the beach last weekend.

"Baby girl?"

"In here."

The closet door opened and Gideon grinned at me, a fragrant mug in his hand. "Aren't you ever going to learn how to manage your schedule?"

I grabbed the mug and gulped a mouthful of coffee. "Maybe I like living on the edge."

"And Mama says *I* have a dangerous job." He waggled his brows at the sight of my towel. "Pity you don't have any extra time this morning."

"And too bad you have to get Marilee to school. So off with you, soldier, so I can get my act together."

Chuckling, Gideon lifted his hands in surrender and stepped away from the closet. "Okay, then, I'm heading out. But you're picking up our little bug from school today, right?"

I dropped the blouse I'd been considering. "I'm *what?*"

"Our daughter? You're picking her up this afternoon because I'm leading a training exercise."

For an instant his face went sober and dark, reminding me of the reason he'd been so busy lately. The military had to be planning something, an operation Gideon couldn't even mention to an ordinary civilian like me.

"Sure." My voice lowered to a somber pitch. "I've got it covered."

He nodded, but a hint of uncertainty lingered in his eyes. "Mandy—"

"I've got it, so don't worry." I shooed him out the door. "Tell Marilee I'll see her later."

No bomb blasts in this opening, just a husband and wife trying to get themselves and their daughter out the door one morning. But what have you learned about Mandy from her dialogue?

First, what kind of mother is she?

Does she have a sense of humor?

What kind of wife is she?

What kind of marriage do she and Gideon share?

In their marriage, do they share responsibilities equally?

Is Mandy exceptionally well-organized, or is she one of those people who is more relaxed about daily activities?

Dialogue, narrative, and interior monologue (thoughts) do work together, of course, but together they can do a great job of revealing character by showing and not telling.

Revealing Character through the Eyes of Others

Sometimes you can reveal a character by prodding another character to talk about him. You need to be careful, though, lest this technique become too obvious. You don't want his opinion to become an "As-you-know-Bob," as in this example:

Tom and Bob are talking. They have been friends with Charlie for years.

Leaning over the bench, Tom addressed Bob. "You seen Charlie today?"

Bob nodded. "Saw him over at the clubhouse, standin' at the bar."

"I'm afraid Doug has it in for him." Tom drew a deep breath, then exhaled it through his teeth. "As you know, Charlie has that quick temper. Remember last fall when he decked that caddy? I was afraid Doug had hit his limit then, but what did I know? But this has to be the last straw. "

Bob dipped his head in a slow nod. "Doug's wife always did like them zinnias."

"'Fraid so. And runnin' 'em over was the worst thing Charlie could have done."

Bob picked up the glove that had fallen from the top of his bag. "Looks like our foursome is about to be a threesome."

Having two characters tell each other things they already know is illogical and silly. But if you can get rid of the obvious statements ("As you know, Charlie has that quick temper), you can easily have one character reveal character through dialogue with another character. After removing that "as-you-know-Bob" phrase, the above paragraph would do a fine job of telling us that Charlie has a temper and probably a drinking problem, too. (Would you run over a woman's prize zinnias if you were *sober*?)

Revealing Character Through Setting

An early scene in my book *She Always Wore Red* features a psychiatrist who interviews a private detective in his storefront office. As the detective takes a phone call, the psychiatrist looks around:

Randolph Harris crosses his leg at the knee and runs his fingers along the trouser leg to reinforce the pleat. The private detective across the desk swivels his chair toward the wall and brings the phone closer to his mouth, employing body language intended to remind his guest that he is not part of the telephone conversation.

Randolph folds his hands and struggles to be patient. He set this appointment for one, canceling two patients in order to drive to this shabby strip mall and meet with Dexter Duggan. He expects a modicum of professionalism in return, but no secretary greeted him at the door, nor did the sandy-haired detective invite him into the inner office until five minutes after the appointed time. When the phone rang at six after, Randolph expected Duggan to ignore the call, but instead the man picked up and launched into a whispered conversation.

Randolph heaves an indiscreet sigh and looks around the office. A laminated map of North Carolina hangs above the desk, with pushpins marking the cities of Raleigh, Charlotte, and Asheville. A bookcase against the paneled wall holds rows of phone books, city names printed on the spines above logos of walking fingers. The second shelf holds camera equipment—several old Nikons, long lenses with capped ends, a battered leather bag, a stainless steel canister with a black lid. A couple of framed photographs balance on the lowest shelf, crowded by a pair of mud-caked boots, a Durham Bulls baseball cap, and a smudged Panama hat.

He focuses on the photographs: a smiling boy, probably six or seven, and a bikini-clad woman standing next to a ski boat.

Oh yes, Dexter Duggan is a class act.

The paragraphs above serve two functions: not only do they describe Dexter Duggan and his office, but they also give us a glimpse into the rigid, judgmental mind of Dr. Randolph Harris.

You can do the same thing by simply closing your eyes and picturing your character's environment. What does his office or workspace look like? What's in the trunk of her car? What does she always have in her purse? What photos does he carry in his wallet?

And when you develop characters, remember this: if you ever find yourself running short on story, it will be *because you don't know your characters well enough.* Go back and add more details about your character's lives so you can know them better. Ask them for their secrets, and watch them go about their day. Do that often enough, and you'll have more story than you can handle.

. . .

Deep versus shallow character

What do you get when you squeeze an orange? You don't necessarily get orange juice . . . you get whatever's inside the orange.

In the same way, when life applies pressure and begins to squeeze
your characters, you can get something neither you nor your character ever expected.

I have never thought of myself as an angry person. I would have
described myself as optimistic and naturally cheerful until I agreed
to take a job teaching high school because another teacher had been
dismissed. I was twenty-two, fresh out of college, and I was asked to
teach eleventh and twelfth grade English, which meant I had
students only a few years younger than me.

I'll never forget the day one senior boy looked me in the eye,
smiled, and said, "We got rid of Mr. Smith in two weeks. We can get
rid of you, too."

In that moment, a geyser of anger erupted inside me. As my
internal organs quivered from the sudden rise in my blood pressure,
I thrust out my arm, pointed to the door, and said, "Get out of here.
I'm walking you down to the office."

And I did. But as I walked, I wasn't thinking so much about the
boy's insubordination, disrespect, and insolent smirk. I was thinking
about the sudden eruption of my anger and how I'd never felt
anything like that before. Never. And as I held the door open and
waited for him to slink into the school office, I wondered if I'd ever
be that angry again.

Well. Of course I felt the same eruption when life squeezed me
again. What you get when life squeezes is *whatever's inside*. And while
I didn't scream or slap anyone or curse a blue streak during those
trying times, I think my temper was hot enough to fry an egg.

Agents and editors will tell you that one major problem with
beginner's manuscripts is that the protagonists aren't pressured
enough. And if a main character is not squeezed hard enough, we're
not really going to know him because we're not going to have an
opportunity to see what's inside him.

So when you think you've taken your character to his bleakest moment (a la the plot skeleton), move that event up a rib and make the situation worse. And then make it worse again. And then again. Squeeze him until whatever's inside him is running out all over the place and all the world can see exactly what he's made of. *That's* drama.

Our goal as novelists is to torture our characters so that they bleed onto the page. Sorry to use blood and guts metaphors, but it's the truth—you can't be sorry about pushing your characters to their limits and them pushing them again.

As a mature woman with adult children and a grandchild, I can now confess that in my parenting years I found myself saying and doing things I never would have thought myself capable of saying and doing. I have felt emotions I would not have believed I could feel. I have confessed things to my husband that I could not confess in any public arena.

Why? Because life squeezed me harder than I ever thought it would or could. And I am human.

If I am to create authentic fiction, my job as a writer must be to create characters every bit as human and flawed and capable of being squeezed as I am.

In a Donald Maass workshop I attended, I learned a practical character exercise that helps define three areas in which you can squeeze your protagonist.

"Write," he told our group, "something your protagonist would never, ever think."

We thought about our protagonist and the situations in our story, then we wrote.

"Now write something your protagonist would never, ever say."

We wrote again.

"Now write something your protagonist would never, ever do."

We wrote a third time.

"Now," Don said, "find places in your story where your character can think, say, and do those three things."

Wow.

Remembering that little exercise has kept me writing and my

characters reaching. I have let life push them far beyond what they could endure. I have led them to the bleakest moments I could imagine and left them with no hope other than a weakly whispered prayer.

But then help arrived, and along with it, a lesson.

Creating the Test of Character

How do you squeeze your protagonist so that deep character comes out? It's easy to squeeze him in the latter part of the story because you've probably arranged a series of complications that put him in increasing jeopardy or a time of testing.

You can also apply pressure during the course of the story. The nineteen-seventies brought us a rash of disaster movies featuring ensemble casts: *The Towering Inferno, The Poseidon Adventure, Airport,* and *Earthquake*. Then came the natural disaster movies like *Jaws, Frogs, Piranha,* and *Grizzly*, just to name a few. What did these films have in common? They took an ensemble cast and stripped away the outer character under pressure (from fire, earthquake, bears or frogs), and revealed what lay underneath. The viewers were able to see the politician for what he really was, the agnostic priest who reluctantly returned to God, the fat lady who saved the day, and the sullen loser who tossed aside his enameled mask of not caring to reveal the courage and goodness that lay beneath it. Part of the pleasure for moviegoers was trying to figure out who would survive and who would fall victim to the flames or the killer fish, but viewers found the most pleasure in seeing the characters' facades ripped away like skin from an onion.

But what if you want to squeeze your protagonist at the *beginning* of the story? What if your story is to be about a man who discovers a terrible truth about himself and then has to live with the knowledge of that truth?

Suppose on his way home from work your protagonist comes upon a school bus which has just slid into a retention pond. He jumps out of his car and races toward the bus, then begins yanking children out. The bus is sitting nose down on a shallow ledge, and the remaining children are clustered at the back of the bus, where an air bubble is keeping them alive.

As he swims into the bus, he realizes that gravity is drawing the bus toward the deep part of the lake. The vehicle shudders, and he realizes that he only has time to get two more children.

He surfaces in the air bubble and sees three children gasping for breath—two white, one black.

Or two boys, one girl.

Or two sighted, one blind.

Or two strangers and the son of the man who is making him miserable at work.

With only ten seconds in which to think, which two children does he grab? Your answer—his decision—will speak volumes about his deep character.

And with his decision he will learn things about himself that he hadn't realized before. How does he, an upstanding man in the community, deal with the knowledge of what he has learned? Maybe he grabbed the two white kids because they were closest, and in the aftermath and resulting publicity, he is accused of racism. Does he doubt himself?

If he abandoned the girl, does that mean he values boys more? How does he explain this to his three daughters?

If he grabs the two sighted kids, how can he face the mother of the blind boy, especially after she accuses him of not valuing her son's life?

And if he abandons the son of his rival at work, can he convince himself that he didn't do so purposely? Sometimes we don't know ourselves as well as we think we do.

No matter who he choses, perhaps he feels that his religious beliefs required him to sacrifice himself for those children. Did he show a lack of faith by not diving into the bus yet another time? Couldn't God have worked a miracle? Maybe he was supposed to give his life that day, and he missed his opportunity to be a hero.

Your job is to construct situations like the one above—something that will test your protagonist and then make him deal with his decisions. If he's conflicted, so much the better, because fiction is fueled by conflict.

This situation you create should test your protagonist's core beliefs, his self-worth, his self-image, and all he holds dear. His decisions may test his family and his marriage. He may lose his job. He may put his life at risk.

But that's a story worth reading.

Every Protagonist Needs an Antagonist

If no one ever stood in the way of your protagonist, if he accomplished every goal with no interference or difficulty, you'd have a pretty dull story. Your protagonist needs challenges to stretch and change him throughout his story journey, and that's the role of the antagonist.

Do not confuse *antagonist* with *villain*—they are two different roles, and we'll discuss villains in a moment. An antagonist is simply someone who stands in the way of your protagonist throughout the book or at any point in the book.

In my Fairlawn series, in which Jennifer Graham inherits a funeral home in Florida, her mother, Joella, wants Jennifer to sell the funeral home and remain in Virginia where Joella lives. Her reasons are admittedly selfish—she wants to be close to her daughter and her two grandsons.

But Jennifer can't sell the funeral home, and she begins to consider keeping the place open and learning the mortuary trade. The more Jennifer thinks about the idea, the more antagonistic Joella becomes. She doesn't stop loving her daughter, but she does begin to act more and more often as an antagonist, constantly pointing out reasons why Jennifer should not remain in Florida. By the end of the first book, however, Joella has accepted Jennifer's decision to remain in Mt. Dora, so she is an antagonist no more . . . until book two, when she finds another reason to stand in the way of Jennifer's plans.

So in one scene your antagonist may be the protagonist's loving mother, and in another scene the antagonist is a stubborn real estate agent. The role is up for grabs, and anyone who stands in your protagonist's way can try it on for a scene or two or three.

The role of villain, on the other hand, is more permanent. All villains are antagonists, but not all antagonists are villains. Many books, in fact, have no villains at all.

But if you're writing a mystery or a thriller, there's bound to be a villain, and he will spend the entire book trying to escape, outwit, outrun, and outsmart your protagonist.

This is a good place to ask if you clearly understand the difference between a mystery and a thriller—my experience reveals that most people don't. Both types of book fall until the "suspense" genre, but the two types of book are completely different.

A mystery is a mental puzzle and the reader is in a race against the detective to solve the crime. Both reader and detective are given the same clues at the same time, and a third party usually acts as the narrator, revealing clues to the reader as the detective sees, smells, hears, feels, and/or tastes them. For this reason, it's tricky to write a mystery in first person, because the reader would have access to the detective's reasoning, thus spoiling the reader's fun.

The reader is unaware of the criminal's identity throughout the book, and all is revealed at the end of the story when the detective unmasks the evildoer.

A thriller, on the other hand, isn't a contest. We often know who the murderer or criminal is because we may spend several scenes or chapters in his point of view. We may not know his name, but we know how he operates, what he's thinking, and who his next victim is.

We also know who the protagonist is, though he may not be a professional detective. He may be a lawyer, a writer, or the neighbor next door. But he suspects that something evil is occurring, and he begins to investigate. The villain becomes aware of the protagonist's snooping, and he begins to leave taunting clues for the police and the protagonist. He has more resources and seems to have the upper hand throughout the story, so the protagonist usually seems to have little or no chance of defeating this foe. The reader watches this cat-and-mouse game as the pursuer and the pursued inch closer and closer to each other. At some point the criminal may threaten someone close to the law-abiding protagonist—he may snatch his wife, his child, or his lover. The stakes rise ever higher as the good guy risks everything in order to save those he loves and defeat the man or woman who taunts him.

We wait for the inevitable confrontation, and when it comes, for at least a moment it appears that the villain will win. The protagonist has his bleakest moment, receives help from some unexpected source, and then he wins the battle . . . or at least escapes with his life, having surprised the villain with his courage and resourcefulness. The villain often dies, usually in a gruesome fashion, and the protagonist limps away with his loved ones, scarred but ultimately victorious.

(Of course, this pattern is not without its exceptions, and occasionally the villain does win. But the exceptions are rare.)

See the difference? A mystery is a mental puzzle, a race in which the reader sees if he can figure out the crime along with or before the famous detective. A thriller is a race to an inevitable confrontation between a law-abiding man or woman and a criminal.

The Anti-hero

Perhaps it's a sign of our times, but anti-heroes seem to be more and more popular. Don Draper of AMC's original program *Mad Men* is an advertising executive on New York's Madison Avenue. He's also a liar, a fraud, an adulterer, and a horrible father yet we root for him because he always seems to pull a winning hand out of a lousy deck—and I'm not talking about gambling.

Dexter Morgan, created by novelist Jeff Lindsay, is a cold-blooded, ruthless serial killer who only kills murderers. We root for him because we can support his code, instilled in him by his adoptive father, police officer Harry Morgan, and because we are frustrated when guilty people escape justice. Furthermore, Dexter has a sister, Debra, whom he protects, so we don't believe him when he says he has no feelings and cannot love. We can see good in Dexter, even though he assures us he has a dangerous "dark passenger." He also works as a blood spatter expert in a police department, so he is working for good even as he plans to kill those who escaped justice and will undoubtedly murder again.

Hannibal Lecter, who terrified us in Thomas Harris's novel *The Silence of the Lambs* and the movie of the same name, now has his own television show.

If you are creating a dark hero, an anti-hero, be sure to give him qualities that allow us to support him. Just as every super-hero has his weakness (Superman and kryptonite, for instance), every dark hero must have some admirable quality or talent or hidden virtue. Otherwise, we'll struggle to find any reason to stick around.

Why is Your Villain in the Story?

While you're forming your characters, you should do a complete plot skeleton for your villain. You may not need to finish it to the point of the resolution—because your hero should overpower the villain—but your villain has to have a valid reason for being in the story other than simply being someone who antagonizes your protagonist.

I've heard screenwriting expert Michael Hauge say that many romances fail because there's no real reason for couples in romantic comedies to fall in love other than the fact that the script calls for it. Maybe they have nothing in common, maybe the cute hijinks of the movie take up so much time that we never see their true personalities unfolding. Sometimes Tom Hanks and Meg Ryan fall in love just because they're the only two single people in the film—or so it seems, anyway.

For a romantic movie or novel to work, the hero and heroine should have personalities that will mesh (and your Myers-Briggs report will help you determine if that's true). They should have *some* common interests, and they should be compatible.

In the same way, a villain should have a real reason for focusing on your protagonist and choosing to make his life miserable. Is he the president of the company that fired the villain five years before? Did the protagonist's father kill the villain's son in a hit-and-run and get away without serving jail time? Did the protagonist do something to injure the villain or someone in his family in a former job?

Make sure there's a good reason for the villain to hate your protagonist. Otherwise, the obsession doesn't ring true.

Also, remember that the villain's or criminal's crime will make perfect sense to him—he may even believe that he's doing a good thing. The Nazis who ran the prison camps in World War II had been told that Jews were a sub-human species that did not deserve to live. Millions of women have been told that unborn babies are not fully human and do not feel pain. Some people believe that robbing banks is perfectly justifiable because the banks are insured, so "no one really gets hurt." People cheat on their income taxes and justify their actions by saying that the government wastes so much money, it's better to keep it in our own pockets.

On the reality television show *Bait Car*, police officers leave a nice car parked on the street with the keys and a tiny camera inside. While the camera films everything, people jump into the car and prepare to take off, but many of them repeat a common refrain: "Whoever was stupid enough to leave the keys in the car *deserves* to have his car stolen."

See what I mean? We twist language in some cases and logic in others, but people have an extraordinary willingness to justify their behavior. So if you're writing a villain or just a simple antagonist, give him a good reason—from his perspective—for doing whatever he's doing.

How Many Characters Belong in Your Story?

As few as possible. Readers want to connect emotionally with your story people, and the more characters you involve, the less your reader will bond with them. Sad but true.

Can you have more than one protagonist? Sure, but you're still going to dilute that reader-character bond somewhat. I wrote a story, *The Face*, about a girl and her aunt. They were co-protagonists until . . . well, I don't want to give away the ending.

But in a surprising number of two-protagonist stories (*A Tale of Two Cities, The Face, A Thousand Splendid Suns*), one of the characters dies so the surviving character can take lessons learned and live a better life. Doing that seems to actually blend the two protagonist-reader bonds so that the reader is focused on only one character at the end of the story. It's a method that works very well.

Three protagonists? In *The Fine Art of Insincerity* I wrote of three sisters. Each sister had her own plot skeleton and followed it to the end of the story, but I made the elder sister the protagonist. The book began and ended with Ginger, and I'm sure the reader bonded primarily with her, though I've received several emails from readers who saw themselves in one of the other sisters.

The more major characters you have, the less your reader will bond with them. You can count on that.

What about point-of-view (POV) characters? Perhaps you have only one protagonist, but there are scenes you need to recount and the protagonist isn't anywhere around. So you need another point of view character, someone who can be in the scene and report it to the reader . . .

This happens all the time, and of course you can use another character to relate what happened.

But if this character is never used again in the entire story, the reader might find it odd to be hearing from him in one scene. There are no hard and fast rules here—you can do as you think best, though your editor might disagree with your decision—but ask yourself if that scene might be rendered as well or better with the breathless participant reporting back to the protagonist.

Example: Michael Jones is a British soldier in the Revolutionary

War. He witnesses the murder of a young woman who is engaged to Thomas Oxford (who happens to be your protagonist).

You could write the scene as it happens in story time, from Michael's point of view. But if Michael is never used again as a POV character, it might be better to have a breathless Michael burst into Thomas's tent and report what he has seen.

In fact, I *know* it would be better to have Michael report it to Thomas so the reader can read it from Thomas's point of view. The reader is interested in *Thomas*, not Michael, and they have invested a lot of emotional energy into the romantic relationship between Helen, the young woman, and Thomas. Helen meant next to nothing to Michael, so while the emotional effect of witnessing her murder would upset Michael, the emotional effect upon Thomas would be far greater.

So have the young Michael report to Thomas, and let us be in Thomas's head as he hears the news, and let us see him break down and mourn.

(Or, if he's a scoundrel, let us see him *pretend* to break down and weep while he's privately rejoicing that the man he paid to kill off his fiancé was successful.)

So before you add in extra POV characters, ask yourself if you can find a better way. Most of the time, you can.

In Conclusion

So there you have it. A lesson on characterization, including bad guys and good guys, plus some tips to cut down on the time you spend staring out the window.

Next up: a lesson in point of view, one of the most common problems for new writers, and how point of view can help you deepen characterization even further.

CHARACTER EXERCISES

1. THINK OF A FAVORITE FRIEND OR RELATIVE YOU KNOW WELL. Ask yourself the four definitive Myers-Briggs questions about this person: Are they an introvert or extravert? Would you say they are sensors or intuiters? Are they more thinkers or feelers? Finally, are they filers (judgers) or pilers (perceivers)? Write down the letters of their four categories, and do a quick internet search on their result: INTP, for instance. Read the description of that personality—does it match the person you were considering, or is it slightly off? Try adjusting one letter and see if that result is closer to your friend's personality. When you find the personality profile that matches, you can see how easily this can work for your characters, though it may need a little tweaking.

2. Now that you have a character in mind, write a list of works and phrases he is likely to use due to his profession, education, or hobbies For instance, a photographer may never use the word *picture*, but will refer to his results as *images*. He may constantly adjust the lighting in a room, or remark on the shadows falling across his companion's face. He may speak of seeing the world through a certain lens or remark that a dull friend that his shutter speed is too slow. Do this for several characters, and you'll be able to give each of them unique personalities and dialogue!

3. Create two characters who are destined to fall in love . . . and give them opposite Myers-Briggs personalities. One is an E, one's an I. One's an S, the other's an N. One's a T, the other a F. And one's a J, the other a P. Opposites do attract, but what sort of problems are they likely to have due to their inherent differences? How can you make these problems funny (if you're writing a rom-com), or tragic?

4. You don't have to do a full personality profile on *every* character in your story, but you should to it for all your major characters. Take a moment to do that now, and examine the personalities in light of how they will interact with the other characters. Do you see the potential for conflicts large and small?

5. Come up with one secret for each of your main characters. What is something he or she would rather keep hidden from the world? Now, write a scene where that secret is revealed . How does your character react?

Chapter Three

POINT OF VIEW

I DON'T KNOW OF ANY WRITING TECHNIQUE THAT IGNITES AS many heated debates as point of view. One writer says that first person is cliché, another says it's practically required for genres like teen fiction and women's fiction. One critique group extols the use of "close third" or "subjective third" while another insists there is no such thing. One editor says that no one uses omniscient anymore; another says everyone uses omniscient at one point or another, they just don't realize they're using it.

I didn't write this book to create or undermine rules (because, after all, rules were made to be broken), but to help you understand what point of view is, how to tell when it's working and when it isn't, and how to unlock the secret power point of view brings to a writer's toolbox.

Point of View refers to the perspective from which a story is told, and, like ice cream, it comes in many flavors and varieties: first person, second person, third person. Third person limited, third person objective, third person subjective. Second person, the quirky but flavorful option. And the granddaddy of them all, omniscient.

Third Person Point of View

Can you guess what the most popular ice cream flavor is? Of all the ice cream companies surveyed in a poll taken by the International Ice Cream Association, 92 percent reported that vanilla was their best-selling flavor. Chocolate chip mint and cookies-and-cream tied for second place.

Third person point of view is like vanilla—perhaps the simplest, but also the most popular point of view choice. In this POV a narrator—the author—stands outside the character and relays information. Until he doesn't.

Example:

When Mary woke up, she noticed it was raining.

Mary wouldn't refer to herself as "Mary," so someone else is relating this story—the author, a dispassionate and mostly invisible narrator. Think of him as a video camera. He starts at the edge of Mary's room—*When Mary woke up*—and moves almost immediately into her head, where he reports that she noticed the rain outside.

A third person POV can remain outside the character and report only on the observable facts, or it can move into the character's consciousness. It is, therefore, one of the most practical and versatile POV options.

If you have a paper towel tube handy (a toilet paper roll would work as well), bring it up to your eye and pretend you are looking through the third person camera. If you choose Mary as your POV character in a particular scene, you are *Mary's* camera, and except for that wee bit at the beginning when you were seeing her wake up, you must remain attached to Mary. Therefore you may only record things that Mary can see, hear, taste, touch, smell, feel, or think.

Why do we make an exception for those little phrases at the beginning of a scene? Because the writer has to give the reader some way of knowing whose POV we're venturing into. Without a phrase or some other clue, we could spend a minute or two floundering in confusion.

And that confusion would break the fictive dream, jostle our reader out of the story world, and remind him that a writer is at work. Such breaks are like the moment Toto pulled back the curtain to reveal that the great and powerful Oz was just a little balding man from Kansas. The reader doesn't want to see the writer doing his job, she wants to be swept along by the story.

Our goal as novelists is to create such a mesmerizing fictional world that the reader is unaware of passing time as she finds herself transported to a world with sights, smells, tastes, sensations, people and places of its own. To do that, writers should avoid words that are unclear in context, be careful not to indulge their penchant for purple prose, and find clear ways to let the reader know which camera she's looking through when she begins a new chapter.

Back to Mary: If we describe the scene only through Mary's eyes and thoughts we are using the point of view known as Third Person Limited—*limited* because the scene records the thoughts and experiences of one character only. Editors often recommend this point of view for beginning writers because it's relatively clear and consistent.

Most modern writers (and editors) prefer that POV be limited to one character per scene. Not per chapter; it's not so confining as that. The extra line of white space between scenes silently tells the reader that we have shifted in time, place, or perspective when a new scene begins.

The beauty of third person POV is its versatility. The camera may zoom in for closeups or remain at a distance. As the writer, you can choose to tell us a great deal about what Mary's thinking and feeling without having to italicize her thoughts or write "she thought." The reader intuitively understands that the camera is in her head, so why remind her? Respect your reader's intelligence enough to trust that they'll figure it out.

. . .

When Mary woke up and looked out the window, she saw raindrops like tears upon the glass. She should have known the day would be as gray as her mood. Why did George have to leave her now?

The above paragraph, of course, reveals third person in all its glory. The camera started recording outside Mary, but immediately moved into her head. And here comes the beautiful, powerful part: as the narrator, you are so much in Mary's head that you use her vocabulary and her thoughts to relate the story. By doing so, you are accomplishing many things in a very few words. You are developing character, establishing mood, and providing narrative. So much work in so short a space!

Let me explain: Mary looked out the window and saw raindrops like *tears* upon the glass. The word *tears*, of course, came from me because I wrote that sentence, but I plucked it from my fictional Mary's thoughts. By using that word to describe the rain, what was I revealing about Mary's mood?

Her sadness, of course. Without having to use a narrator's voice to *tell* the reader that Mary was sad, without requiring the narrator to describe her broken heart, I allowed Mary's word choice to reveal her state of mind. That's *showing* versus telling. That's making every word work.

How would Mary have described the rain if she had awakened in a happy mood? Like *diamonds*? Like *jewels* or *crystals*? You bet. She might have even described the sky like "the grey of a soft blanket."

The example continues with thoughts that have come straight from Mary's head, but they've been translated into third person:

She should have known the day would be as gray as her mood. Why did George have to leave her now?

· · ·

Twenty years ago, the standard practice for writing interior monologue (thoughts) was to put the thought in italics and switch to first person. Writers believed this gave the writing a more intimate peek into a person's mind, and beaucoup writers handled thoughts this way.

But writing practices change, and today's readers want faster and smoother—we are a technological generation. We're accustomed to getting information instantly, we see words as images that play on the backs of our eyelids, and we want our reading experience to be as seamless as possible. So cut the unnecessary italics (and prevent your reader from squinting) and don't switch from third person to first. Why force your reader to change gears when he can simply keep reading what he already knows is coming from the character's consciousness?

So reserve italics for their proper use: emphasis, foreign phrases, and book titles. You don't need to employ them for a character's thoughts.

Third Person At a Distance

Sometimes, perhaps for reasons of prolonging suspense, you don't want your reader to know what the character is thinking. If you were writing in first person, in which the reader expects to be privy to all a character's pertinent thoughts and memories, you would be denying the reader what he had every right to know. In third person, however, you can simply withdraw the camera and switch from a "close up" to a shot a little farther back. We are still seeing things through the perspective of one character, but the tone is more like that of a detached observer.

Some writers call this detached POV "third person objective." In its purest form, the camera would never zoom in for the close up, never tell us what Mary was thinking, and would maintain an emotional distance from the character: think of it as the reporting of a fly on the wall.

. . .

When Mary woke up, she saw rain pelting the window. She got out of bed and dressed quickly.

The above example is emotionally neutral. It is a simple recitation of facts: who, what, where. Mary woke up in her bedroom (we assume), then got dressed. No emotion-laden words to describe the rain, no interior monologue to relate what she's thinking and feeling.

This may be the preferred technique in some stories where a certain detachment serves the plot (perhaps a detective story?), but I'm not sure the payoff is worth sacrificing the bond that develops when the reader has full access to a character's consciousness (third person subjective.) Why not give yourself the best of both worlds and use "third person all-purpose?"

If anyone else enters the scene written in third person limited, we should *not* have access to that character's thoughts or feelings.

Mary lowered her feet to the floor when Mother came into the room. "Why are you sleeping so late?" Mother asked, wondering why her daughter looked so pale. A bruise marked Mary's forehead.

Have you figured out why the above example is incorrect? With the phrase *wondering why her daughter looked so pale,* the camera has jumped into Mother's head and the writer is relating *Mom's* thoughts —and that's a problem because this is Mary's scene. Another problem exists in the next sentence: *A bruise marked Mary's forehead.* This is incorrect for a Mary POV scene because Mary can't see what's on her forehead, only Mother can.

But all is not lost. If you want to get in all of that information, go right ahead and include it. But do it from Mary's POV.

· · ·

Mary lowered her feet to the floor when Mother came into the room. "Why are you sleeping so late?" Mother asked. "You don't look well . . . and how did you get that bruise on your forehead?"

When a writer moves from one character's POV to another's in the same scene, this is often called "head-hopping" or "turning on a dime." Oddly enough, "head-hopping" is usually condemned in writer's circles while "turning on a dime" is accepted, but they are the same thing. And the writing will be clearer and less confusing for the reader if you don't jerk her around from one head to another.

(Note: like the use of interior monologue without italics, this is a style that has developed in the last twenty years. Many older writers —many of them best-selling novelists—have been happily head-hopping for years, and I doubt they'll change. Why should they, when they've enjoyed success writing the way they learned to write? But you should know that the preferred style these days is limited POV—one POV character per scene.)

When an editor points out that a writer is using more than one POV per scene, some writers will defend their technique by saying that they're simply using the omniscient voice. But head-hopping is not omniscient voice; omniscient is something else entirely. More on that later.

Take a look at these impromptu examples:

Todd looked up as she came through the doorway. Mary hadn't changed at all. Despite the passing of fifteen years that had left him as worn out as a slipper that had been chewed on and dragged through the mud, Mary looked as young and carefree as she had at graduation.

He subconsciously flexed his jaw and straightened his spine. Maybe she'd remember him.

. . .

See the problem? Common little words—like *subconsciously*—can creep into our prose when we're writing in the flow, but if we stop and think about it, we realize that we can't be in Todd's consciousness while something subconscious is going on. Subconscious actions take place below a person's consciousness, so that POV camera is all over the place in that example.

Why not just delete the word *subconsciously?* Makes things a lot easier for you and your reader.

Here's another situation to consider:

Jenna lowered her head into her hands and wept silently. Tomorrow had to be better. Her situation had to improve. Because she couldn't handle another day like today.

Little did she know what life had to offer in the next twenty-four hours.

Ah—that last sentence did *not* come from Jenna's head. It's the clear voice of a narrator, and how can it belong in a book that is written in third person?

Some writers will defend a sentence like this, calling it the literary equivalent of a camera pulling away at the end of a scene. I see their logic, but whenever I'm reading a book and come across something like this, it always jars me. But, to be fair, writers make the most critical readers. So while this does make me lift a brow, it probably wouldn't bother the average reader.

I wouldn't make a habit of ending a scene in a narrator's voice, but I also wouldn't mind the occasional use of an omniscient exit line. After all, we often begin scenes with omniscient entrance lines, so fair is fair.

So there you have it: third person, the vanilla ice cream of the literary world. Everyone loves it, it is amazingly versatile, and it works in practically any genre. You can't go wrong with third person, but you might find a better option with another POV choice.

. . .

First Person Point of View

If third person is vanilla ice cream, first person is chocolate mint chip. People who love it adore it, and some genres almost require it. It is de rigueur in most novels for teenage girls (*Twilight*, *The Hunger Games*, *Matched*, *The Fault in Our Stars*, just to name a few recent titles) and chick lit, and easily accepted in women's fiction.

First person allows you to tell the story in the character's own voice, but without the distance you find when you relate those feelings in third person. You can cover the same emotional territory in first person as in third, but using "I" instead of "she" imparts a greater emotional intimacy.

Let's listen to Mary when the camera begins the story in her head and *stays* in her head:

When I woke up I noticed it was raining. Rivulets streaked the windowpanes like tears, and the sky was as gray as my mood. Why did George have to leave me now?

Compare that to our third person version:

When Mary woke up and looked out the window, she saw raindrops like tears upon the glass. She should have known the day would be as gray as her mood. Why did George have to leave her now?

Do you see the difference?

The only drawback to using first person is that in its purest form, using first person requires that the *entire book* be written in first person. So if I were writing in Mary's first person POV and I wanted to include a scene where George confesses himself to Father Tom, I couldn't include it in the novel because Mary wasn't present at the confessional.

I could, of course, have George go to Mary later and tell her about what happened when he went to confession. Or I could have Father Tom break the sanctity of the confessional and tell Mary what George said—and those are valid options, especially if this is the only scene I need that can't be covered by Mary in her first person POV.

Like millions of other girls and women, I read the Twilight series and was swept into another world populated by benign vampires and teenage love. But, like millions of other girls and women, I was always a little mystified as to what Edward saw in awkward, fumbling Bella. I accepted his declarations of love as true, but something inside me kept wondering why Bella had captured his heart . . .

Then Stephenie Meyer began writing *Midnight Sun*. It was the same story of *Twilight*—Edward and Bella meet for the first time at Forks High School—but all the scenes were from Edward's point of view. (Meyer never finished the book, by the way, but copies of the partial manuscript are available online.)

You might think a novel that covers the same territory would be dull and repetitive, but I found it fascinating and so did thousands of other readers. It was the same story, yes, but this time we saw events through Edward's perspective. We learned more of his personal history, and—finally!—we saw what attracted him to Bella. He watched her, he saw that she had come to Forks to help out her mother, he saw that she was sensitive and an old soul . . . she was *selfless*.

And after reading all that, I found myself wishing that Meyer had written *Twilight* in third person, so we could get scenes from Edward *and* Bella. We could have seen events from both perspectives in one book, and to my way of thinking, the characterization would have gone even deeper.

But who am I to argue with success of Myer's books? My wish will remain just that—a whimsical thought. But I think this example does illustrate how first person works—in its purest form, first person POV creates the strongest bond possible between reader and protagonist. But its principal drawback is that it doesn't allow the reader to bond as deeply with the other characters because we will never see things from their point of view.

What About Mixed POV?

Some writers—myself included—have compromised with the stringent use of first-person-only in a book. I'm sure mixed POV has existed in many books, but I first noticed it in the novels of Diana Gabaldon. Her Outlander series features a female physician, Claire, who travels back through time and falls in love with Jaime, an eighteenth-century Scotsman. All of Claire's scenes are written in first person—lots of intimacy—and everyone else's scenes (and the books feature a huge cast of characters) are written in third person POV.

Did this use of mixed point of view lessen my enjoyment of Gabaldon's story? Not in the least. Did it jar me from the fictive dream? Not a bit.

So I began to used mixed POV myself. I used it in *The Immortal*, *The Novelist*, and in *The Note*. I've probably used it in other books I can't remember, but I've used it often enough to know that mixed POV is not a big deal if done consistently.

If you're going to mix POV, then you should choose a character, assign him a POV, and stick to it. Don't write Missy Shaw in first person in chapter one and in third person in chapter four. Stick to your pattern throughout the book or you're bound to confuse your reader.

I recently read a novel that violated this principle—and reading the book drove me crazy. I never felt connected with the protagonist and I was never sure who I was reading about until well into each scene. I'm not sure what the writer was doing—maybe trying to be inventive?—but his disjointed approach didn't work for me. Others might call it genius, but for me it's not about how creative and unusual the writing is. I care first and foremost about the strength of the story, and this particular story was so fragmented that I nearly stopped caring about the characters.

Second Person Point of View

Second Person Point of View is the bubble gum flavor of ice cream. It's delicious, but a bit annoying because you have to work on holding the bubble gum in your mouth while trying to swallow the ice cream and cone. You end up asking yourself if the flavor was worth the effort.

Here's our example with Mary:

You woke up to rain this morning. Water streaked your windowpanes like tears, and your heart felt as gray as the sky outside. Why did George have to get all freaky and leave you now? Because he was a jerk, that's why. Or maybe he just didn't like you.

I've never written in second person, but a friend of mine has, so it's not as rare as you might think. It's still a bit odd, and whether or not your reader will bond with the protagonist probably depends upon whether your reader accepts this quirky POV. I've had Amazon readers remark that they put a book down because they didn't like my (occasional) novels in present tense, so I have to wonder how many readers would put up with something as unusual as second person POV. I would end up asking myself if the flavor was worth the effort.

Omniscient POV

Omniscient POV is often called the "God view" because the unseen narrator sees and knows all—or as much as the writer wants him to know:

. . .

In the house on Forty-second Street, at six-fifteen in the morning, Mary Jones opened her eyes and thought the raindrops on her window looked like tears. Why had George chosen to leave her now? He had his reasons, of course, none of which were known to Mary. But in his heart of hearts, he knew he would never be the man she needed. Or wanted. Because she could never accept his secret. And secrets, as the sages say, have a way of bubbling to the surface.

Did you notice the swift movement of the POV camera? It is swooping everywhere. First it hovers outside Mary Jones's house, then it moves into her bedroom and into her head, where it notes that she thought the raindrops looked like tears. The omniscient narrator then relates her silent thought: why had George chosen to leave her now?

The camera/narrator then flies outside of Mary's head and dives into George's, because the narrator knows about George's reasons and knows that Mary doesn't know what George was really thinking.

But the narrator knows. He knows that George feels inferior, and that he will never be the kind of man Mary needs or wants. The narrator also knows that George has a secret . . . and we assume that the narrator knows what the secret is.

Then the narrator pulls away from George and speaks directly to the reader. *Secrets, as the sages say, have a way of bubbling to the surface.*

Can't you just hear the snide smile in his voice? That last line isn't from Mary's head or George's; it's the narrator enticing us with a teasing promise of secrets and suspense to come.

An omniscient narrator has a distinct voice. A writer who merely head-hops within a scene, jumping from head to head, is not writing in omniscient, he's simply leap-frogging from character to character.

The omniscient point of view, according to my favorite handbook to literature, is:

. . .

A term used to describe the point of view in a work of fiction in
which the author is capable of knowing, seeing, and telling whatever
he or she wishes in the story, and exercises this freedom at will. It is
characterized by freedom in shifting from the exterior world to the
inner selves of a number of characters and by a freedom in movement in both time and place; but to an even **greater extent it is
characterized by the freedom of the author to comment
upon the meaning of actions and to state the thematic intentions of the story whenever and wherever the author desires**.
(Emphasis added.)

Omniscient was a common POV in the time of Dickens, who gave
us this possibly-the-most-famous-of-all-omniscient-openings:

It was the best of times, it was the worst of times, it was the age of
wisdom, it was the age of foolishness, it was the epoch of belief, it
was the epoch of incredulity, it was the season of Light, it was the
season of Darkness, it was the spring of hope, it was the winter of
despair, we had everything before us, we had nothing before us, we
were all going direct to Heaven, we were all going direct the other
way—in short, the period was so far like the present period, that
some of its noisiest authorities insisted on its being received, for
good or for evil, in the superlative degree of comparison only.

So begins Charles Dickens' tale of two look-alikes in two cities, a
sweeping story that spans two countries and two men's hearts. His
omniscient voice is that of an orator: big, bold, and poetic. He
narrates more gently when he is writing scenes, but at the ending,
when his unlikely and self-sacrificing hero is about to mount the
steps to the guillotine, he resumes his poetic tone once more:

. . .

They said of him, about the city that night, that it was the peacefullest man's face ever beheld there. Many added that he looked sublime and prophetic.

This is the narrator's voice; he is telling us about a scene as though he were a reporter gathering impressions and quotes from people in the crowd.

One of my favorite omniscient novels is William Goldman's *The Princess Bride*. After opening the book you'll likely have to wade through several letters, forewords, and acknowledgements to even find the beginning of this novel, but it's worth the search:

The year that Buttercup was born, the most beautiful woman in the world was a French scullery maid named Annette. Annette worked in Paris for the Duke and Duchess de Guiche, and it did not escape the Duke's notice that someone extraordinary was polishing the pewter. The Duke's notice did not escape the notice of the Duchess either, who was not very beautiful and not very rich, but plenty smart. The Duchess set about studying Annette and shortly found her adversary's tragic flaw.

Chocolate.

And so begins the tale of Buttercup and Wesley, but the omniscient narrator feels free to tell us about Annette and her employers, his agent, his wife, and many other adventures as he lets the tale unwind. Furthermore, he tells a historic tale in modern lingo, and his deliciously droll voice adds charm that would be lost if William Goldman had chosen to tell the story in straight third or even first person. Unless, perhaps, Goldman had decided to turn Wesley into a wry commentator on modern society.

Margaret Mitchell uses an omniscient point of view in *Gone with the Wind,* telling us right away that

. . .

Scarlett O'Hara was not beautiful, but men seldom realized it when caught by her charm as the Tarleton twins were. In her face were too sharply blended the delicate features of her mother, a Coast aristocrat of French descent, and the heavy ones of her florid Irish father. But it was an arresting face, pointed of chin, square of jaw.

Disclaimer: I should tell you that *Gone with the Wind* is one of my favorite books. I first read it in the fifth grade, and have read it many times since. I have sections memorized. I used to read it aloud, playing the parts of Scarlett and Rhett. I learned how to flirt from reading this book.

But it wasn't until many years later that I realized the power of point of view as revealed in *GWTW*.

Margaret Mitchell uses omniscient point of view to open the book and many chapters and scenes, especially when reporting on news of the war—news and details that Scarlett wouldn't have known.

But after Mitchell is finished with her reporting, she usually dives immediately into Scarlett's head and remains there for the rest of the scene. In fact, we are in Scarlett's head 99 percent of the time. Every once in a while, when Scarlett is not present, Mitchell will dip into Melanie's head, Wade Hampton's, or continue with her narrative, but I don't think she ever allows us access to Rhett Butler's or Ashley's thoughts. We have only their words to tell us what they are thinking, and neither of those two men want Scarlett to know the truth. Ashley doesn't want Scarlett to know his love is a mixture of lust and admiration, and Rhett doesn't want Scarlett to know he loves her passionately—because she'd use his love against him if she knew. So he teases her and lies to her and makes sly jests. We never know whether or not take him seriously, and neither does Scarlett.

And that is why the book is far, far better than the movie.

In the classic film, Rhett Butler frequently expresses his love for

Scarlett. And because the unblinking camera is a neutral observer, movie watchers have no reason to doubt his sincerity. He *behaves* like he loves Scarlett, so why should we doubt him?

But in the book, every time Rhett expresses his love for Scarlett, we have access to her thoughts so we know she doesn't believe him. She dismisses him so completely—he's trying to get something from her, he's only saying that to make her angry, he's already told her he's not a marrying man—that we dismiss him, too.

And on that foggy night after Melanie's death, as Scarlett walks back to her lonely mansion in Atlanta, she has the mother of all epiphanies—why, Rhett really *does* love her! He sacrificed for her, and spoiled her, and risked his life for her because his love was *real*. And all of his posturing and protesting and pretending that he didn't care for her was only an act to protect his vulnerable heart.

Scarlett realizes that she has been a fool, so she runs home to Rhett, only to find that the years of her indifference and selfishness have worn out his love. He's too exhausted and broken to care anymore.

But Scarlett is forever confident—she *will* win him back. Because she refuses to be defeated. And tomorrow *is* another day.

Do you see the difference POV makes? By keeping the reader out of Rhett Butler's head, Margaret Mitchell persuaded us that Scarlett was right—Rhett didn't love her. Perhaps, as he intimated, he wanted her the way a collector wants a pretty doll to set on a shelf.

So Scarlett's epiphany results in a shock of understanding for the reader, too.

In the movie, however, we believe Rhett when he goes around saying, "I love ya, Scarlett," so the epiphany is not nearly as powerful as it is in the book.

Your choices regarding point of view—which POV to use, and whose POV to reveal—can make a tremendous impact on your story.

"Deep POV"

Lately I've been hearing a lot from writer's groups about "deep

POV" as if it were a special Thing Unto Itself. Many writers are frustrated because they think they should be writing in "deep POV," and there are times when a deeper point of view is appropriate. But the power of point of view lies in its flexibility, and a good writer understands that point of view is rather like the gears on a car: you often need several gears in order to get where you're going.

For instance, let's consider our Mary-getting-up example:

When Mary woke up and looked out the window, she saw raindrops like tears upon the glass. She should have known the day would be as gray as her mood. Why did George have to leave her now?

Technically, this scene moves through at least three points of view. The first sentence is in third person, because the camera sees Mary sitting on the bed. The second sentence moves into Mary's head—close third person—and the third sentence gives us Mary's direct thoughts—deep POV.

You need all three "gears" to move the reader from outside Mary into her direct thoughts.

You could start in deep POV if you wanted to:

Why did George have to leave her now? Mary made a fist, then shoved it against her mouth, struggling to hold back tears. He was a jerk, that's why. And she was an idiot for believing his lies.

Technically, the camera moves from Mary's direct thoughts, out to third person (so the camera can show the reader Mary's action), and then back into Mary's direct thoughts. Or perhaps that second sentence could be considered "close third," because Mary is consciously choosing to make a fist and bring it to her mouth. But honestly, call it what you will—the important consideration is that the second sentence makes the scene clear for the reader, and that's why we are writing novels in the first place: to communicate something to the reader.

All point of view choices lie somewhere on a continuum—you can have distant first, second, or third person if you want to have a detached character. You can also have "deep" first, second, or third person. You control how much information you want to reveal.

At the far end of the POV spectrum, of course, lies stream of consciousness writing—where you write down everything your character thinks and feels. A point of view this deep wearies the reader quickly, because our thoughts are often random and scattered. It's a good technique to have in your toolbox, but I only use it if my characters are either drunk or feverish, and then for only a couple of paragraphs.

What does it look like? Something like this:

Mary swam up from sleep as a soft pitter patter eased into her consciousness. What was that, a clock? No—rain on the window. Rain—ugh. They needed it, though. Flowers were dry, and the water bill too high last month. What day was it? Tuesday. No, Wednesday. She smiled. Her favorite show aired on Wednesdays.

She rolled over. Breakfast? Out of Lucky Charms. Pop Tarts on the top shelf of the pantry, if Mom hadn't eaten them. She'd have to feed the dogs and refill their Tupperware container, which meant a trip to the garage in her bare feet—watch for dead roaches.

The pattering was louder now. Rain. She blinked, then focused her eyes until the plaster swirls on the ceiling came into focus. A sense of sadness washed over her—confusing. Why was she sad? Oh—George left. Yesterday. The memory of his face, his sad eyes. Why had he decided to leave her now?

Stream of consciousness is as deep as you can go, and it's exhausting, scattered, and lengthy. Readers don't want to know everything about our characters, so we trim conversations, omit uneventful trips to the bathroom, and we rarely reveal every thought in our characters' heads. Part of our job is writing only the bits that are going to influence the *story*. If something in your story isn't working to advance plot or deepen character, it should edited out.

Which POV to Use?

Before deciding upon a point of view, check out other examples in your genre. Chick Lit, for one example, is usually written in first person, present tense. A lot of young adult novels use first person. Magical realism (*Like Water for Chocolate*, *Perfume*) almost always calls for omniscient point of view. You can certainly ignore these guidelines, but you do so at your own risk. Editors and readers may prefer books that abide by the traditional blueprint for the genre.

Third person works well for stories with many characters. Each character will have his own perspective, and readers can learn about their goals (which may conflict with your protagonist's) through POV character's thoughts, actions, and dialogue.

One word of warning here: if there's one thing I've learned from my book club, it's this: the more point of view characters you use, the more you will dilute the bond between your reader and your characters. When we read a book with only one POV character, we bond deeply with that character. That bond is weakened, however, when we introduce someone else—it literally becomes a case of divided loyalties. On and on it goes, until the reader gets worn out by trying to keep up with the cast of POV characters.

I try to limit the number of point of view characters to five or less. Notice I didn't limit the *number of characters*—you will need as many as it takes to tell the story—but the number of characters *through whom* you tell the story.

(Practical hint: I always create a timeline that looks like an Excel chart. The rows are filled in with scene details, and the columns give me spaces to jot down POV character/date and time/weather/mood/events of the scene/etc. I assign each POV character a certain color, so with a glance at my chart I can tell if I'm using a minor character too often, forgetting a major character for too long, or using a POV character so rarely that I should eliminate his POV altogether. You may find this tip useful—or the thought of constructing an Excel chart may give you hives. In that case, ignore this paragraph and read on.)

Third Person can also be quite intimate if you "zoom in" as we did in the example with Mary. It may not be quite as intimate as first person, but it can come pretty close. Furthermore, you can use this "zoom" feature with any POV character, not just the protagonist, as you would be if you were writing in the pure first person form.

Third person is also useful if you're writing a mystery or thriller and you don't want to reveal clues to the reader too soon. If you're writing in First Person, the reader expects to have complete access to the protagonist's thoughts, feelings, and memories. In Third Person, it's permissible to withhold certain thoughts, feelings, and memories if it serves your plot. In Sherlock Holmes novels, for instance, the story is told not by Holmes, but by Watson . . . because Sir Arthur Conan Doyle didn't want the reader to be privy to Holmes' deductive reasoning until the unmasking of the criminal. It's much more fun to leave the reader in suspense until the detective explains everything.

First Person works well for stories where the main character needs to give readers full access to angst. Readers live with the main character throughout the story and have immediate access to the protagonist's thoughts and feelings. Make sure, however, that you have created a *likeable* protagonist. Readers won't want to spend an entire book in the head of someone they despise.

One tendency to guard against in First Person POV is the temptation to get caught up in stream-of-consciousness writing (recording every thought that pops into a character's head), that the pace becomes sluggish and the story becomes crowded with ruminations that do nothing to advance plot or deepen character. If paragraphs do not move story events forward or shine a light on some unrevealed aspect of your protagonist, highlight and hit the delete key.

(Really, I can think of only two occasions when you should let yourself yield to a stream-of-consciousness passage: when a character is drunk, suffering from a high fever, or both. If any of those situations apply, go for it.)

If you want to use omniscient point of view, you'll need a good reason for doing so. This POV is not as popular today as it was generations ago, but it occasionally pops up in best-sellers (though I just grabbed a handful of recent best-sellers from my bookshelf and couldn't find an omniscient POV among them).

Probably the most important consideration in deciding upon which POV to use is the story itself. What do you want to reveal? What do you want to hide?

In my book *The Note*, I knew that my protagonist, Peyton MacGruder, had once tried to kill herself while pregnant. She had subsequently spent time and gave birth in a mental hospital. Her father, acting as her legal guardian while she was incapacitated, signed papers surrendering her baby to an adoption agency, and the child was placed with a family.

I knew these things by the time I started my second draft, but I didn't want my reader to know them until the end of the book. So which POV did I choose?

Third person. If I'd used first person, my reader would have expected to have full access to my character's thoughts and memories. And since Peyton wouldn't have been able to look at a baby without shivering at the memory of the infant taken from her, I would have had a hard time justifying my slamming the door on her memories until the end of the book.

On the other hand, in my novel *The Pearl*, I knew I would be writing about a mother who lost her precious five-year-old son in a freak accident. She would then be approached by an organized group who would offer to clone the son she'd lost. I knew my readers would find this not only troubling, but highly unbelievable, so I wanted to make them feel every emotion, think every thought, weigh every option, and understand exactly why my protagonist would agree to cloning. I needed them to have full access to her angst, so I chose to write her scenes in first person POV.

You shouldn't just flip a coin when deciding your point of view—consider the genre, the story, and whether or not your protagonist will be in every scene. Those are the key considerations.

Special Situations

I was critiquing manuscripts at a writers' conference when a woman came up with her story. I asked about the protagonist, and she said he was a child.

"So this is a children's book?" I asked.

"Oh, no. It's an adult book. It's about these children who find a dead body. It's based on something that happened in my childhood."

I took her manuscript and skimmed the first few paragraphs. "How old is this child?"

"About seven."

I shook my head. "I see a problem here. You've got this seven-year-old using words only an adult would know. You've said he's a kid, but he's talking like a grown-up."

She frowned. "Then how am I supposed to write this story?"

She had inadvertently stumbled across a problem related to point of view: if your point of view character is a child, then nearly all the words you use in that scene *should be the words of a child*. Everything in the scene ostensibly comes from his head, so you'll have to use a child's vocabulary to write the scene. If you do it well, you'll create a very convincing character.

The same principle applies if you're writing a scene in the point of view of a recent immigrant . . . a highly educated doctor . . . a Southern socialite . . . or an overachieving lawyer.

All of us have certain phrases we use because we picked them up in our profession, our background, or from our region. Make sure the scenes featuring particular characters feature lingo and language they would use and nothing that they wouldn't.

By the way—if you don't want to restrict your adult book

featuring children to a child's vocabulary, consider Harper Lee's *To Kill a Mockingbird*.

When he was nearly thirteen, my brother Jem got his arm badly broken at the elbow. When it healed, and Jem's fears of never being able to play football were assuaged, he was seldom self-conscious about his injury. . . .

When enough years had gone by to enable us to look back on them, we sometimes discussed the events leading to his accident. I maintain that the Ewells started it all, but Jem, who was four years my senior, said it started long before that. He said it began the summer Dill came to us, when Dill first gave us the idea of making Boo Radley come out.

Scout tells the story of what happened to her as a young girl, but she tells the story as an adult looking back. Harper Lee was free to use a full adult's vocabulary, understanding, and emotions. This technique—often called an *envelope story* because the ending wraps back around to the beginning—opens with an adult's voice and transports the reader back to a particular time in the narrator's youth. It usually returns to the adult's voice at the ending, sealing the "envelope." The technique is probably the best and most popular way to tell an adult story about something that happened to a child.

While I was writing *Journey*, a novel set in ancient Egypt, I noticed that several of the ancient pharaohs had blind harpists among the court musicians. So I decided to write a blind harpist into my book, and I made her the love interest of two rival brothers.

Well—easier said than done. Almost immediately I realized that I faced a challenge—in every scene from the harpist's point of view, I could not refer to anything visual because she couldn't see it. I would have to describe places and people only by using sounds, smells, sensations, tastes, and feelings.

. . .

Jendayi followed her handmaid through the palace halls and tried to deny the sour feeling in the pit of her stomach. She was glad Pharaoh would not be summoning her to play again tonight, for nothing but loneliness, longing, and pain could pour from her harp now.

She heard Akil's shuffling steps behind her and lowered her head, knowing he would be angry if he read her feelings on her face . . .

Life itself haunted her, for living seemed an exercise she often heard about but would never really experience. She ate, slept, drank, and played in the lonely blackness of the blind; every day looked like every night. Each time she rose from her bed she slipped into a tunic that felt like the one she had worn the day before; the sounds that rose and fell around her were the same sounds that had kept her company since the days of her childhood. The people who moved along the fringes of her world raised their voices when speaking as if she were deaf, or they were quick to assume that because she did not make eye contact with them, they could not make contact with her . . .

Notice all the sensual details *other* than images? When one sense is disallowed, you have to make the most of the others.

If you find yourself faced with a point of view challenge in your novel, don't worry—just close your eyes, slip into the skin of that POV character, and write the story as he would tell it.

If you have the opportunity, you should read novelist Mark Haddon's *The Curious Incident of the Dog in the Night-Time*. This novel features an autistic boy as the protagonist and first person point of view character. Haddon does a wonderful job of writing in the voice of an autistic British boy. Not only is it a good story, it's a beautiful example of point of view handled well.

Here's the first paragraph:

It was 7 minutes after midnight. The dog was lying on the grass in the middle of the lawn in front of Mrs. Shears's house. Its eyes were closed. It looked as if it was running on its side, the way dogs run when they think they are chasing a cat in a dream. But the dog was not running or asleep. The dog was dead. There was a garden fork sticking out of the dog. The points of the fork must have gone all the way through the dog and into the ground because the fork had not fallen over. I decided that the dog was probably killed with the fork because I could not see any other wounds in the dog and I do not think you would stick a garden fork into a dog after it had died for some other reason like cancer, for example, or a road accident. But I could not be certain about this.

Isn't that beautiful writing? Notice that Haddon uses no contractions, a feature of colloquial language that would be foreign to this child, and the boy speaks in complete, factual sentences. Already we understand that we are inside the mind of a very unique person.

The Foolproof Way to Determine the Best POV

Still uncertain about which point of view you should use in your novel? Don't let uncertainty stop you, but start writing. Write a scene in first person, if that's a viable option, and read it aloud. Then write it in third person and read aloud. Finally, try writing it in omniscient and read it aloud.

Which scene was easiest to write? In which did the story seem to flow most naturally? Which scene sounded best when you read it aloud?

Which point of view suits your story best? If you've chosen first person and you are planning to include important scenes where your protagonist will not be present, can you have the events of that scene recounted later? Or can you choose another character to write in first or third person and use them, in that particular POV, throughout the novel?

Most important, which scene appeals to you most? Can you write the entire story in that point of view?

More than once I have finished an entire novel in one point of view, then turned around and changed it to something else. You'll know when you hit upon the point of view that works best.

Point of view can be tricky until you get used to practicing it, then it will come more naturally. As you grow more relaxed with the technique and learn to submerge yourself into your characters' thoughts and feelings, point of view will become a powerful weapon in your writer's arsenal.

Why write:

Joe Smith propped his foot on the lower bleacher and watched his son on the field. He smiled as happiness rose within him, bringing tears to his eyes and embarrassing him in front of his friend, Tom Harris. Tom glanced his way, then handed him a handkerchief, keeping his blue eyes on the baseball diamond.

"Yeah," Tom said, obviously understanding the emotion that had moved Joe and the resulting embarrassment. "I know."

When you could write:

Joe Smith propped his foot on the lower bleacher and watched his son through foolish tears.

Tom glanced his way, then handed him a handkerchief. "Yeah." He kept his blue gaze on the diamond. "I know."

Go find an empty paper towel roll. Then sit at your computer, dive into your character's point of view, and write something wonderful.

POV EXERCISES

1. Do you remember the story of the Three Little pigs? If you've forgotten it, here it is:

Once upon a time there was an old mother pig who had three little pigs and not enough food to feed them. So she sent them out into the world to seek their fortunes.

The first little pig built his house out of straw because it was cheap. The second little pig built his house out of sticks because they were easy to find. The third little pig built his house with bricks.

The next day, a wolf happened to pass by the road where the three little pigs live. When he saw the straw house, he knocked on the door and said: "Little pig, little pig, let me come in!"

But the little pig answered: "Not by the hairs on my chinny-chin-chin!"

Then the wolf showed his teeth and said: "Then I'll huff and I'll puff and I'll blow your house in!"

So he huffed and he puffed and he blew the house in! The wolf opened his jaws, but the first little pig escaped and ran to the second little pig.'s house.

The wolf came to the second house. His mouth began to water as he thought about having two fine pigs for supper. So he knocked on the door and said: "Little pigs, little pigs, let me come in!"

But the little pigs answered: "Not by the hairs on our chinny-chin-chins!"

"Then I'll huff and I'll puff and blow your house in!"

So the wolf huffed and he puffed and he blew the house in! The wolf tried to catch the pigs at once, but the little pigs scrambled away as fast as their little feet would carry them.

The little pigs made it to the brick house and told their brother what had happened. Then the wolf knocked on the door and said, "Little pigs, little pigs, let me come in!"

And the little pigs answered, "Not by the hairs on our chinny-chin-chins!"

"Then I'll huff and I'll puff and I'll blow your house in!"

The wolf huffed and he puffed and puffed and huffed, but he couldn't blow this house in. So he sat down to think.

While the wolf was thinking, the third little pig made a blazing fire in the fireplace and put on a big pot of water. So when the wolf decided to climb down the chimney, he landed in a pot of boiling water! The little pigs slammed the lid on the pot and knew the wolf would never bother them again.

Your assignment: write the story in omniscient point of view. Don't just copy the story above, but tell it in your unique voice as an omniscient narrator.

2. Now that you've written the story in omniscient—the way the story is traditionally told— write the story from the POV of the little pig who loved straw. Why did he love straw? What was he thinking as he built his house? Feel free to give us his thoughts and feelings as the story unfolds.

3. Now write the story from the POV of the stick-loving little pig. What was he saying, thinking, and feeling as they built their homes? How did his feelings change when the wolf appeared?

4. Now write the story from the POV of the little pig who used bricks to write the story. Why did he love bricks? Where and how

did he learn that brick is a superior building material? Who taught him to lay bricks? How did he feel when the wolf approached, and how did he treat his brothers when they ran to his house?

5. Finally, write same story in the wolf's voice of view. How did he feel when he approached the house of straw? How had his feelings changed by the time he reached the house of sticks? How frustrated was he when he reached the brick house? Had he experienced a brick house before? Had his mother or father ever warned him about brick houses . . . or pigs? How did he feel when he slipped down the chimney?

You can add a lot to *any* story by varying the viewpoint and revealing the history, character, and personality of each of the POV characters. If you are ever having trouble deciding which POV character to use, write the scene with one character's POV, then write it again using the opposing character's POV. Which scene is more effective? Use that one.

Chapter Four

TRACK DOWN THE WEASEL WORDS

Suppose Joe's car battery dies. He takes it to a mechanic who tells him to come back in an hour. Joe does, and finds the mechanic smiling as he wipes his hands on a towel. "Good to see you," he says. "You'll be happy to know that your bill comes to $2500.00."

Joe gasps. "Twenty-five hundred dollars! What kind of battery did you put in?"

"An ordinary one," the mechanic says. "But I also threw in 250 unnecessary parts."

Makes no sense, does it? Joe doesn't want to pay for parts he doesn't need. And extra parts won't help his car run better. In fact, unnecessary parts will only clunk around under the hood, possibly destroying his engine.

Joe demands that the extra parts be removed, the bill be reduced, and he vows never to visit that mechanic again.

Now let's say Joe writes an article for *Southern Life*. He sends it to the editor, who sends it back post haste. Upset by her rejection of what Joe considered an excellent piece, he breaks every rule of writer's etiquette and calls to ask why she rejected his work.

"I liked your topic," she says, "but your writing was all over the place and I don't have time to rewrite every article that comes in.

You used too many words to make one or two points, and I'm not paying for writing that doesn't work."

In short, Joe and his mechanic have the same problem.

Ever since man has been putting pen to paper, the goal of the disciplined writer has been to say as much as possible in as few words as possible. We look for verbs with punch, descriptive nouns, and we scratch out dozens of adverbs and adjectives.

My favorite English teacher, the late Janet Williams, used to tell us that we could pay ourselves a quarter for every word we could cut out of our compositions. Back in those days we were tossing in every word we could think up to fill the required amount of pages, so her advice went against our natural instincts. But for those of us who took writing seriously, her advice proved to be golden.

And over the years, I have amassed a mountain of quarters by heeding her advice. I've been writing professionally for thirty years, publishing over 120 books as well as hundreds of magazine articles. Why? Because along the way I've learned to write tight.

You can, too.

This lesson is a collection of easy-to-remember guidelines, tips, and techniques to help you improve your novel, short story, nonfiction article or book, or term paper. Not every section will apply to your project, but many of them will apply to any kind of writing.

So settle back, grab a marker or pencil, and get ready to revise your manuscript. You'll be amazed at how easy it is to track down the weasel words that eat away at the effectiveness of your writing.

Prologues

If you've written a prologue or introduction to your book or novel, set your emotions aside and look at it with a critical eye. If it

- reveals what you're going to repeat in a later chapter
- steals material from an exciting scene in an effort to hook the reader
- consists of historical backstory to "set the stage"

- adds no real value to the work as a whole,

delete it. And when you delete it, don't just hit the delete key—I know how painful that can be. Instead, create a folder on your computer or in your desk and label it "Cut Materials." By placing cut sections in that folder, you're not annihilating them, you're reserving them in case you need them again.

Which you probably won't.

Why?

If your prologue or introduction only told the reader what you were going to tell him anyway, think of a way you can do that without actually using the same words. Use a quote that echoes the theme. Look for an anecdote to illustrate an important principle of your book or article. Find another way to entice the reader and prepare him without actually repeating the material you're going to use later.

If your work is fiction and your prologue or introduction consisted of an excerpt from an exciting scene near the end of your book, find another interesting way to open your story. You don't have to open with a car chase, a bomb, or a kidnapping, but you do have to arouse the reader's sympathy and interest. How? Have your character do something interesting, and put something at risk if your character fails. The reader will keep reading because he wants to know if your character will succeed in getting out of the house in time for his important job interview.

I don't know how many times I've had the TV on as background noise and I'll inadvertently become interested in some mindless, idiotic show. My husband will call me, and I'll say, "Just a minute. I have to find out if Toni makes it to the prom or not."

Do I really care about Toni and her prom? Not in the least, because they have nothing to do with my real life. But the TV writers have hooked me with the material, I sympathize with Toni, and I want to stick around long enough to see if she makes it to her school dance.

If your prologue or introduction is historical information (in a novel, it's called 'backstory'), you can usually cut it without a second thought. I don't know any faster way to put a reader to sleep than to regale him with historical information. If, however, this information is brief, active, and extremely well-written, you could make a good case for keeping it.

If you cut your prologue or introduction because it adds no real value to the work, put it in the "cut materials" folder and let it rest in peace. You'll earn a pile of quarters for your brave sacrifice.

Your Opening Paragraphs

While we're looking at the beginning of your manuscript, let's take a moment to think like a book buyer. What is the first thing a browsing reader sees that might entice him to pick up your book?

Ten points if you answered "the spine." Unfortunately, we don't have much control over the spine, so there's not much to worry about unless you are also designing your own cover.

So what's the next area that a potential book buyer considers? Right, the front cover. It may be unfortunate, but people *do* judge a book by its cover, so do your best to make sure yours looks good. If you're publishing with a traditional publisher, this, too, might be out of your control, but if you're self-publishing you will need to hire a good graphic artist to design a cover for you. I have made covers for a few of my e-books and, frankly, they looked amateurish. I learned my lesson, and now try to leave cover design to the professionals.

The next thing a potential book buyer looks at? Back cover copy, usually, and though publishers rarely ask for it, I always submit potential back cover copy along with my manuscript. No one at the publishing house knows my book as well as I do, so I figure that I can at least give them some copy to adjust as they try to create an enticing back cover.

Now we're down to factors we control completely: what's the next thing a potential book buyer examines? The first page. He flips past the front matter and reads the first sentence or two, and that's it. Studies have shown that potential buyers spend less than six seconds looking at that first page, and in that six seconds they make up their minds about whether or not to buy the book.

So don't waste your opening line. It may be the most important sentence in your entire manuscript.

Writers have come up with all sorts of memorable openings, from Snoopy's infamous "It was a dark and stormy night" to Melville's "Call me Ishmael."

My personal favorite first line comes from Jodi Picoult's *Second Glance*: "Ross Wakeman succeeded the first time he tried to kill himself, but not the second or the third."*

Isn't that delicious? Wouldn't you keep reading? I sure would—and did.

I can't give you a formula for writing a killer first sentence, but I can give you some guidelines. First, avoid weather reports and descriptions of landscapes or furniture. Second, include a person and a provocative question.

That's it. Make sure your first sentence is active, not static, and that someone is doing something.

Whenever I teach fiction classes over several sessions, I always have my students write their first line on a piece of paper and hand it to me. I then read each of those sentences to the class, asking for honest responses: hands up high for "Yes, I'd keep reading," hands slightly raised for "maybe I'd keep reading," and no uplifted hands at all for "it's not working for me."

It's an eye-opening experience when writers see how real people receive their first line.

So spend extra time—as much as you need—on that first line. It's more important than you may realize.

After the First Line

You can't coast after you come up with that killer first sentence. The rest of the first scene must be top-notch, too. You keep a reader

---

* Jodi Picoult, *Second Glance* (New York: Washington Square Press, 2008).

reading by withholding information. You tell him what he needs to know, but not a mite more.

The following probably applies more to fiction than nonfiction writers, but the principle is the same: don't dump a lot of details on your nonfiction reader in the beginning. Tell him what he needs to know, but only when he needs to know it.

If, like a lot of beginning novelists, you try to explain everything as you move through the material, you'll do a great job of eradicating all suspense from your book. Memorize this: you don't want to answer all the reader's questions, you want to raise questions in his mind. Think of it as "baiting" the reader. Your job is to toss out little hooks to snag his interest and keep him reading. You can't do that if you've explained everything.

My novel *Magdalene* opens with these paragraphs:

> Silence, as heavy as doom, wraps itself around me as two guards lead me into the lower-level judgment hall. When I fold my hands, the *chink* of my chains disturbs the quiet.
>
> My judge, Flavius Gemellus, senior centurion of the *Cohors Secunda Italica Civum Romanorum*, looks up from the rolls of parchment on his desk, his eyes narrow. I don't blame him for being annoyed. I am not a Roman citizen, so I have no right to a trial. Besides, I have confessed and am ready to die.*

When I teach this material in person, I read the above passage and ask my students to quickly lift their hands when I've read something that makes them ask a question. Let's look at these paragraphs again, and I'll mark the places where I usually see a flutter of hands:

> Silence, as heavy as doom, wraps itself around me as two guards lead me into the lower-level judgment hall. *[Where is she?]* When I fold my hands, the *chink* of my chains disturbs the quiet. *[Why is she in chains?]*

---

* Angela Hunt, *Magdalene* (Wheaton, IL: Tyndale House Publishers, 2006).

My judge, Flavius Gemellus, senior centurion of the *Cohors Secunda Italica Civum Romanorum*, looks up from the rolls of parchment on his desk, his eyes narrow. I don't blame him for being annoyed. I am not a Roman citizen, so I have no right to a trial. *[Why is she on trial?]* Besides, I have confessed and am ready to die. *[Why would anyone confess, and why is she ready to die?]*

Do you see how it's done? As a storyteller, your task is to put questions in the reader's mind, not to reveal everything up front. Editors will often write RUE in the margins of a manuscript—the letters stand for *resist the urge to explain*. Respect your reader's intelligence enough to let them figure things out, and don't reveal anything the reader doesn't absolutely need to know.

One note: Hooking the reader is not the same thing as leaving your reader in confusion. The reader isn't confused after reading the above passage; he's only asking questions. If the reader is confused because your writing makes no sense, he's likely to put your work down and not pick it up again.

Backstory—anything in a novel or short story that happens before the present story time—should be reserved for the back of the story. Too many beginning writers start out with something vital and interesting, but in chapter two they give us what I call the "backstory dump," which tells us about everything that occurred between the time Grandpa arrived in this country to when Papa died last year. The reader doesn't need to know all of that in chapter two, if they need to know it at all. So put all of it in your "cut materials" file, and later, when you need your protagonist to reflect on an emotional moment from the past, pull out that brief snippet about Papa dying and flesh it out into a scene. Let us see Papa propped up on his pillows, his face pale and sunken; let our heroine feel his callused hand as she grasps it. Then let him whisper words she will never forget.

Do you see? If you change some backstory into flashbacks and use them after we are fully engaged with the character, we will be much more emotionally involved with your characters. And that's our aim.

Now let's move from big picture revisions to some of the little details. From macro to micro.

What are Weasel Words?

They are words that clutter up your manuscript. Some of them are common to almost everyone who speaks English; others are unique to each writer. For instance, after I handed in one book, the editor called and said I was using *pull* too much.

I was flabbergasted. "Pull?"

"Yes," she said. "You have people *pulling* into driveways, *pulling* onto roads, *pulling* things from their purses and pockets. The word is all over the place."

I shook my head. "I didn't realize."

But I went back and did a search for the word *pull* in my manuscript—and there it was, sprinkled like paprika every few paragraphs. I deleted some, changed some to *turned*, others to *took*, others to *tugged*. But now I'm much more aware of my use of the word *pull*.

Tools for Tracking

The best tool for tracking down your weasel words is your word processing program's search and replace feature. If you write in any of the standard programs—Word, Word Perfect, Scrivener, Pages— you will find *search* (or *find*) and *replace*. When you're searching for a particular weasel word, ask your program to search for the word with spaces before and after it (unless it's a word likely to be used several times at the end of a sentence. In that case, you'll want to omit the last space).

For instance, if I was searching for *it*, I would enter [space]it[space] in the search box. Then I'd enter [space]IT[space] in the *replace* box. If you forget to add the spaces, the program will capi-

WRITING LESSONS FROM THE FRONT

talize every instance of *it* in your book, and you'll have to manually change them back to what they should be.

That's what I do for every weasel word on my list. I use search and replace to find the word or phrase (with spaces), then I replace it with the exact same word or phrase, except in all capital letters (also with spaces before and after). This doesn't change any of my prose, but those weasel words now LOOM on the page and catch my attention as I work through subsequent drafts. And every time I see one, I stop and ask myself if I can make the sentence better without that word. If I can, great. If I can't—or if it would make the sentence too convoluted—the sentence remains as it was.

Identifying the Weasel Words

The first weasel word is one I first noticed the year I taught high school English. I'd never thought of it as a weasel word, but suddenly there it was, all over my students' papers. I grew weary of circling it with my bright red pen, and over and over again I drew little weasel faces in the margins of their papers.

A very small, very overused word. Can you guess what it is?

Yes! IT!

It is so common we really don't think about it, but sometimes we fall into patterns that result in what I call "vague its." This particular species of *it* has infested many a sentence. When you find one of these, the best thing to do is shoot it and start over by asking, "What am I really trying to say here?"

Example: *Mary wore a blue dress with flowers on it.*

Does that *it* cause you to stop or slow down in any way? Can you tell immediately what *it* represents?

Yes, the blue dress. You shouldn't have to think too long about that *it*, so it's a good *it*. You could keep it, though you could earn some quarters by writing:

Mary wore a blue flowered dress.

The *it* that weakens your prose is found in sentences like this:

It is hard to get a drivers' license.

Hmm. What does that first *it* stand for? You have to think a moment, don't you? *It* has no apparent connection to anything else in the sentence, the paragraph, or the world.

So back up and say what you're really trying to say:

Getting a driver's license is hard. Or complicated. Or whatever you really meant.

What about this example:

"You don't understand," Mom said, sniffling. "It's so hard to live without your Dad."

In the second example, the questionable *it* is found in dialogue, and we loosen up when considering dialogue because people talk in all kinds of ways. If your character doesn't use proper grammar when she's crying and upset, she's just like the rest of us. Welcome her to the human race, and let her keep her undefined *it*.

Pardoning Reasonable Weasels

Please understand that the principles I'm presenting in this book are not hard and fast rules. I'm not saying all prologues are wrong or every *it* should be condemned or it's always wrong to use italics. Writing is part craft and part art, and I would never want to infringe on anyone's art . . . as long as they knew what they were doing. But when people make a word mess and call it art, well . . . I'm not likely to read it.

Doesn't mean everyone else will feel the same way.

So if you want to write *It's the way he smiled that made me love him*, no one's going to demand that you be tarred and feathered by the writer police.

But as you sit down to revise and edit your manuscript, it's a good idea to search for *[space]it[space]* and replace it with the same term, but in capital letters. Look at each of the *its* you find in your manuscript, and see if each one is clearly related to the word it represents. If so, fine, no problem. But if you have a disturbing number of the noisome vague *its*, perhaps you should consider their eradication.

. . .

Passive Verbs

We are a video generation. We have grown up with film and television and instant-everything. We microwave and keep the Internet at our fingertips. We Google for information, we call up maps in our cars, and we can even send emails through our refrigerators.

So why wouldn't you want words that move at the speed of life?

You're probably familiar with the *to be* verbs: *is are am was* and *were*. These are passive words, and sometimes they have their place. Sometimes you want to say "The sky was a blue dome overhead" and be done with it.

But at other times we pull out the passive verbs when other perfectly active and visual words are within arm's reach.

If I write *the cat was on the table*, what do you see the cat doing as the sentence plays out in your mind? You're not really sure, are you, because the verb *was* is a wimpy little verb that doesn't pull much weight. If you do a search/replace and replace every *was* with *WAS*, you'll be able to go through your manuscript and replace every wimpy *was* with a hunky anything else.

You could write:

> The cat yawned on the table
>> The cat reclined on the table
>> The cat retched on the table
>> The cat curled itself on the table
>> The cat lay on the table
>> The cat died on the table
>> The cat stretched on the table
>> . . . the possibilities are endless.

I always search for *was* and *were* in every draft and replace them with capitals because I want to see if I can find something better. Sometimes I stick with the simple *was*. Most of the time I find a better, more active way to write my sentence.

If I'm writing in present tense, of course, I search for *am* and *is* as well. I won't replace every active verb, but at least I consider its replacement. That consideration is what teaches us to write tighter.

Weak Adjectives and Enabling Adverbs

An adverb, almost by definition, is employed to support a verb that isn't doing its job. So be brave and search for ly[space], replace it with LY[space], and you should corral a small herd of shifty adverbs. For each of them, either see if you can replace the weak verb with something stronger, or simply cut the adverb. You'll earn a stack of quarters and do your manuscript a big favor.

Someone once reminded me that Jesus taught people by using nouns and strong verbs . . . and we all know how long people have been repeating *his* stories.

Cut the Obvious

True story: on at least two occasions I have taken novels that had gone out of print and sold them to another publisher. But before I handed in the old manuscript to a new publisher, I asked if I could edit them again. Why? "Because," I told one of my editors, "I write tighter now, and I want to improve it."

On those two occasions, I took the manuscript and without deleting a single line of the plot, I cut over nine thousand words from the book. How? By cutting out statements of the obvious like She stood ~~from her chair~~. Three words, three quarters.

He clapped ~~his hands~~. (What else is he going to clap, unless he's a walrus?)

They ~~all~~ stood ~~to their feet~~. (Ditto. Unless they stand on something else, lose the unnecessary words.)

She nodded ~~her head in agreement~~. (A nod means agreement.)

He stood ~~up~~. She crouched ~~down~~. (You can almost always get rid of *up* and *down*.)

She scratched her head ~~with her hand~~. (Unless she's using her ballpoint pen to take care of the itch.)

She ~~reached out and~~ accepted the trophy.

Do you see how quickly those unnecessary words can add up? So spare a few trees and develop a sense for seeing extraneous verbiage. Then cut, cut, cut.

The Thing about That

I overuse *that* all the time. It slips into my language, my thoughts, and my writing. So whenever I start to cull the weasel words, I do a search for *that*, replace it with THAT, and then carefully consider every THAT I come across. I don't know a test for it except to read the sentence without it—if the sentence makes sense without the THAT, I take it out. If the sentence seems to be missing something important, I leave the *that*. Very simple.

Miscellaneous Weasel Words

Other weasels on almost every list of overused words are *just, very, rather, began to, started to, some, "of the," "there was,"* and *suddenly.*

Just is used too much. You may want to leave it in dialogue, because people do use it in casual conversation, but in nonfiction writing or narrative, you'll probably want to omit *just.* Or replace it with *simply* where applicable.

Very often comes off as amateurish unless it's in a character's dialogue. Remember—the more concise the writing, the stronger the writing, so your sentence will probably be stronger without words like *very.*

Why write *he began to run* or *he started to eat,* when you could write *he ran* or *he ate?* Unless you purposely want someone to be in the process of beginning an activity, the simple past tense will do. But if you want to write:

As he began to eat, a shot rang out, shattering his pasta bowl,

Then *began to* is best.

"Of the" is often used in format titles (The Sword of the Lord and of Gideon), but if you find yourself writing *he hid inside the cloak of the knight,* then ditch the *of the* and write *he hid inside the knight's cloak.* Much, much cleaner.

"There was" is a passive verb linked to a nothing word. So if you find those constructions in your book and you didn't write it for a purposeful reason, cut the nothing words and figure out what you're trying to say. Instead of

There was a peaceful haze over the valley . . .

write

A peaceful haze hovered over the valley.

Suddenly: In fiction, if you are writing and a shot rings out, to your characters it has rung out *suddenly* whether you use the word or not. See for yourself:

She bent to breathe in the scent of the sweet flowers. "Thank you for the lovely bouquet," she told the little girl. She pressed a kiss to the child's forehead and slipped her fingers around the beribboned stems, ready to hand the flowers to her waiting attendant—

A shot rang out.

She turned, saw horror on her attendant's face, and felt a dull pressure in her back, but that had to be the result of walking all day, from bending to receive dozens of little bouquets, from kissing children and shaking hands and smiling until her jaws ached like they ached now, but no, the pain as lower, but it wasn't pain exactly, it was pressure, and then she heard a splatting sound and felt some thing splash her shoes, probably the children, maybe a child had spilled a bottle of water, but as she looked down she saw that the water was red, as red as her dress, as red as the single rose the prince had left on her pillow this morning—

Sorry—I got a little carried away.

Do you see how you don't need *suddenly* to write a sudden action? If it occurs unexpectedly, it will *feel* sudden.

And I wrote that run-on sentence-paragraph to illustrate something about story time. As a writer, you are the one who controls the passage of time in your story. You can press years into a single sentence—*Years passed, and time did not heal all wounds*—or you can take a single moment, even a second, and draw it out for effect. This is a handy trick if you are writing a car crash, someone being shot or wounded, or the moment when your protagonist receives the shock of bad news.

If you've experienced a moment of tragedy, you can probably remember how it felt: time slowed down, giving you time to record every thought and notice the oddest details. To create the same experience on the written page, write the scene and don't stop the momentum by inserting a period. I wouldn't drag a moment out forever, but you can definitely make time slow to a crawl during dramatic moments. Simply feel free to ignore everything you ever learned in English class and glory in the run-on sentence.

Your Own Personal Weasel Words

Earlier, I told you about the editor pointed out my overuse of the word *pull*. We all have our own personal weasel words, and you may go through phases where you use certain words more than others.

Be especially aware of the body language signals you write—I tend to overuse brows, and sometimes I find eyebrow calisthenics on my pages. Brows are wrinkling, slanting, knitting, lifting, arching, twisting, and lowering. So whether you have a tendency to overuse smiles, shrugs, brows, noses, or whatever, be aware of it. Try to limit yourself to one or two of those expressions per chapter. Or at least per page.

What I Learned From Sol Stein

One of the most useful writing tips I learned from Sol Stein (I highly recommend his books *Stein on Writing* and *How to Grow a Novel*), was this:

$$1 + 1 = 1/2$$
$$1 + 1 + 1 = 1/3$$

That's not the math you learned in school, but it works well in writing. What Stein is warning us about is overwriting, saying the same thing again and again, using different words to repeat ourselves. Like I did in that last sentence.

I usually fall prey to this tendency when I'm on a roll and the writing is going well. I'm in the groove, the words are flying from my fingertips, and I'm letting it all come out. Problem is, the stuff coming out is the same thought translated into different words.

> He felt angry and frustrated, boiling mad, as frustrated as a dog in a room full of fire hydrants.

When you find that you're piling on layers of the same idea or emotion, choose the best phrase and cut the others. Trust your reader—he'll get it the first time.

Exclamation Points

Unless a character's house is on fire or he's running for his life, you will probably want to lose them. Too many exclamation points come across as amateurish—as though you're working too hard to convey an emotion or sense of urgency. So reserve them for truly dire circumstances, if you use them at all.

Find more elegant ways to convey emotion or urgency through dialogue, interior monologue, or action. And remember—sometimes an emotion is stronger if it's understated. Quiet can be intense.

Scene: Sherry's six-year-old daughter is missing when Sherry tries to pick her up from school.

> Somehow Sherry found herself in the school office, where what seemed like dozens of people offered her a seat, a glass of water, a telephone. Why wouldn't they offer something useful?!
>
> The principal, Mrs. Jones, hurried into the room, breathing hard. "I've just spoken to your daughter's teacher," she said, planting her arm on the tall counter. "And she says a man picked

your daughter up ten minutes ago. She assumed he was your husband."

"My husband is dead!" Sherry heard the words rip from her own throat. "And Lily wouldn't go with anybody because I've taught her about stranger danger. Someone has taken her! She's been kidnapped!"

"Calm down, I'm sure there's a logical explanation—"

"You don't know what you're talking about!" Sherry turned and ran from the office in a blind panic.

That's certainly one approach—and one where exclamation points could be justified. But take a moment to consider the opposite tack:

Somehow Sherry found herself in the school office, where what seemed like dozens of people offered her a seat, a glass of water, a telephone. Why wouldn't they offer something useful? Why wouldn't one of them calmly step forward and explain where Lily was, and how there'd been a simple misunderstanding—

The principal, Mrs. Jones, hurried into the room, breathing hard. "I've just spoken to your daughter's teacher—"

"Lily," Sherry said, her voice muffled by the pounding of blood in her ears. "Her name is Lily."

"Of course it is." Mrs. Jones made an effort to smile. "The teacher says a man picked Lily up ten minutes ago. She assumed he was your husband."

Her husband? Sherry stared at the principal as the room shifted and her pulse quickened. "My husband—" her voice faltered—"my husband died four years ago. In Afghanistan."

"I'm so sorry." The principal pressed her hand to her ample chest. "Let me get you a telephone and a place to sit. I'm sure you want to call around and see if Lily could have gone home with one of her friends—"

Sherry cut her off with an uplifted hand. "I have a phone. And I'm calling the police."

You may disagree, but I find the second scene much more powerful—and the scene doesn't have a single exclamation point.

Other Punctuation Problems: Em Dashes and Ellipses

Some of my writing students probably think I'm being way too picky when I bring up em dashes and ellipses, but I've read enough beginners' manuscripts to know that this area ought to be addressed. If you want your manuscript to rise above the average submission in the slush pile, you should learn to use these punctuation marks properly.

First, know what they are. An em dash is a long hyphen. If you type two hyphens in most word processing programs, the auto correct will automatically insert an em dash (unless that feature has been turned off).

You use em dashes in a couple of ways. First, you can use an em dash to insert a parenthetical phrase.

All manuscripts—including this one—need to be proofread. Just be sure to use an em dash at the beginning and the end of the inserted phrase. Lots of writers make the mistake of using an em dash at the beginning, and a comma where the second em dash should go.

Another use for an em dash, particularly in fiction, is to indicate when someone has been interrupted.

> "Let me tell you a story," Grandpa said, settling back in his chair. "It all began when your grandma was out to get a hog. She had no sooner—"
>
> "Come and eat," Grandma called from the kitchen. "Last one in has to hear the end of that silly story."

In nonfiction, an ellipsis (. . .) is used to indicate the omission of a word or phrase, line or paragraph, from within a quoted text. Four dots are used at the end of a quote to indicate that the original quote continued.

In fiction, an ellipsis is the three dots you often see in dialogue or narrative. Three dots—no period—are used at the end of a sentence in dialogue when a character is trailing off in thought.

> "Seems like only yesterday I was sixteen and dreaming of my first ball gown . . ."

Three dots within a passage of dialogue can be used to indicate a pause in the character's words. This is useful if you want to slow down the reader and add a dreamy quality to the character's speech:

> "Seems like only yesterday I was dreaming of my first ball gown . . . of course that was before my daddy decided no daughter of his would ever take up dancin'."

Sophisticated Sentence Structure

In general, I can think of three principles that will guide you as you construct or revise sentences. Writing a sentence may seem like the easiest thing in the world, but when you begin to wrestle with sentences that contain three or four clauses, getting the structure right can be tricky.

The Pencil Principle: if you consider that a pencil has three parts —the tip, the eraser, and the middle, you can order them by priority: the tip is the most important, the eraser is the second most important, and the middle belongs in last place (though it would be hard to use a pencil without one).

Similarly, the most important segment of your sentence belongs at the end, like the pencil tip. The second most important belongs at the beginning, with the eraser, and the least important can go in the middle.

Example: In one of my books I found myself juggling these three elements:

My angel
Fed acid
To Ramirez.

If I wanted to stress that my angel fed Ramirez *acid*, I'd use my angel first, acid last.

If I wanted to stress that my angel fed acid to *Ramirez*, of all people, I'd use my angel first, Ramirez last.

If I wanted to stress that poor Ramirez ate acid from my *angel*, I'd use Ramirez first, my angel last.

Another principle to keep in mind when you're considering sentence structure is feeling-action-speech order, or the FAS principle. Suppose you want to work with these three elements:

"Get out of here!"
He slammed his fist on the desk.
Anger rose within him.

Which works best for you?

1.) "Get out of here!" He slammed his fist on the desk. Anger rose within him.

2.) Anger rose within him. He slammed his fist on the desk. "Get out of here!"

3.) He slammed his fist on the desk. "Get out of here!" Anger rose within him.

Feeling, action, and then speech, as in example two—will usually work best. In fact, if the emotion is evident in the action, you can save yourself a few quarters and cut the emotional line. Or combine them. Your choice.

He slammed his fist on the desk ~~as anger rose within him~~. "Get out of here!"

Yet another principle of sentence structure to consider is what I call "the –ing thing." Because writers like to vary their sentence structure, instead of writing:

Noun verb subject. Noun verb subject. Noun verb subject.
　Bill ate the hamburger. It tasted good. Bill loved his burger.

Sometimes they will write:

Verbing, noun subject.
　Loving his burger, Bill ate all of it.

The problem arises when writers automatically change the structure without thinking about what they've written:
Smiling, Tom accepted Brenda's invitation is a perfectly good sentence.
Slamming the door behind him, Tom stomped toward the gas station is not. The –ing phrase implies continuous action, and Tom can't be slamming the door behind him while he's stomping toward the gas station. This needs to be changed to:
After slamming the door, Tom stomped toward the gas station
OR
Tom slammed the door, then stomped toward the gas station.
So do a search for your –ing phrases. If they begin a sentence, make sure your active character can do the actions of both phrases simultaneously.

Dialogue Do's and Don'ts

In middle and high school, our English teachers rejoiced when we got jiggy with colorful speech attributions. We had characters chortling, laughing, chuffing, retorting, explaining, bellowing, and burping responses to one another. And our teachers smiled and gave us good grades for our creativity.

If you try the same thing in professional writing, your work will be returned to you faster than a blink. When you write dialogue, whether in fiction or nonfiction, your best bet is to use the word *said* in speaker attributions. Better yet, don't use anything at all, but indicate who's speaking by body movement.

Let's look at a bit that could be part of a nonfiction interview:

> I met up with the two cupcake bakers at their shop on East Avenue. Martha wore a blue apron, Bettye wore pink.
>
> "I always did like girly things," Bettye said, wiping the counter with practiced ease. "Martha's always liked blue."
>
> Martha swiped a stray hank of hair out of her eyes. "I'm not a tomboy; don't you write that. I just like the sea, that's all. It seems cool, and it can get awful hot when you're standin' next to an oven."

In the first paragraph, I used the word *said* and it probably slid right by without stirring even a ripple of recognition in your mind. *Said* is like the word *the*—it's almost invisible when we're reading.

In the third paragraph, it's clear from the physical action (Martha swiping hair out of her face) that this is going to be a Martha paragraph, so any dialogue that follows will come from her. No speaker attribution is needed.

When you're writing dialogue—whether it's in a polished professional article or in the funkiest fiction—try to avoid people growling, giggling, or gasping in their speaker attributions.

Dialogue Explanations

Another situation to avoid whenever possible is dialogue that contains explanations. Like this: "What's wrong?" she asked, confused.

The woman's confusion should be evident in *what she said*, not in the writer's clumsy way of *telling* us she is confused. Remember the old adage *show, don't tell?* This may be brief telling, but it's still telling.

If you really want to add a bit more to emphasize her confusion, do it with description, not a speaker attribution.

> Her eyes clouded as she looked from Tom to Mary. "What's wrong? What aren't you telling me?"

Make sure the confusion is evident in the description and in the dialogue itself.

Dialogue Adverbs

We've already talked about adverbs, and as weak as they are, they're even weaker in speech attributions.

In an early draft of a novel, I once wrote:

> "No slave holder is ever going to sit at my table," Mrs. Haynes said emphatically.

Okay, all is forgivable in a first draft. Writing is revising; we know that. So we get rid of the adverbs after *said.*

Said emphatically. Said angrily. Said softly. Said impetuously.

I could fill a page with said + adverbs, and they'd all be awful. Why spend two quarters when you can keep one? Instead of *said softly,* write *whispered.*

Said angrily? Yelled. (And a note of caution here—we don't want to go too overboard, lest we get into people screaming, roaring, screeching . . . you get the picture.)

Sometimes it's better to spend a few quarters to evoke a visual image: *"I hate her," she said, her upper lip curling.*

As to my example, I ended up writing:

> "No slave holder is ever going to sit at my table." Mrs. Haynes

unfolded her napkin with an emphatic snap. "You can be assured of that."

Yes, it's more words, but I traded an adverb for a sensory detail—the snap of the napkin—and that's a trade well made.

Listen to Your Dialogue

I always encourage writers to listen to their dialogue as the computer reads it aloud. In hearing it, you will notice things you might not have noticed as you read it on the page.

(If you work on a Mac, speech capability is built in. If you work on a PC, you can download the free Adobe Reader and use it to have the computer read your manuscript aloud.)

First, does it sound like natural speech? Do your speakers use contractions, run-on sentences, and contradict each other? Real people do. And while it's true that dialogue is not exact speech, but an *approximation* of real speech, a lot of beginners' dialogue is neither.

Writers often drop character names into dialogue to help clarify things for the reader, but how often do you actually say the name of the person you're talking to? Not often, I'd bet. So delete names in your dialogue if they seem superfluous.

Look at this exchange:

"Hi, Bob. How are you?"

"Just fine, thanks. And you? How're the wife and kids?"

"Well, Marge had the flu, as you know, and little Billy needs braces. Plus we just found out the roof leaks, so we will be needing to raid the savings account again. Seems like we just can't get ahead."

"Well, it's nothing to be ashamed of. Everyone goes through tight spots. Now I've got to run. I'll see you later."

"Okay. Nice seeing you."

"Nice seeing you, too."

Snooze-a-rama! Heaven help us if all books were written as badly as that.

First, see all those routine greetings? The "how are you"s and "See you laters?" Get rid of them; they're accomplishing nothing. You could just as easily write:

> Bob and Tom met at the corner. After greeting Tom, Bob looked his friend directly in the eye and asked if they were having financial difficulties.
>
> "Why would you ask that?"
>
> Bob shrugged. "It's nothing to be ashamed of. Everyone goes through tight spots."

See what I mean? Cut to the chase every time. Those little pleasantries mean nothing—unless they're highly unusual and you want the reader to notice how stilted someone is during the usual pleasantries.

Second, watch out for the "as you know, Bob"s that often occur in beginning novelists' dialogue. Do not have your characters telling each other things they already know. Nothing more obviously shows the writer at work than exposition planted in a conversation.

If you need to get exposition into dialogue so your reader will know what's going on, one of the most common ways is to have someone new come to town. This new person wouldn't know the town history or what happened to a particular character, so a native can show the newbie around and fill him in. You see this tactic employed all the time in books and films, and it works well.

I remember watching one of the muppet movies—I forget which —and Kermit the Frog was talking to actress Diana Rigg. She was relating the long and convoluted history of other characters when he interrupted: "Excuse me—why are you telling me all this?"

She lifted one shoulder in an elegant shrug. "It's exposition. It has to go *somewhere*."

And away they went.

Don't be so obvious. Do your best to find a creative way to impart information your reader needs to know.

Third, listen to the computer read your dialogue because the computer will not add emotion the way your mind will when you read it. The computer's slightly robotic voice can be a benefit if it reveals where your dialogue lacks emotional depth.

Free tip: one way to show that a character's native language is *not* English is to eliminate all the contractions from his dialogue. The dialogue then becomes stiff and stilted, just as it would if the character were just learning English.

Do not remove contractions from the dialogue of *all* your characters or they'll all sound stiff!

No Ping Pong Allowed

If you look carefully at your dialogue, you may find that you are writing "on the nose"—with no subtlety or subtext. And that for every conversational "ping," the other character answers with an appropriate "pong."

Real conversation isn't like that . . . unless it's deadly boring.

Consider this exchange:

Tom carried the bag of groceries into the kitchen where Brenda waited.

"Did you get the catsup?" she asked without looking up.

"Yes, I did. Heinz. Because I know you like it."

"I like any kind. As long as it's on sale."

"Well, this one wasn't."

"On sale?"

"Right. But the mustard was twenty cents off. And by the way, I saw Melissa standing over in produce."

"Melissa?" Brenda finally looked up. "Did she speak?"

"Sure she did. She said hi and I said hi and then she asked if I'd seen Toby."

"Well?"

"I hadn't seen Toby."

"Did you tell her that?"

"Well, she asked, didn't she?"

ZZZzzzzzzzzz. Let's try again.

Tom carried the groceries into the kitchen where Brenda waited.

"Catsup?" she asked without looking up.

"Heinz. Because you won't eat anything else."

"I like any kind, as long as it's on sale."

"I saw Melissa standing over in produce."

"Was it?" She turned, finally. "Was the catsup on sale?"

"Did you hear me? I saw Melissa." He bent closer to look into her eyes. "She asked if I'd seen Toby."

Brenda blinked. "You must think I'm some kind of tightwad."

Tom slammed his fist onto the counter. "Good grief, Brenda, how long are you going to ignore that missing kid?"

Ah . . . much better. The first passage is an exercise in tedium; the second crackles with suspense. There are undercurrents and questions are flying through the reader's mind. Why is Brenda so concerned about the cost of catsup? Who's Melissa, and why doesn't Brenda want to hear about her? Why is Tom so upset? And who in the heck is Toby?

(I don't know the answers to any of those questions. If you do, feel free to finish the story.)

Don't let your dialogue click back and forth like a metronome. Keep it off-balance, and you'll keep your characters off-balance. Keep your characters off-balance and you'll keep your readers off-balance. And that's a good thing because it add suspense to any novel.

Don't write dialogue phonetically.

Years ago writers would approximate the sound of spoken speech

by writing dialogue the way it sounded. Who can forget Mammy's
speech in *Gone With the Wind*:?

> "Ef you doan care 'bout how folks talks 'bout dis fambly, Ah does,"
> she rumbled. "Ah ain' gwine stand by an' have eve'body at de pahty
> sayin' how you ain' fotched up right. Ah has tole you an' tole you dat
> you kin allus tell a lady by dat she eat lak a bird. An' Ah ain' aimin'
> ter have you go ter Mist' Wilkes' an' eat lak a fe'el han' an' gobble lak
> a hawg."*

We don't write dialogue phonetically anymore for several reasons:
it's hard to read, it breaks the fictive dream, and it's not politically
correct. It's fine to drop a 'g' occasionally, or change *got to* to *gotta*,
especially if it results in a more natural speech for your character, but
please resist the urge to spell things the way they sound.

If you want to signify that a character is from a different country,
read some books written in that country and get a feel for the way
the natives use language. For instance, I wrote a series of books in
Ireland and spent some time there doing research. I kept a little
notebook and would jot down little phrases I heard people use in
ordinary conversation. I also copied down unique road signs because
they gave me additional colorful vocabulary. (For instance, on the
side of a rocky hill in the U.S. you'd see a sign saying "Watch for
falling rocks." In Ireland, in the same situation I saw, "Mind your
windscreen.")

In her novel *The Help*, Kathryn Stockett did an amazing job of
creating the sound and rhythm of southern black speech with word
choice. Here's a paragraph from the first chapter:

> By the time she a year old, Mae Mobley following me around every-
> where I go. Five o'clock would come round and she'd be hanging on
> my Dr. Scholl shoe, dragging over the floor, crying like I weren't

---

* Margaret Mitchell, *Gone With the Wind* (New York: MacMillan Company, 1936),
p. 54.

never coming back. Miss Leefolt, she'd narrow up her eyes at me like I done something wrong, unhitch that crying baby off my foot. I reckon that's the risk you run, letting somebody else raise you chilluns.*

By sprinkling your character's conversation with unique phrases —whether picked up in another country, another profession, or another social group—you will singularize your characters. Soon your readers will know which character is speaking by the words he uses . . . or so we hope. Creating particular and unique characters is one of our goal as writers.

Be Kind to Yourself and Avoid Dinnertime Dialogue

I'm not saying that you should never write a scene where people talk and eat at the same time. I was merely searching for a way to describe a difficult situation to write. I stumbled into it once, and I'll never do it again.

In my novel *The Canopy*, I wrote a scene where ten characters sat around a dinner table and discussed their expedition into the jungle. Not only where there ten people, but they were from different countries—a Russian, an Englishman, a couple of Americans, a Peruvian, a Frenchman, and others I've forgotten. Because it would have been beyond awful to end every bit of dialogue with "so-and-so said," I resorted to bits of body language to make it clear who was speaking. So characters were casting looks, passing plantains, shrugging, dropping spoons, picking up spoons, waving forks, dropping napkins, picking up napkins—well, you get the picture.

To make matters worse, my friend Bill Myers and I recorded the book for audio, using accents for each of the characters. Bill read all the male POV scenes and dialogue, and I read all the female scenes and dialogue. But when we got to the dinner table scene, with all the

---

* Kathryn Stockett, *The Help* (New York: Berkley Trade, 2011).

characters talking at once, I think Bill was tempted to bash me over the head with the manuscript. Talk about a challenge!

So do yourself a favor—if at all possible limit conversations in your book to two or three people at a time. You'll be glad you did. Besides, when you're at a banquet, who do you really talk to? The people on either side of you, right? So it is natural to keep dialogue between a few.

One day you'll thank me for that little tip.

Interior Monologue

I spent a lot of time on this in *Lessons from the Writing Front: Point of View*, but I'll review it here because it's an important part of getting your manuscript ready for submission.

When you are using a limited point of view—one POV per scene —the things you write are limited to what your POV character sees, hears, tastes, touches, senses, knows, and feels. So if he thinks *I want to get out of here*, you do not need to write *he thought* afterward. Neither do you need to place his thoughts in italics.

Because you're in limited third person, the things you're writing come from his head, so the reader intuits that the thoughts come from the character's consciousness. You don't need to remind him. You don't need to write *he thought, he mused, or he recollected*. You don't need to put it in quotes (they're only for spoken speech) or in bold. You simply write it.

> Johnson walked into the room he'd left ten years before. No one had disturbed the furniture as far as he could tell, but the upholstery looked faded from the sun. Right over there, on that row of tile in front of the fireplace, Lydia had looked him in the eye and said she loved him. Really loved him. And she meant it—he read sincerity in her eyes and in the curve of her mouth. But then she walked away, looking for her rich third cousin, and then she'd married him, despite Johnson's pleas.
>
> What a fraud.

Poor guy. He walks into a room and we see what he sees because we're looking through his eyes. We then access his memories, of a day ten years earlier when Lydia had told him she loved him and then ran after some rich guy. And then we hear, straight from Johnson's brain, what he thinks of the lady: what a fraud. (I know, John's thought is pretty tame. But what can I say? He's a laid back kind of guy.)

So spare yourself some quarters and cut all the "he thoughts" if they are signaling interior monologue. If you find a "he wondered," you can usually turn the sentence into a question.

From:

He wondered if she had ever loved him.

to

Had she ever loved him?

If you ever have characters mumbling under their breaths because you're really trying to slip the reader some information, please change it to interior monologue instead--unless your character is drunk or suffering from a mental illness.

If you have pages and pages of interior monologue, you probably need to take some of it out and turn it into a scene. If your character drifts back in time for more than a page or so, you'd probably be better off if you lift out that memory and turn it into a full-fledged flashback, a separate scene . . . and then insert it only when (and not a moment before) the reader needs to know that information. If the reader doesn't need to know the information, place it in your "cut materials" folder. Where it can wait. And rest in peace.

Two Hads Will Do It

One final foolproof way for novelists to spruce up their scenes and earn a few quarters.

A *flashback* is a full scene that takes place before the present story time. A *recollection* is a little snippet that takes place within a present time scene. The scene I created earlier about Johnson and Lydia contained a brief recollection.

> Johnson walked into the room he'd left ten years before. No one had disturbed the furniture as far as he could tell, but the upholstery looked faded from the sun. Right over there, on that row of tile in front of the fireplace, Lydia **had** looked him in the eye and said she loved him. Really loved him. And she meant it—he read sincerity in her eyes and in the curve of her mouth. But then she walked away, looking for her rich third cousin, and then she **had** married him, despite Johnson's pleas.
>
> What a fraud.

What I want you to notice are the two *hads*. The first is the key that takes us back to the day when Lydia looked him in the eye . . . and the second, pertaining to Lydia's marrying her cousin, brings us back to present story time.

You do not need *hads* any where else in the recollection. Novice writers might have written:

> . . . Lydia **had** looked him in the eye and said she loved him. Really loved him. And she **had** meant it—he **had** read sincerity in her eyes and in the curve of her mouth. But then she **had** walked away, looking for her third rich cousin, and then she **had** married him . . .

When inserting a recollection, remember that the first *had* takes you back, the second brings you forward. Simple and elegant.

A flash back can work the same way, depending on how it's structured. You could indicate the start of a flashback by inserting the date in front of the scene:

January 3, 1517.

The wind blew steadily at the mouth of the cave, pushing the men back.

In this case you don't need any *hads* at all, because the date tells the reader that this scene took place before the present story time (assuming that present story time is after January 1517).

Or you could write the scene and use a *had* to take the reader back and another to bring her forward:

> She **had** turned ten that month, and remembered little about her party except that Uncle Jack brought a bouquet of red balloons . . .
>
> . . .
>
> But she **had** been a child then, and now she was a woman grown. And now 'twas time to put away childish things.

In Summation

Self-editing is an art, but revision is necessary. I write my novels in at least five drafts, and I never feel that they are 100 percent perfect. My friend novelist Alton Gansky once reminded me that if a novel is 100,000 words and 99.9 percent perfect, it still contains 100 errors.

What makes revision even more challenging is that we're not searching for concrete "errors" like typos. We are looking for ways to make language clearer, to amplify the art, to ratchet up the emotional experience, and solidify a theme. We are working to focus the total effect of our work, and sometimes we are only guessing at what is best.

So I hope these few guidelines, pointers, and tips have been helpful as you set about revising your work. I will leave you with two additional thoughts:

If you find a section of your book isn't working—if it isn't deepening character or advancing plot in fiction, or if it isn't providing more information or motivating your reader in nonfiction--you need to place it in your "cut materials" file and leave it there for several days. If you forget about it, it probably wasn't supposed to be included in your book.

And always remember that writing is a craft and an art. The more you learn, the more you realize you need to learn, and that's what makes writing so amazing and challenging.

So go ahead—get back to work on your manuscript and make it the best it can be. We're waiting to see what you do with it.

WEASEL WORD EXERCISES

Learning to write well involves purposeful practice, so here's your chance to whack out some weasel words!

This scene is from the second draft of my novel She's In a Better Place. You should know why some words are capitalized—they're my weasel words.

I climb the stairs and glance to the left. Light streams from Bugs's and Clay's room, so I check on my youngest son first.

"Hey, bud," I call, finding Bugs hunched over a video game in bed. "Shouldn't this lamp be out?"

He LOOKs up and grins, displaying an adorable gap where his front teeth should be. "I WAS waiting on you to kiss me good night."

"Sure you were." I set the video game on the nightstand, then sit on the edge of the mattress. "Anything special you want to pray about?"

He presses his lips together as if in deep thought, then shakes his head. "Nothin'."

"Okay. You want to pray, or shall I?"

He closes his eyes. "Dear God, please bless Mr. Gerald and Lydia and McLane and Jeff and my teacher and the preacher and the dead guy downstairs. Bless Skeeter and Grandma, too. Help us not to catch the measles. In Jesus' name, Amen."

My seven-year-old son's generous heart never fails to touch a soft spot within my heart. Though we haven't seen my sister McLane and her husband, Jeff, in almost a year, Bugs never fails to remember them in prayer.

I PULL the covers up to his chin as he snuggles beneath the quilt. "Someone at school have the measles?"

"Maybe. Claire had bumps. Miss Dickson didn't know what they were, but she said they might be measles."

"I doubt it. I'm pretty sure your friends have all been vaccinated."

"What's fascinated?"

"*Vaccinated.* You've all had shots against measles."

I kiss his forehead—careful to note THAT his skin feels normal, not fevered—and turn out the lamp. I leave the door open, though, because Bugs likes the hallway light left on until he falls asleep.

How would you change the above passage? Would you change the weasel words or let them stand?

Here's how that passage appeared in the final book. You'll note that I changed or cut some weasel words and left others alone.

I climb the stairs and glance to the left. Light streams from Bugs's and Clay's rooms, so I check on my youngest son first.

"Hey, bud." I find Bugs in bed, hunched over a video game. "Shouldn't this lamp be out?"

He grins, displaying an adorable gap where his front teeth should be. "I was waiting on you to kiss me good night."

"Sure you were." I set the video game on the nightstand and sit on the edge of the mattress. "Anything special you want to pray about?"

He presses his lips together as if in deep thought, then shakes his head. "Nothin'."

WRITING LESSONS FROM THE FRONT

"Okay. You want to pray, or shall I?"

He closes his eyes. "Dear God, please bless Mr. Gerald and Lydia and McLane and Jeff and my teacher and the preacher. Bless Skeeter and Grandma, too. Help us not to catch the measles. In Jesus' name, Amen."

My seven-year-old's generous nature never fails to touch a soft spot within my heart. Though we haven't seen my sister McLane and her husband in almost a year, Bugs never fails to remember them in prayer.

I pull the covers up to his chin as he snuggles beneath the quilt. "Someone at school have the measles?"

"Maybe. Claire had bumps. Miss Dickson didn't know what they were, but she said they might be measles."

"I doubt it. I'm pretty sure your friends have all been vaccinated."

"Have I been fascinated?"

"Vaccinated. Yes, you've had a shot to protect you from measles and lots of other serious diseases."

I kiss his forehead—letting my lips linger a moment to be sure his skin feels normal, not fevered—and turn out the lamp. I leave the door open because Bugs likes the hallway light left on until he falls asleep.

2. Do a search for *your* weasel words in your current writing project, fiction or nonfiction. Print out the page with those words in capital letters. How will you change them? Don't forget to check your HADs in recollections!

3. What are some of your commonly overused words? We all have our pet words: mine are look, pull, smile, nod, and anything to do with eyebrows. Write your pet weasel words on a notecard and tape it to your computer. Never finish a draft without looking for those words and seeing if you can replace or cut them when they've been used too frequently.

4. Finally, do a search for the "no duh" phrases like *stood to his/her feet, clapped her hands, waved her hand, sat down, stood up, fiction novel,*

unique oddity, or anything else that's redundant. Train yourself to notice these things by routinely eradicating them. How many redundancies did you find in your work?

Chapter Five

EVOKING EMOTION

I WAS A SINGER BEFORE I BECAME A WRITER. I SPENT A YEAR traveling throughout the United States as part of a ten-member vocal ensemble whose specialty was *a capella* arrangements and "God and Country" music.

Our director was and is a marvel—a great storyteller, an amazing musician, a teacher, a caring minister, and a disciplined mind. One day he said something I knew to be true: "It's all in the music," he said, talking about a wonderful arrangement of "God Bless America" we'd just rehearsed. "You can write in a standing ovation if you know what you're doing."

I listened in amazement. He was right; every time we sang "God Bless America" people rose to their feet at a certain point, applauding the entire time. How *did* he do it?

Years passed. I came off the road, got married, had children, raised a family and began to write. I learned about plotting, creating characters, and the art of revision. I studied every craft book I could find because I wanted my books to be the best they could be.

One day I was talking to a friend who ran a novelist's retreat where I often taught. I pointed out that I knew musicians who could write music that unfailingly evoked specific emotions and actions— so why couldn't we do the same thing in our writing?

"That sounds like a great class," she said. "Why don't you teach it?"

Gulp. I knew how to write scenes that moved my readers, but *how* did I do it? And how could I explain it to others?

For several days the question badgered me. I did an Internet search and found dozens of websites where writers were told to write "to evoke emotion," but I could not find much concrete advice on how to do that. Occasionally I found a page that reminded me to use details or music, description and memories, but those were things I used all the time. So how was I supposed to teach others how to evoke emotion?

Finally I turned my thoughts to what makes me cry. What moves *me*? And even though I am a rational, practical person at the core, I also feel deeply and can cry easily provided something moves me.

So what moves me? What makes me laugh? What makes me cry?

I came up with an answer in a flash: country music. Not those beer-drinkin', I-lost-my-cheatin'-lover kinds of songs, but the ballads that tell a story in three and a half minutes. Songs about old married couples and parents and kids, moms with prodigal daughters and dads raising hard-headed sons. Those kinds of songs.

I can't tell you how many times I've been driving down the road barely able to see because I've been bawling over some country song on the radio.

So why did those songs move me so much and so quickly?

I decided to analyze them, and in analyzing them I think I've come up with some common denominators we can translate into writing. So yes, we can write to deliberately evoke emotion. And while we may not make every reader cry, we can certainly touch their hearts and deepen the impact of our books. And isn't that what we want to do?

In his wonderful book *Stein on Writing*, Sol Stein says, ". . . the fiction writer's primary job . . . is creating an emotional experience for the reader." E. L. Doctorow once wrote, "Good writing is supposed to evoke sensation in the reader, not the fact that it's raining, but the feeling of being rained upon."

Our readers ought to be so submerged in our stories that they feel the wind on their faces, smell the fresh-cut grass, and shudder at the ominous sound of distant footsteps in the empty house. They are not supposed to see the writer at work, so it is our job to be invisible —just like an orchestra conductor at work.

The Key to Evoking Emotion

As I prepared my class on evoking emotion, I realized that the task boiled down to one simple principle: in order to evoke emotion in a limited amount of time and space, *you must tap into the well of emotion that already exists in the reader.*

In 1992, when Alexandra Ripley's *Scarlett* was released, I was among the thousands of readers who couldn't wait to read the official sequel to *Gone with the Wind.* I began to read only a few minutes after the book arrived at my house, and within a few pages I was sobbing . . . because Mammy died.

Was I sobbing because Alexandra Ripley made Mammy seem so appealing and wonderful that I fell in love with her within the space of a few pages? With no disrespect intended for Ms. Ripley, no. I wept because I had fallen in love with Mammy in Margaret Mitchell's *Gone with the Wind.* Mammy and I had bonded in the many times I read GWTW, and when she died in *Scarlett*, I cried as though I had lost a real friend.

Alexandra Ripley didn't lay the emotional groundwork for my tears; Margaret Mitchell did. But Ms. Ripley was smart enough to tap into what Mitchell had established and keep me reading the rest of her book.

That is our task as writers. We have to keep our reader in mind and try to think of the emotional situations in their lives. How can we tap into those feelings and memories? To do this, we have to be aware of the culture our readers live in, and we have to be willing to lay bare our own emotional histories. I've had personal and family traumas of my own, and whenever a reader says, "I could tell you've been through something just like the story in your book," I know I've done my job.

This May be Unusual, But . . .

As much as I appreciate the writer's art, I also realize that a picture—especially a *moving* picture—is worth a thousand words. So I would like you to watch a few videos as you study this writing lesson. You can move on without watching the videos, of course, but you'll get much more out of this lesson if you participate fully—and that means sitting back and watching a few YouTube vids. (Of course, if you're reading the e-book version of this lesson and have access to wi-fi, this will be easy.)

Ready? We're about to get interactive.

If you haven't seen Beyonce's version of "Single Ladies," take a few seconds to look at this. You don't have to watch the entire thing. Just a couple of seconds will do, enough to get the general idea. (If the link doesn't work, search for *Beyonce Single Ladies* on youtube.com.)

http://www.youtube.com/watch?v=eREH27Zc7NY

Got the idea? Okay—now look at this parody of "Single Ladies." And *do* watch all of this one. (If the link doesn't work, search for *wrinkled ladies* on youtube.com.)

http://www.youtube.com/watch?v=NCvHgppVey4

What did you think? Did you smile? I love Anita Renfroe's version; I love the look, the moves, and that bit about growing wrinkles of our own . . .

Part of my laughter, of course, comes from the fact that I'm over fifty and I relate personally to everything Anita sang. In fact, at this stage of my life, I relate a lot more to Anita than to Beyonce. Maybe you do, too.

What, specifically, did we find funny about the wrinkled ladies?

First, it was a parody. Exactly like the Beyonce video, and yet nothing like it.

Second, humor always contains an element of truth, and the wrinkled ladies song was truth exaggerated. Yes, we're all going to wrinkle eventually, but we're not going to dance around in leotards in celebration of that fact.

Third, those ladies were celebrating themselves in an unusual way. We laughed, but we laughed *with* them, not *at* them. Most of us who are of a certain age were thinking we'd fit right in if we were dancing on that soundstage.

Fourth—humor usually contains an element of the unexpected. Most people try to hide their wrinkles and their no-longer-slim bodies, yet those women were celebrating every bulge and bump and asking for a "bowl of sugar, put some cream on it, don't be mad when you see your skin don't fit." I love it!

When considering how to put a program together, I have learned that laughter is the key that unlocks a listener's—or a reader's—heart. People have walls around their hearts, most folks tend to be guarded. If we want to reach inside their hearts and get through the wall, laughter is the way to do it.

So one of the first emotions you need to evoke in your book or story is humor. Find a place—preferably up front—where you can make your reader laugh or smile.

"But it's a murder mystery," you may be muttering. "People are dying all over the place."

People were dying all over the place in *Jaws*, too, but Spielberg remembered to add humor. Sheriff Brody was always joking—with a straight face—that they needed a bigger boat. That oft-repeated line broke the tension and made it possible for audiences to sit through the tension and the gore of violent shark attacks.

When I was planning to write my Fairlawn series, about a woman who inherits a funeral home, I knew I'd have to overcome a certain "ick" factor. So I gave my protagonist a full dose of the heebie jeebies and made her squeamish about the operations of a funeral home. This enabled me to ease my protagonist—and my reader— into the funeral industry, gently explaining why it's important, how the work is accomplished, and how it can be considered a ministry and not a gruesome job. By the end of the third book, Jennifer is a mortician herself.

I also made certain that for every grim story line, I had an equally humorous storyline. In one book a woman has a "Red Hat" funeral, complete with kazoos, and in another book a woman plans a fake funeral so she can lie in the coffin and hear what her friends really think about her.

Humor is important. So plan on including something to make your reader chuckle.

Maybe you need to add another character to your story, a small child or a quirky maiden aunt, who can be the focus of a humorous storyline. Or maybe you need to heighten your protagonist's sense of humor. The next time you read a book or watch a movie, look for the funny bits and notice where they are placed. They're present for a reason—to break the tension and make the reader/viewer smile.

Now we're going to look at a second video: "God Bless America," the arrangement I mentioned earlier. You'll probably be listening alone, so you're not likely to stand up and cheer, but see if you can determine the point where audiences always rose to their feet—and why. (If the link doesn't work, search for *Re'Generation: God Bless America* on youtube.com).

Here's the link:
   http://www.youtube.com/watch?v=LvRt6I6Doow

. . .

Did you watch all of the video? How did it move you? Let's analyze why.

We saw beautiful images of people and places we could all identify or identify *with*: small children, grandparents, little babies, nonconformist teens. We saw the central prairies, the rocky western coast, southern live oaks, and the rugged northeastern coasts. We saw Chinatown in D.C., several Washington memorials, quiet forests and high-tech highways. We had humor—adorable tiny ballerinas and a boy praying with his dog. We saw our men in military uniform and war memorials for those who did not come home alive. The tones of the images—majestic, cute, beautiful, pastoral—varied as well. Surely some of those images touched all of us in some way.

We also felt the appeal of patriotism. Those of us who love this country for its ideals felt a tug at our heartstrings—we *do* beg God to bless America, to forgive her failures and bless her for her attempts to do good. We were also moved by the beauty of a well-know and well-beloved song. "God Bless America" isn't our national anthem, but the song is a national favorite.

Those elements can translate into words, more or less. We can describe warriors and pioneers and community leaders. We can transport our characters to beautiful landscapes and historic monuments and fill them with the spirit of patriotism.

But let's look at the musical devices the song used to create an effects. First, the volume—sections of the song were *forte*, very loud, with singers at full volume and trumpets trumpeting. Other sections were *a capella* and actually spoken in whispers: the prayers of "God bless America."

Did you find the place where audiences always rose to their feet? The standing ovation always occurred near the end, as the key change led into a chorus of "America the Beautiful." That key change literally lifted people out of their chairs because they were carried along by music which moved *upward*.

Can we translate musical volume and key changes into written words? More on that topic later.

For now, let's look at another video. (If the link doesn't work, search for *Christian the Lion I will always love you* on youtube.com.)

http://www.youtube.com/watch?v=KCb64TjNZ54

I don't know about you, but I can be feeling as dry as a milk bucket under a bull until this video plays. Then the waterworks start and I can't stop them.

Part of this video's effectiveness, of course, lies in the song. There are several other vids about Christian the Lion on YouTube, and they're not nearly as effective because the song doesn't work as well as "I Will Always Love You." And we can't ignore that poignant pause—total silence for a couple of beats as the lion looks at the two men and then charges. Will he attack them? No—he hugs them! Our tension and nervous anticipation is rewarded many times over as the lion frolics and displays his obvious affection for the two men he knew as a cub.

We love this video for many reasons. First, it demonstrates that animals have memories and form real bonds with their humans. (Score one for the animal lovers!) Second, seeing real love and joy and delight uplifts the viewer. We want to rejoice with those who rejoice, so seeing this joyful reunion lifts our spirits. Third, we have a clear sense that we are seeing selfless love. Animals have no ulterior motives (or not in this case, anyway). The lion isn't being affectionate to get a treat. He's running toward the men because he's happy to see them and because he has bonded to them. Isn't that what love is?

As a Christian, I find this video moving for two additional reasons. It reminds me of the biblical promise that one day in the future, the lion will lay down with the lamb. Animals will no longer hunt and kill each other, and the natural fear they feel toward man will be erased.

And how can anyone who's familiar with C.S. Lewis's parables look at a lion and not think of Aslan, the powerful and loving lion who symbolizes Christ? This video not only comforts and delights me in the present, but it reminds me of the future and makes me homesick for heaven.

How can these things be translated into written words? Think about the themes—love, joy, selfless giving. We are moved when we see these ideals portrayed in scenes, whether they're in films or novels. As our society grows darker and more selfish, stories of strangers who sacrifice for another person grow more rare. I get teary-eyed when I read newspaper accounts of firemen who help free kittens from sewer drains, or businessmen who stop traffic so a mother duck and her babies can cross a highway. We *hunger* for stories about virtuous acts.

What do we see on TV? What genres are top-sellers in our book-stores? Crime stories, murder mysteries, horror films. We are surrounded by darkness in reality and our entertainment, so it's no wonder that our spirits lift when we encounter a rare moment of goodness.

I can hear some of you sputtering now. You don't want to write a saccharine story that's all sweetness and light. You want your books to feel real and gritty, populated by characters who face real problems.

That's fine. But remember the power of the positive moment. The darker your story world is, the brighter the light shining in it.

This next video is a fun family romp, but it teaches us a lot about what moves people. (If the link below doesn't work, search for *Rodney Atkins Watching You* on youtube.com).

http://www.youtube.com/watch?v=oqYUns2YQik

I particularly like this video because it's upbeat—proving that you can elicit emotion without getting maudlin about it. What did you find moving?

The first thing I notice is the simple power of story. This is a complete story with a beginning, middle, and ending. The dad sees his kid do something, realizes that the child is imitating what he's seen Daddy do, and then the father prays to ask for help and forgiveness. Later that night, when the little buckaroo prays on his own, Dad realizes that maybe he's doing some things right.

Delightful lesson learned in a positive way, and a welcome reminder that our children are always watching us.

Did you notice the use of humor? The video is filled with images to make people smile—the boy and his dad clowning around on the porch, the kid making faces at the camera, the boy wagging his finger as the father does the same thing to his child. Humor, right at the start and throughout the video.

How did the video make this lesson pertain to almost every adult who watches it? I saw dozens of items common to most American homes: the wall marked with lines to indicate a child's growth, pictures held up by magnets on the refrigerator door, the mention of happy meals and chicken nuggets. How many of us have or have had those things in our homes? The sight of these common elements helps the viewer tap into his or her own emotional well, so the video grabs us almost immediately.

And how many of us who are parents haven't had a moment when we regretted saying or doing something in front of our child? The songwriter tapped into something else we've all experienced: parental guilt. We know what we ought to do, but so many times we fall short. We want to be good parents, but we're human and we make mistakes. I believe every parent has felt the pang of remorse at least once in his parenting career. The feeling is particularly acute when it's our child who points out our mistake, as in this video.

But perhaps the most moving force in this short clip is the simple portrayal of the love between a father and his son. We see love in their hugs, smiles, and joking around. And if we have felt that kind of love at any point in our lives, we will look back, remember, and feel the same thing. And that's a beautiful illustration of how the songwriter evoked emotion by tapping into the viewer's own emotional well.

One more video, and then we'll get to the application of these insights. If the link below doesn't work, search for *Brad Paisley He Didn't Have to Be* on youtube.com.

You might want to have a couple of tissues handy.

http://www.youtube.com/watch?v=BjO1F6oCab8

Excuse me while I blow my nose. There. That particular video gets me every time. Why?

Once again, we're told a story with a beginning, middle, and end. Unfortunately, it's a familiar story about a fatherless boy who feels abandoned—that is, until a wonderful man falls in love with his mother and wants to include him in the new family. The boy moves from abandonment to acceptance, and once again we rejoice in a bright moment of goodness in a sad situation.

I particularly appreciate that love is beautifully depicted without once being mentioned. He doesn't sing about love, love, love, but you see it in every frame of the film and every line of the song. Talk about showing and not telling!

In quick clips we see photos of the family together, the step-dad teaching the boy how to throw and hit a ball and how to ride a bike, and we glimpse all the memories of growing up with a loving dad. Those of us who had similar childhoods will be moved by the memory of our fathers, and those who didn't have a loving father may feel a longing for something they never had.

I think all parents remember how helpless and insecure we felt when someone placed a new baby into our arms. We had no idea what the future would hold, and somewhere in the back of our minds we may have worried that we would mess up this tiny human being. We felt vulnerable and helpless to a degree, yet this man looks to the man standing beside him—the man who didn't have to be his father, but chose to be.

. . .

Keep Your Reader in Mind

A few years ago I taught a writing course at Taylor University. When I taught this material, I showed the same videos I've featured here . . . and noticed something. A few of my students were visibly moved at the Christian the Lion clip, but few of them had any emotional reaction to the later videos.

Why? I had to smile when the answer struck me. Most of them were young people in their late teens or early twenties, and they'd had pets, so they related to the love between the lion and the two Englishmen. But only a couple of the older students were parents, so the majority of them simply watched the family-centered videos and smiled.

They had no emotional memories of having a baby . . . raising a child . . . or making a mistake as a parent. I learned a lesson in that class—when writing an emotional scene, keep the emotional experiences of your most likely reader firmly in mind.

We've Identified the Elements—How Do They Translate to Writing?

How can we create beautiful music in our written scenes? How can we create dramatic, poignant pauses like the one in "Christian the Lion?"

How do we raise and lower the volume of a scene? How do we "change keys" or move from a full orchestra to a whisper?

How do we portray emotion without getting sappy about it? How do we portray a noble value like love, self-sacrifice, loyalty, joy, or goodness in a way that's believable and real?

Most important, how do we identify and tap into the well of emotion within our readers?

(When I teach this lesson at workshops, I analyze passages from other novelists, but here I'll use excerpts from my own work so I won't have to deal with copyright and permissions issues. I hope you will excuse what must look like flagrant self-promotion.)

My novel, *Unspoken*, features a protagonist, Glee, and my favorite character: Sema, a gorilla. Glee has raised Sema since the gorilla's infancy and considers the animal her child. Furthermore, Glee has taught Sema sign language, so the gorilla communicates with her. Sema has a personality all her own—she loves Glee, she hates all species of cats, and she is not above name-calling when the mood suits her.

Not only is Sema occasionally funny (Stinky nut! Is one of her favorite exclamations), but I inserted humor into the book after a particularly tense scene where Sema drowns in the moat around the zoo's gorilla enclosure and is then resuscitated. After her near death experience, Sema begins to sign about a "shiny man" she sees. Not seeing any "shiny man," Glee is convinced that Sema suffered brain damage while she was deprived of oxygen, so she and a friend sneak Sema out of the zoo and into a clinic for an MRI.

Later, Glee reluctantly leads Sema to a public pavilion where she is to "perform" for a group of visitors to the zoo. I have inserted brackets to make note of elements that heighten the emotion. (You might want to read this twice, ignoring the bracketed information the first time, and studying it the second.)

As soon as we moved from the exit and into the sun, Sema straightened and walked bipedally, **slipping her hand into mine. [Any parent who has ever walked hand in hand with her child will identify with this.]** The gesture caught me by surprise—as eager as she was, I had expected her to practically pull me down the path. But perhaps this excursion frightened her—after all, the last time she ventured into the depths of the zoo, she'd been drowning.

We strolled beneath the sprawling limbs of a live oak, lacy with gilded spring leaves. The asphalt path baked in a golden sunshine that hinted of a warmer afternoon to come. **[Notice that the scene begins on a quiet note, with leisurely descriptive sentences.]**

On Sunday mornings, when the only individuals stirring were khaki-clothed employees and animals, Thousand Oaks seemed a welcoming place. Whenever Sema saw something interesting, she stopped on the path and sank to a squatting position as her hands flew in various questions.

Her curiosity didn't surprise me. Though she had glimpsed all sorts of situations through television and travel in my car, she had never seen so many wheeled refreshment stands, souvenir kiosks, and symbols. A sign stood at each intersection along our path, and cartoon images of animals adorned each wooden marker. Sema wanted to know about every species. **[Again, any parent who has ever patiently answered their child's questions will identify.]**

She pointed to a picture of a pink flamingo. *Lip stick bird?*

I laughed. "He is the color of lipstick, isn't he? And he has long legs. He's called—" I hesitated, not knowing the sign for *flamingo.* "Well, we'll find the sign later."

She pointed to a picture of a wombat, one of the most popular animals in the Australian Outback exhibit. *Fur pig?* **[Little bits of humor are inserted here as preparation for the drama that lies ahead.]**

"Um, I think that's a . . ." I paused to think of a sign, then combined a *W* with the sign for *pig*, hand beneath the chin with flapping fingers. "Wombat." Any marsupial expert would chastise me for implying that wombats and pigs were related, but Sema had made the connection, not me.

The wind picked up, sending a wave of oak leaves toward us with a sound like scattering seashells. **[The wind is picking up—mood music to indicate the approach of something ominous. Similar to a faster tempo in music.]** I glanced at the sky, knowing that spring winds often brought sudden showers. A cloudbank had risen behind the crest of the oak behind us and the air had become thick and damp. **[More mood music to establish an increasingly threatening atmosphere despite the light conversation they're having.]**

"Come on, sweetie, we need to move on. Remember my surprise?

We're almost there." **[Glee's use of endearments reminds readers of their children.]**

Glee give toy?

"Not a toy, my girl, something else. I'll explain after we look at a few books."

Obediently, Sema took my outstretched hand. We continued our steady walk along the path that led to the amphitheater where local high school bands played on Saturday afternoons and the community college chorale sang on summer nights. How many guests would the amphitheater hold, two hundred? Since Matthews had insisted on this location, he must be expecting a crowd.

I looked around. In the distance, a custodian pushed a wheeled garbage can toward one of the brick restrooms while a hungry sea gull hovered above the man's head, probably hoping for a scrap. The custodian hadn't noticed us, and I didn't want to attract his attention. Better to get Sema calmly situated backstage before anyone else began to mill about.

Aware of the passing time, I tugged on Sema's arm, urging her forward. She walked slowly, rocking on her hips, her head swiveling to check out sights and sounds she'd never had an opportunity to investigate. A flock of sparrows moved as one over our heads, then looped back to settle on the branches of an oak ahead of us.

"Look there." I pointed toward the birds. "All those little friends have come to say hello."

Without warning, the stillness of the setting shivered into bits, the echoes of a siren scattering the sparrows. Sema's fingers tightened around mine as I looked around. What was this, a fire drill? **[Like any alarmed parent, Glee is thinking of her charge—and the scattering sparrows reinforce the idea that she needs to flee.]**

I searched the sky and saw no signs of smoke, but the wail continued, lancing the silence, drilling straight into my head. "Come on, Sema." I tugged her toward the amphitheater. "We need to hurry."

She jerked her hand from mine. Amazed at this unexpected display of rebellion, **[another phrase that will remind parents of a similar situation in their lives]** I turned, a rebuke on my tongue, and saw the white tiger crouching beside an overturned garbage can no more than twenty feet away. The cat lay flat against the asphalt, his hindquarters twitching, his golden eyes focused on us. Sema uttered no sound at all, but the rank odor of fear rose from her glands and invaded my nostrils. **[Sensory details—in this case, the sense of smell—heightens emotional involvement in the scene.]**

What should we do? Some rational part of my brain, the small portion not occupied with immediate panic, told me to face the creature and wave my arms in an effort to make myself look bigger and more intimidating, but who could listen to reason when faced with a man-eater? Instinct screamed *run!*, but I couldn't run. I had to think of Sema, whose African cousins occasionally faced leopards. According to gorilla researchers, *sometimes* the gorilla won the encounter—

[Long run-on sentences stretch out the story moment and give us access to Glee's frantic thoughts. Anyone who has ever been in a similar frightening situation will relate to this.]

But tigers were four times heavier and stronger than leopards, and Sema had not been reared in the wild. Neither did she like cats, not even Nana's calico.

"Sema." I struggled to push words past the lump of ice in my throat. "Sweetie, don't move." **[Sensory detail—cold ice in her throat, coupled with another endearment for Sema.]**

The wind pushed at my hair, bringing with it the sound of cars on the highway. Hard to believe civilization and salvation lay a few feet away and we were standing in one of the nation's most cosmopolitan areas— **[When faced with panic, some part of the brain does keep ticking off odd little details . . .]**

The tiger's whiskers quivered with the ghost of a growl. The low sound scraped across my nerves, but as long as he didn't charge, we might be able to escape. **[More mood music. The sound**

scraping across her nerves could well be the scrape of a bow across a cello . . .}

I glanced toward the restroom, where the custodian had disappeared. If I screamed, he would come running. He carried a radio, all the maintenance crew did, and he would call for help. In the worst case scenario, I might have to wrestle with the tiger, but if I screamed loud enough, the animal might run away.

"Sema," I strengthened my voice and slipped the loop of her leash from my wrist, "see the big tree ahead of us? I want you to run to the tree. Run as fast as you can, okay? Climb up in the tree and don't come down until you see Brad."

I wasn't sure she understood until she released my hand. I looked down, grateful that my words had taken hold, but Sema only lifted her arms and pulled the bent fingers of both hands across her face. In a barely comprehendible flash I realized she was signing *tiger*. But this wasn't the cuddly tiger of her Winnie the Pooh book; this one could kill us. **{Any parent or child who has read Winnie the Pool will relate.}**

I ignored her sign. "Ready to run, Sema? Okay—*go!*"

The tiger charged at the sound of my shout. I pushed at Sema's shoulder, thinking she would run to the tree while I waved my arms and drew the cat's attention, but Sema, my brave girl, ran straight toward the beast. **{*My brave girl*—making Sema human makes her seem like the reader's daughter as well.}**

I froze as terror lodged in my throat, making it impossible to utter another cry. The heavy air filled with the shrill sounds of screams and snarls as the tiger took Sema down. My sweet girl exhibited traits I'd never seen in her, flashing her canines as she roared. The powerful stink of fear blew over me as the two combatants rolled on the thin grass, teeth flashing, claws ripping, blood flowing. **{This scene began on a quiet note, but the crescendo has brought us to a loud battle. Notice the insertion of smells, sounds, and sights.}**

The world had shrunk to a black and white blur when I heard sharp sounds, one shot followed by another. The tiger roared again, then collapsed. Sema rose unsteadily to a standing position, looked at me, then folded gently at the knees and toppled backward. **[The loud, frantic fight is over, interrupted by the crack of a gun. And suddenly . . . silence.]**

Both animals lay on the grass beside the path. The tiger's side rose and fell in one last shudder. Sema lay flat, her eyes wide, her gaze focused on the spreading limbs of the treetop canopy overhead. **[We are quiet again, more references to the peaceful trees that were mentioned at the beginning of the scene. But the situation has changed.]**

"Sema!" I sank to the ground and frantically ran my hands over her torso. **[Every parent who has ever had a child suffer injury will remember this feeling.]** Had she been shot, too? My palm came away wet and red when I brushed her chest; gouts of blood pumped from a gash on her neck. She might have wounds on her back as well, but I didn't want to move her until help arrived.

"Help!" I couldn't seem to draw in enough air to push a shout out of my throat. "Could someone please help me?" **[When the worst happens, life seems to stop.]**

From somewhere to my right a pair of men ran forward, but I dared not take my eyes off Sema for more than an instant. Her hands rose as though she wanted to say something, but I shook my head.

"Be still, Sema, until help comes. Someone will be here in a minute. You know how I've always taught you to be patient?" My voice cracked. "You need to be patient now." **[Note the physical details—voice cracking, pretending to be brave and confident.]**

Love shone in her eyes as her face settled into lines of content-ment. Such emotions are difficult for humans to falsify; I now believe it is impossible for animals to lie about love.

Her hands rose again. *Sema go.*

"Sure, sweetie, we're going home in a few days. We'll be back in the trailer before you know it, and I'm going to take care of you until you feel better. We'll be able to read and play and watch movies—"

Shiny man say . . . her hands faltered . . . *Sema go now.*

"No, Sema, not now, don't do this. You don't have to go anywhere. You stay with me, stay here, so I can take care of you. Don't you even think about leaving, girlie, because Brad's going to help me take care of you and I know you like Brad. Together we're going to make sure nothing like this ever happens again—" **[Glee's sentences grow choppier as her panic rises. She's rambling and she knows it, but she'll do or say anything to stave off what she fears most.]**

Sema happy. Sema love.

Her head lolled to the right and the spark of life slipped from her eyes. Emptiness rushed in to fill her face and I didn't need a doctor to tell me her heart had stopped. **[More physical details.]**

Swallowing the sob that rose in my throat, I pulled her closer, pillowing her head in my lap. In that moment I understood the mystifying behavior of elephants and gorillas that lose loved ones—I wanted to pound on her chest, slap the dullness from her eyes, do anything I could to catch the spirit of life and force it back into her body.

But it had gone. I sat on the grass, numb to everything, as color ran out of the world and the clouds began to weep. **[The scene ends on another quiet note, accompanied by the "mood music" of a quiet sky weeping in consolation.]**

Do you see how you can cobble the things we've discovered into a scene? You can vary the volume by moving from slow-paced passages to faster-paced events. You can change the tempo by varying sentence and word length. You can add mood music to enhance whatever you're describing. And, perhaps most important, you can tap into your reader's emotional memories by writing about things they've thought, said, and done.

Did you notice that Glee did not weep in the scene above? The clouds did, but nowhere did I mention Glee weeping. I could have written *I sat on the grass and sobbed,* but that would have been too "on the nose." Much better to pull back and let the world weep for Glee and Sema.

An actor friend of mine once explained a dramatic trick that works well in fiction. "Sometimes," he said, "an actor will noticeably choke back tears . . . and the audience will feel compelled to supply the emotion the actor is repressing." So if you want your reader to feel grief or hilarity or anger, have your character struggle to rein in his grief or his laughter or his urge to knock someone's block off. The reader will then feel the emotion your character is struggling to restrain. In the scene above, Glee does not weep, but the clouds do, and so will the reader . . . I hope.

Here's another scene, this one from *The Fine Art of Insincerity*, featuring another emotion revealed only through interior monologue. I've condensed it a bit.

There's a baby.

My husband is having a baby. With another woman. A difficult situation involving one interloper has become an impossible situation involving two. **[Notice the short sentences and sentence fragments. She is angry, so long, flowing sentences wouldn't have matched her mindset.]**

Michael's latest confession has left me anxious and bewildered, too agitated to sleep. I'm still awake when I finally hear the front door close, followed by the roar of a car engine and the pop of tires over gravel. I'd heard voices from downstairs, so one of my sisters must have talked to Michael before he left. I can't imagine what was said. **[Notice the physical details—specific sounds. When a scene is mostly internal, you need external details to keep it anchored.]**

I hope he thinks about what he's done to our family on the drive home.

Still . . . in the solitude of my room I have to admit I had hoped Michael would say something that would help me make sense of this situation. **[Now she's calming down, so the sentences**

lengthen and begin to flow.] At first I'd clung to the hope that he'd tell me the woman was going through a divorce of her own, so he'd been a friend and counselor, nothing more. But he and this woman have created a baby . . . and, knowing Michael, he will want to do the best thing for all concerned. Which leaves me to do . . . what, exactly? **[Notice the use of ellipses. These create a pause in the flow of interior monologue, allowing her comments to feel more natural and thoughtful.]**

I lie in the darkness, staring at the moonlit walls while my imagination cobbles together possible outcomes: obviously, I could divorce him, release him to marry his lover and be a father to her child. I would be left alone and our sons would lose a lot of respect for their father. They're old enough to understand what Michael did, and they might not want to forgive him. **[Clearly, this woman is more thinker than feeler, but she's still feeling plenty. But the practical side of her nature is planning for the future. Your reader has probably had nights where she lay awake in bed and thought about her marriage or her children. Anyone who has ever passed a sleepless night will relate to this.]**

. . . A blush burns my cheek. How tawdry it all is! The story will spread around the college, our neighborhood, our church. People who love Michael might hear the rumor and grant him the benefit of the doubt, but the baby will be proof of his guilt. And as our friends whisper over dinner tables and cell phones, people will speculate about what I might have done to drive him away. Did I neglect him? Was I frigid or overbearing? People who know me will assume it's all my fault, that my organization and list-making drove bookish Michael straight into another woman's arms. What they don't know is that Michael *appreciates* my organization skills—they're responsible for keeping our family stable.

I don't think I did anything to drive Michael away, but my opinion doesn't matter. People will talk. The only way I can preserve my reputation is to remain steady and behave as normally as possible. Since I didn't cheat, why should I suffer?

Nothing about this is fair.

Perhaps I shouldn't surrender the high ground. Michael's the one who strayed, so he should be the one to leave the house. But when should he leave? If I tell him to leave until we settle the situation, where will he go if not to the other woman? And once he's ensconced in her house or apartment, how am I to get him back . . . if I *want* him back? Do I? Do I want him at all?

Right now I can't imagine ever wanting him again. My brain, which has always benefited from a fertile imagination, is supplying me with all sorts of unpleasant mental images: Michael walking with a leggy young professor on campus, driving her home in his car, entering her apartment, falling into her bed. It takes no effort to imagine him in her arms, skin against skin, to hear the endearments he might have whispered in her ear. **[What wronged wife hasn't imagined the physical details of an affair? And rare is the reader who doesn't care what people think.]**

I grit my teeth and roll over to face the wall, dropping the curtain on my dark visions. My husband has been with another woman. Why? Was I not enough for him? Am I no longer attractive? I'm not the waif he married, but I've borne him two children. I've stood by Michael's side for twenty-seven years, fretting with him over employment cuts at the college and family financial crises. I've stayed up with him while we struggled to figure out how we were going to finance two boys in college. I've spent a half dozen nights in a hospital easy chair, watching over Michael's son as he recovered from an emergency appendectomy. I've put miles on this body for Michael and his children, and I've done my best to hold back the ravages of time. **[What woman hasn't doubted her beauty? We may pretend that we don't care about aging, but we do. Any woman over forty will relate to Ginger's thoughts.]**

Obviously, I didn't do enough. I faced a competitor I didn't even know existed, but now she's standing between me and my husband, between Michael and our sons. She's bringing a new life into the world, a life Michael will be responsible for—

I groan at the thought of adding child support payments to an already-stretched budget. And college! And orthodontia and education expenses and a regular allowance—all the things children want and need. If Michael sets up his own place, he will not only have to pay for an apartment and utilities, but he will have to pay child support to the other woman. He might be forced to move into her apartment simply for financial reasons.

Yet the alternative is inconceivable. How can I stay with a man who betrayed me? Whose actions will tell the world that I didn't satisfy his needs? Staying with Michael might mean I would be forced to endure this woman's child in my home on weekends, summers, and alternate holidays. I would have to open my heart and life to the child of a woman who stole what belonged to me, the right to enjoy my husband's body. The right to occupy first priority in his heart. **[The intact, two-parent family is no longer the status quo in America. So most readers will relate to these questions about step-parenting.]**

. . . I bury my face in my pillow as a rush of angry tears bubbles up from an untapped well within me. I wish I could cry prettily, but I have never been able to manage it. Hollywood actresses seem to weep effortlessly—tears flow from their mascaraed eyes and roll down perfectly sculpted cheeks. My tears spurt like geysers, accompanied by a red nose, a stuffy head, and labored breathing. In seconds I am such a sniffling, blubbering mess that I have to employ a dozen tissues to keep my airways clear. **[Again, every woman in the world will relate to this. Yes, she's crying and I'm describing it, but so realistically that every female reader understands. Not a whiff of sentimentality here.]**

Finally I fall back onto the bed, exhausted. I still don't have any answers, but at least I don't have to handle the shock of this discovery at home. Few people know me on St. Simons, so no one will care if I burst into tears in the middle of Fish Fever Lane or the Harris Teeter grocery store. Here I don't have to face my neighbors, my coworkers at church, or my friends. Here I won't have to face Michael . . . and I'll be able to process my thoughts without interference.

. . . As I close my eyes, a new thought strikes: for twenty-seven years, Michael and I have stopped what we were doing and headed to bed at eleven o'clock. I have drifted off to sleep with him by my side.

If he's gone . . . who's going to remind me to go to bed? **[A thought shared by every divorced woman and widow. And notice the emotional shift—from angry and short in the beginning, to this self-pitying whisper.]**

One more scene, and this one is brief. From my book *The Novelist,* about a woman who's, well, a novelist. She is struggling with her young adult son, and in one scene she flashes back to a time when he was learning to walk:

When Zack was fourteen months old, he fell and hit his chin on the edge of a chair. I picked him up and wiped him off, but the sight of gaping flesh made me wince. I knew he'd need stitches. **[Every parent with a son will relate to this—it's a common accident with rambunctious little boys.]**

I drove carefully to the emergency room, then held my baby on my lap as a doctor confirmed my suspicions. "Not a big deal," the physician told me. "Two stitches will do the trick." **[Notice the low "volume" of this scene. Despite the accident, everything is quiet and calm.]**

"Will it, you know, leave a scar?"

The doctor smiled. "Think of it as a badge of boyhood. I'll bet seventy percent of the men in this building have a similar scar on their chins. It's just one of those things." **[The reader is agreeing.]**

Zack, who had calmed by that time, seemed more intent on studying the stethoscope around the doctor's neck than in listening to this positive prognosis. **[A visual image all mothers of babies will remember from their own lives.]**

The nurse lifted Zack from my lap. He began to cry, stiffening his little body and reaching for me as the nurse wrestled him onto a papoose board. I stood and folded my arms, every nerve tensing as they restrained my son's arms and legs with wide Velcro bands. **[Many readers will recognize this sight or this helpless and frustrated feeling. Notice the folded arms—she has erected a wall between herself and what's happening on the exam table.]**

I bit my lip as my chin quivered. I've never been tied down like that, but I could imagine how helpless my little guy was feeling. The boy only had about ten words in his vocabulary, so he couldn't even verbalize his fears. **[Mom wants to cry, but doesn't dare. The audience supplies the missing emotion and concern.]**

I couldn't watch. I turned my head, studying a table loaded with medical instruments, as Zack shifted from screams to frenzied shrieks of the one word he had always used to summon help: "Mama! Ma-ma! Ma-ma!" **[Every mom or dad will relate to this frustrated reaction to the scream of a frightened child in pain. The volume has increased as well—from soft to screaming loud.]**

One book I found especially helpful when learning how to portray emotions was Ann Hood's *Creating Character Emotions*. The most important thing I learned while reading Hood's book is that emotions are not one-dimensional—strong feelings are almost always a blend of feelings. Anger, for instance, can be a blend of shock, anger, reproach, and helplessness. Shame can combine guilt, disgrace, embarrassment, and unworthiness. So if your character is in love, he may display signs of jealousy, sorrow, hope, desire, lust, fear, and even hate . . . sometimes in rapid succession.

Try to avoid having a character *tell* us what he's feeling—show us what he's feeling instead. We can't use photographs or drawings, but we have an entire dictionary of lovely words at our disposal, so go to it.

Body Language

I'm a sucker for body language books. Not only does a knowledge of body language allow me to entertain myself at parties, but it's an indispensable tool when I write.

In communication, only 7 percent of understanding derives from what is actually spoken. Thirty-eight percent comes from tone of voice, and a whopping 55 percent comes from the silent speech signals otherwise known as body language.

You should get a book on basic body language and memorize a few poses. Most you will translate instinctively. For instance, someone who stands with their arms folded across their chest is actually erecting a wall between himself and the outside world. Arms folded plus fists clenched may signify anger behind the wall.

One arm folded and one arm hanging down is what I consider the typical "middle school" pose. The person wants to be relaxed and accepted, but the other arm is in a defensive position just in case. At a glance, this person looks awkward and unsure.

Men who stand with their feet apart and thumbs tucked into belt or waistband, fingers pointing toward the crotch—well, if you think about it, that posture is self-explanatory. It's what I think of as *cowboy cocky*.

A woman who plays with her hair in the presence of a man is literally preening—she's attracted to the man. If she sits on the sofa with a foot tucked beneath her, her bent knee will most likely be pointed toward the man who has piqued her interest. If she kicks off her shoe while in this pose, well, she's *definitely* telegraphing her attraction to him.

A person who's insecure about a certain body part may touch it several times in the course of a situation—a bald man may rub his head, for example. A liar may tug on his ear or rub his nose. He may avoid direct eye contact, but other liars can look anyone in the eye and utter the boldest fabrications imaginable.

A boss who comes out from behind his desk and sits on the edge to look down at his employee may be subtly pointing out that he is *over* the employee. That he's a "bigger" man. Or woman, as the case may be.

The man or woman who touches your arm while you're talking is asking to cut into the conversation. You may be talking too much.

Body language is not an exact science—a girl may have her arms folded because she's cold—but it's useful to writers because if you use it in your dialogue and scenes, the reader will subconsciously pick up on these cues. So don't add body language merely as beats to break up extended passages of dialogue; make them count. Like this:

Sylvia heard laughter from the next room. She had welcomed Charles and Melanie ten minutes before, and both said their respective spouses were on the way. "Harry always has to work late," Melanie had said, her lower lip protruding as she walked toward the living room, "but he'll make it."

Sylvia put three glasses of iced tea on a tray and lifted it, then paused beneath the plastered archway. Charles and Melanie were both sitting on the sofa, but Charles was leaning away from Mel. Melanie had turned toward him, one elbow on the back of the sofa, the other playing with strands of her long blonde hair. She flipped her hair over her shoulder and leaned toward Charles, forcing him to slant so far over the sofa's arm that Sylvia feared he might fall.

"Come on, Charlie," Melanie purred, apparently oblivious to Sylvia's presence. "Just give me your hand. I want to look at your life-line, that's all."

Sylvia snorted beneath her breath. Poor old Harry couldn't arrive soon enough.

Sentiment versus Sentimentality

When a poem, song, or book is described as *sentimental*, it's not a compliment. The word usually describes something that goes after an emotional reaction without subtlety or finesse. The writer takes shortcuts and resorts to clichéd images. My dictionary says that a sentimental piece of literature, music, or art is "self-indulgent."

Some novelists are known for writing sentimental work. Their books can make me cry, too, but I hate myself for doing it. Shortcuts are fine if you only have three minutes for a music video, but novelists have no time constraint. We have hundreds of pages in which to establish genuine emotional content and context, so we have no reason to opt for sentimental shorthand.

For example: If you wanted to show how deeply a man loves his wife, what would you have him do? The lazy writer would have him bring home (I bet you've already supplied the answer) . . . a dozen red roses.

Fine, but how cliché is that?

In my book *The Fine Art of Insincerity*, the husband brings his wife a dozen red roses, but I turned the cliché on its head. Later my protagonist learns her husband is having a baby with another woman. She tells us:

He has showered me with red roses . . . and every petal was a lie.

In your book, if you want to show how much a harried husband loves his wife, skip the roses and search for something unusual in the characters' backstory.

For instance, let's say Tom and Cathy have been married thirty years. They're like most long-married couples: comfortable with each other, but not exactly passionate. In an early chapter plant a brief mention of Cathy's childhood, months of which were spent on Clearwater Beach with her grandmother. Later have her reminisce about those sunny days and how much she loved that beach. Still later, have her find a picture of herself and her grandmother sitting in the sand with a beach bucket and shovel. Have Cathy brush away a tear while Tom silently looks on.

Then Cathy discovers a lump—and learns that she has breast cancer. Despite Tom's protests, she worries that he won't find her desirable any more. She is no longer young, she's put on a few pounds, and all day Tom is surrounded by young and pretty women at the Honda dealership where he works.

Later, when she awakens from a successful mastectomy, have Tom *not* be by her side. How does she react? With despair? Anger? Grief? Does his absence confirm her fears about no longer being desirable and beautiful?

But then Tom rushes in with a big bag in his hand. When she asks what he's carrying, he sheepishly pulls out the photo of her and Grandma, now freshly restored. He sets it on the hospital bed table, then creates a tableau of plastic beach bucket, shovel, and a small plastic bag of white sand, tied at the top with a ribbon stamped *Wish you could be in Clearwater Beach.*

Clearly, the man has gone to great lengths to make her happy.

Cathy struggles to restrain her tears, but she reaches out to him and he gently takes her in his arms.

That's how you depict love. And if you want to practice what you're learning here, choose a scene from the above storyline and write it up—perhaps the scene where Cathy learns that her breast lump was a malignant cancer. Try to incorporate as many emotion-evoking methods as you can.

How'd you do?

In Summation

Use your characters' qualities and histories to create three-dimensional scenes, and write with your readers' emotions and memories in mind.

Establishing honest sentiment is a lot harder than tossing in a dash of clichéd sentimentality, but if you are writing the Tom and

Cathy story, your reader will never look at a plastic beach bucket without thinking of your characters.

Never go for the obvious. Work hard to think of something unexpected.

Not everyone cries as easily as I do, but it never hurts to weep while you write. Robert Frost said, "No tears in the writer, no tears in the reader. No surprise in the writer, no surprise in the reader."

Dig deep into *your* emotional well when you write. Call up the emotions you felt when you got married, when your first child was born, when you lost your job, when you were betrayed, when you lost someone you loved.

Once you've called up those feelings, don't just write, "I felt sad. Really sad." Instead, depict your sadness in a fresh way, using language that's sharp and clear and clean.

Look for metaphors that illustrate how something feels through comparison: An empty house paired with a death in the family. A gap in the line of Christmas stockings on the mantle paired with an estranged son no one ever mentions. A skittish stray dog paired with a foster child who has been abused.

If you feel emotion as you write, your reader will, too.

The average person might find this odd, but every time tragedy strikes my family, I find my fingers itching for paper and pen even as my brain tries to cope with the situation. I want to write down everything I'm feeling, every single emotion, because some day I will use it. I want to record concrete details—what things looked and smelled like, how my stomach turned over, or how my fingers tingled as a rush of adrenaline ebbed away.

As a firm believer in the providence of God, I believe everything happens for a reason. And because I'm a writer, everything is fodder for my life in pages.

So start keeping a journal. You can write in it every day if you like, but I'd rather you reach for it when you're feeling great emotions. Record those impressions, feelings, insights, and physical reactions. One day you will use them.

Are you ready? If you've read the **Writing Lessons from the**

Front in order, you should have a skeleton for your plot, a cast of terrific characters, a point of view established, and a plan for revising your manuscript. Now, during revision, you will be able to make sure your scenes evoke the emotion you want the reader to experience. I hope you're willing to do this important work . . . because that's the entire purpose of an novel.

Remember what Sol Stein said? The novelist's primary job is to *create an emotional experience for the reader.*

I've created a checklist to help you make sure you use every tool at your disposal. Feel free to copy it for your own use but please don't mass produce and pass it out at conferences and meetings.

These books are brief for a reason, you know—I don't want you to spend most of your time reading how-to books. I want you to spend most of your time writing, Put what you've learned into practice. *That's* the best way to improve.

So go ahead—get back to work on your manuscript and make it the best it can be. The world is waiting to laugh and cry with your characters.

EVOKING EMOTION EXERCISES

1. WRITE THE FOLLOWING THREE SCENES:

Scene A: A teenage girl says goodbye to her boyfriend and goes into the house. A moment later she answers the door—her boyfriend is there, and he tells her he has just run over her beloved dog.

Scene B: A mother receives a telegram telling her that her son has just been killed in a training exercise at Fort Brag.

Scene C: A young girl who has stayed up late every night for a week to finish her science fair project stands by her display and hears that the principal's daughter has just won first prize at the event.

Now evaluate your scenes:

1. Have you written lots of sensory details in your scenes? Things your character sees, smells, feels, hears, and/or tastes?

2. Have you made certain to fully develop your protagonist's emotional reactions?

3. Have you reached for clichéd symbols or phrases? Or have you taken the time to imbue an object or someone's words with great meaning?

4. Have you kept in mind that many emotions are mixed with other emotions? What is the chief emotion your character feels in each scene? _____ What other feelings are mixed with this one? _____

5. What sort of personal emotional memories will your reader think of when he or she reads this scene? What stage of life is your likely reader in? Childhood? Young adulthood? Young parent? Middle aged parent? Senior adult? Given your reader's probable life experiences, how can you write or edit this scene to better tap into your reader's emotional memory? What images can you include? What sounds? Smells? Sensations?

6. What is present in the scene (landscape, weather, furnishings, background noise) that could provide "mood music" in the background of this scene?

7. How does the volume of this scene change? If this is a "loud" scene, would it be more effective if you brought the volume down to a whisper? How can you do that?

Does the scene start softly and end with a bang? Does it start soft, become loud, and return to a quiet ending? If it were a musical piece, what sort of piece would it be?

Is the scene all on one level? Find a way to either ratchet up the volume or tone it down as the scene draws to a close.

8. How does dialogue enhance the emotional impact of this scene? Should your characters say more or less? Should their voices crack with grief or laughter? Should they be direct, or should they take pains to talk about everything but the one topic uppermost in their minds?

Is their body language appropriate for what they are thinking and feeling in this scene? What are they communicating through their body language?

9. Could memories enhance the emotional impact of this scene? Could your protagonist or point of view character have a memory flash through his mind? (But try to avoid flashbacks in the first chapters of the book. That's where you want to focus on moving forward.)

10. Who will be the most emotionally affected by this scene? To whom is the reader most closely bonded? Is this the best point of view character for this scene? Would the scene be more or less

moving if events were recorded from another character's perspective?

Chapter Six

PLANS AND PROCESSES TO GET YOUR BOOK WRITTEN

I'VE ALWAYS FELT THAT BEING A WRITER IS ANALOGOUS TO BEING A builder. A builder must know how to use the right tool at the right place in the right way, and he must know how to read and follow a blueprint. If he can do those things well, he can build anything from a doghouse to a Victorian mansion.

If a writer knows how to use the right tool at the right place in the right way, and if he knows how to read and follow the "blueprint" of every genre, he can write anything from a picture book to an epic novel.

I've been a professional writer for over thirty years, and I've written just about everything, including picture books and catalog copy and novels and collaborations and biographies and poetry and how-to books. I've always struggled to do my best, and I learned along the way.

You can, too.

This book will cover areas and concepts you should consider before, during, and after the writing. This lesson details the work a writer should do *away* from his or her manuscript—conceptualizing, identifying the genre, research, scheduling, drafting, critiquing, and publishing. So whether you want to write nonfiction or fiction, you should find something of value within these pages.

. . .

Nonfiction

Nonfiction is a broad umbrella that covers many different types
of books, but the chief goal of nonfiction writers always seems to be
to impart information. People who want to learn something head to
the nonfiction section of their libraries and bookstores where they
browse such diverse topics as how to feed their horses and how to
find the best bargains at Disney World.

Yet nonfiction offers far more than how-to books. Biographies
and autobiographies (memoirs) also fall into this category, as well as
titles intended to persuade, entertain, and inform (including reference and textbooks). But no matter what your nonfiction topic,
remember that *your book should have take-away value for the reader.*

I've met many beginning writers at conferences who simply want
to tell their story. They've been through something unusual or traumatic, and they're convinced that other people will find their story
fascinating.

Well . . . maybe and maybe not. What people often fail to realize
is that everyone has a story, and we are most keenly interested in our
own stories. So if you want me to read and enjoy your story, I need to
feel that I will somehow benefit from it.

Will I be entertained? Will I be inspired? Will I be challenged?
Will I learn what you learned so I don't have to endure what you
endured?

Will I learn the importance of trying to keep a marriage
together? Or the wisdom of leaving an abusive husband? Will you
offer me helpful tips and resources so I can accomplish what you
accomplished?

If you're writing a biography, is the subject truly noteworthy?
Does he or she provide an inspiring example for others? Could he or
she be a role model?

If you're writing a book on the history of aviation, have you
mingled enough true stories among the facts and diagrams that a

layman would keep reading? People love to read about other people, so have you included interviews and anecdotes about brave pilots?

If you want to tell your life story, remember to think of your reader first and last. Even if you think the book will probably be of interest only to your grandchildren, ask yourself what they can learn from your life and then speak to them in such a way that they'll put down their iPads and cell phones to read your book.

No matter what your topic, take a minute to complete this little exercise:

My reader will receive _____from my book.

I hope that blank was easy to fill in. Because if you're struggling to find a reason people would want to read your book, a publisher will struggle to find a reason to buy it.

I cut my teeth writing nonfiction. My novels, in fact, are almost always based in fact (which probably explains why I've never written a fantasy).

One of my first published books was on the topic of adoption. My husband and I worked so hard to adopt our children, I thought other couples would benefit from hearing our story.

But I quickly realized that *every* adoptive couple has a story, and many were just as interesting as ours. So my book had to offer something extra. I couldn't simply write up our story and call it quits.

I had to offer other interested couples a few practical tools. So in the back of the book I included a list of private adoption agencies from all fifty states. I also included a bibliography for further reading, and if the Internet had been around in those days, I would have included a list of helpful websites.

The take-away value of your book will depend, of course, on your topic and the type of nonfiction you are writing. But generally, personal stories do not sell unless

- you are a celebrity
- you have a large TV or radio platform
- or you offer tremendous take-away value for the reader.

"But I'm not worried about selling my book to a publisher," you may say. "I'm going to self-publish it."

Doesn't matter; the same rules apply. Unless you want your book to sit on Amazon with a scattering of five star reviews from your relatives and one-star reviews from everyone else, make sure you remember this: people will read, enjoy, and recommend your book only if they have received value from it.

Take a moment to let that sink in.

Maybe another moment.

Got it?

Okay. Now that you have considered and defined the value readers will gain from your book, visit the following website and locate your topic within the library Dewey Decimal system:

http://www.library.illinois.edu/ugl/about/dewey.html

If you wanted to write a book on the history and development of pretzels, you would find your book placed at 641, under "Food and Drink."

If you have trouble deciding where your book would go, is it because you simply don't know where the library would put it, or is it because you haven't identified a clear topic? You could answer the first question by calling your local library and posing the question to a reference librarian. To answer the second question, you probably need to clarify the concept of your book and determine who would benefit most from it.

Because I heard this often at writers' conferences, I know some of you want to write the true story of your parents or grandparents but "in novel form." If that's your situation, ask yourself a couple of basic questions. First—are you willing to change the order of story events to tell a better story? (Fiction has to make sense; real life doesn't.) Second, are you going to change any names or fictionalize any part of the story?

If you are going to bend the truth a bit, you should either say so in an author's note at the end (*The author has taken liberties with certain dates, places, and identities in order to protect the innocent* . . .) or you could write the book as a novel.

If you write the book as a novel, however, you shouldn't insist on recording events "just as they happened." Ever wonder why most novels and movies have a notice that they were *based upon* actual events" instead of claiming to be true stories? Because actual events rarely fit the blueprint for writing a screenplay, so history may need to be tweaked.

The Oscar-winning film "Chariots of Fire," for example, was based upon the true biography of Eric Liddell, an Olympic runner who later became a missionary to China. In the movie, Liddell's sister Jennie was portrayed as a bit of a nag—she didn't want him to focus on his running and was always chiding him about the Olympics. But in real life, Jennie Liddell was tremendously supportive of her brother. Why did the filmmakers cast her in such a negative light?

Because fiction thrives on conflict and the story falls flat without it. Poor Jennie's reputation was sacrificed to story.

On the other hand, if you want to stick to the facts and record events as they actually happened, you can certainly do it in the *style* of a novel, you simply write what's called "creative nonfiction." Let me illustrate:

Factual reporting:

Melvin and Belinda Brown, my grandparents, arrived at Ellis Island in 1852. Melvin had been sick with the whooping cough while aboard ship, and Belinda had grown thin with running all over the ship seeking medicine for him. They settled in Philadelphia after Belinda saw the city's name on a poster and told Melvin she liked it.

Creative nonfiction style:

On a summer day in 1852, Melvin Brown stood at the railing of the S. S. Minnow and watched the Statue of Liberty appear on the horizon. "Look there," he told his wife Belinda, nudging her with his elbow.

He glanced at her wan face and frowned. She had worn herself to a nub caring for him when he was sick, and for a while he worried that she'd catch the whooping cough herself. But his wife was stronger than she looked, and he could only be thankful that they'd both survived the crossing.

Later, as they walked down the ramp that led to Ellis Island, Belinda squeezed his arm and pointed to a poster featuring tall buildings and wide streets. "Phil-a-del-phi-a," she said, sounding out the word. "What a pretty name. If they let us choose, let's settle there."

How could he refuse? He owed her his life.

He covered her hand with his. "Whatever you want, dearest."

Writing in creative nonfiction, of course, means that you have to take a few liberties. You may know that your grandparents Melvin and Belinda Brown arrived on a ship in 1852, but you don't know what Melvin actually said to her or if they watched the Statue of Liberty as they pulled into port. What you do in those cases is write what you believe is *plausible or likely*—and it's probably a good idea at the end of the book to include an author's note saying that you've "filled in the gaps" where necessary. But if you're writing creative nonfiction, you shouldn't change any major events you know to be true. When you do that on a large scale, you're writing fiction.

Always remember that *story* is valuable even in nonfiction. I was taken to church regularly as a child, and in those days most churches didn't offer programs geared to children. So I had to sit in the worship service with all the adults, and I'm pretty sure I had my head in my mother's lap for many a sermon. I slept, or tried to sleep, while she played with my hair or read her Bible along with the pastor.

But even as a preschooler, I remember sitting straight up, eyes wide, the minute the preacher launched into a story. He'd say, "The other night . . ." and I perked up. Everyone else did, too. Or he'd tell a story about his childhood or one of his friends.

I can't remember much about those early sermons, but I do

remember loving the preacher's stories. Humans are hard-wired to appreciate story, so it's a good idea to pepper your nonfiction book with anecdotes. Even something as simple as a recipe book—a collection of baking formulas and directions—can benefit from stories to introduce each recipe.

My husband loves "American Pickers" on the History Channel. I couldn't see what he found so fascinating about Mike and Frank picking through old junk until I watched a couple of episodes. It's not the junk that attracts people, but the *stories* people tell. After hearing those stories, those piles of junk become heaps of treasure.

So even in nonfiction, don't ignore the power of story. You'd be leaving a valuable writer's tool on the shelf.

Writing a Life Story

If you're writing the story of someone's life—your or someone else's—you may find the plot skeleton lesson useful. All good stories have the same bone structure, so you may discover that the life story you want to tell naturally fits the skeleton.

I've never written my life story (boring!), but I've written about episodes in my life and that's what I'd recommend to you, too. No one wants to read about every event in anyone's lifespan because we all go through long periods where nothing noteworthy happens. But everyone has stories about a specific event or time when something unusual happened—and that's a story worth writing.

On several occasions I've been hired to write a celebrity's story as a collaborative work. I've written with Deanna Favre, wife to football player Brett Favre; Mandisa; Heather Whitestone, Miss America 1995; Gayle Haggard; and a couple whose frozen embryo was inadvertently transferred to another woman. In each situation, my client experienced an event that proved to be the "inciting incident" for a story. They formed goals, they faced complications, they endured bleakest moments and received help. And they learned lessons and made decisions that changed their lives forever, and those are the values and lessons the reader takes away from their stories.

All of the above terms will be familiar to you if you've read *The Plot Skeleton*, and if you haven't that little book will help you structure your story, too. Focus your story on one event, identify the plot elements that will make this story compelling and memorable, and identify the life lessons learned through this event. And there you have all the elements needed for a compelling life story.

Fiction

Fiction, of course, is all about story. A novel is a fictional exploration of a universal truth—as viewed by the author—consisting of narrative prose, a plot, a setting, and a theme. A novel is usually one character's story—it may offer a large cast and several point of view characters, but still, one character is dominant. A novel is a microcosm that says, "this is how the world is."

I wish I could come up with a more succinct definition, but I've tried. Since *truth* is a relative term these days, the author's worldview definitely comes into play. And though novels are fiction, meaning the events are not actual, novels focus on true characters, lessons, and moral values. A novel that does not present both sides to a moral argument descends to the level of propaganda.

My novel *The Pearl* deals with cloning after a woman's five-year-old son is killed in a freak accident. Because she is a radio personality, a group known for promoting cloning offers to clone her son. She is so desperate to regain her beloved child that she considers the offer.

When I began writing *The Pearl*, I knew that as a Christian I ought to be opposed to cloning, but why? I wasn't sure. After all, if we can clone a liver and transplant it into a dying man, why not support cloning?

So I had my protagonist do some serious investigation in the matter, and I was careful to uncover as many pro-cloning as anti-cloning arguments.

At the end of the story, it's not facts and figures that make her decide to turn down the cloning offer. She says no because she sees firsthand what the technology leads to when combined with selfish human desires. If I had completely avoided the pro-cloning side of the argument, I don't think it would have been an honest book.

The purpose of a novel is not to impart facts (although learning new things is often a pleasant side effect of reading fiction), but to evoke emotion.

Let's break this down. Novels usually have one protagonist. A novel with two protagonists (*A Thousand Splendid Suns, A Tale of Two Cities, The Face*), will often feature a main character who sacrifices himself for the other, so only one character remains at the ending. Why only one?

I once decided to try my hand at an "ensemble novel." In *Uncharted*, I would feature six main characters, and I would give all of them equal weight. No character would be more important than the others.

Which meant I was dealing with six different plotlines, or plot skeletons. Which meant I had six different inciting incidents, six different goals, six different characters facing complications . . . you get the idea.

When I had finished the rough draft, I had a long book that felt repetitive. I carried it with me to a writer's workshop led by Donald Maass, who wisely pointed out that even in an ensemble cast, one character needs to be predominant. So I chose one out of the six, recast the story from her perspective, and that move turned a convoluted story into an especially haunting one.

By having six main characters, I was also diluting my reader's bond with the protagonist. Readers want to identify with the main character, and if a writer has more than one strong main character, readers literally divide their loyalties. This dilutes the reading experience. The closer you want to bind your reader to your protagonist, the shorter your list of point of view characters should be.

Likewise, the broader the topic, the smaller your point of view needs to be. Someone once said, "If you want to write about war, write about one man's war."

I remember sitting my friend Lori Copeland's living room on

September 11, 2001. I had been about to go to the airport to fly home, but after the planes crashed into the Twin Towers, I realized I wouldn't be going anywhere.

As we sat in silence watching the formerly awesome towers crumble into dust, I remember thinking that the situation was overwhelming, simply too awful. How could anyone ever write about it? The tragedy, the devastation, the horror of all those people struggling for their lives in three separate locations . . .

Yet people have written successfully about 9/11 . . . through the eyes of *one* person. When a tragedy or situation is so huge you struggle to grasp all its implications, go into the head of one person affected by the event and write the story from his or her perspective.

I once had only a few minutes to talk to a woman about her manuscript in progress. Hoping she'd be succinct, I asked the usual opening question: "What's your story about?"

"It's about a woman," she answered, "who is abducted."

"Ah." I nodded. "So the book's about how she tries to get away from her kidnappers?"

The woman shook her head. "She spends most of the book locked up in an old house. But there's this detective—"

"So the story is about the detective and how he tries to outwit the kidnapper?"

She shook her head again. "The woman's boyfriend is a lawyer, and he's tied in with the kidnappers . . ."

"So it's the boyfriend's story, and he's frustrated by the police and trying to find her—"

She shook her head a third time.

At that point, I understood her problem—she couldn't pinpoint her protagonist. If you can't identify whose story you're telling, you need to go back to the starting line and ask yourself *whose point of view will help me write the most dramatic and emotional story?* I've gone back and started again, and believe me, it's worth the retreat.

Look over your cast of story characters and choose one to be the protagonist. The other characters will still play a role, of course, but the story should focus on one person—his hopes, fears, struggles, and desires.

Evaluating Your Idea

The late Gary Provost used to say that great ideas are like WAGS —and I've never forgotten his acronym. As you consider whether your story idea is strong enough for a full novel, consider these four elements:

W: World. Would this story transport the reader to another world? I don't mean Pluto or Mars, but any world the reader would find interesting. The world of high finance. The world of the Amazon rain forest. The world of a gorilla's zookeeper. The world of a woman with breast cancer. The world of ancient Persia.

People read to escape their ordinary lives, so don't let your protagonist spend most of his time in the ordinary world.

Lars and the Real Girl is one of my favorite movies. The film is set in a small town somewhere in Minnesota, and it's an ordinary small town until Lars, a painfully shy young man, orders a life-size anatomically correct adult doll . . . and believes she's real. The entire town enters into a kindly conspiracy to support Lars's delusion until, as his psychiatrist says, "he doesn't need it any more." The little town may look ordinary, but it's not because it's a community where Bianca the doll goes to church, reads to sick children at the hospital, and occupies a seat on the school board.

So wherever your story takes us, make sure it's a world your reader is likely to find different and interesting.

A: Active characters. Make certain your protagonist is not a navel-gazer. He or she must be willing to get up and do something to reach his goal.

I nearly wrote myself into a corner when I began to write *The Awakening,* a novel about a woman who suffers from agoraphobia. Aurora lived in the top floor of a Manhattan apartment building, and she hadn't stepped foot outside the building in over ten years. And there I was, writing a story about a woman too frightened to go anywhere or do anything.

So I had to make an adjustment. And that leads us to the next letter:

G: Goals. Active characters set goals, and if you are familiar with the plot skeleton, you'll recognize this event as one that occurs just after the inciting incident. As I was writing *The Awakening*, I sent Aurora to the rooftop, where she heard an audible voice from out of nowhere—her inciting incident. After hearing that voice—and believing that perhaps someone cared—she set the goal of trying to go down five additional steps of the staircase each day. An insignificant goal for most people, but Aurora wasn't most people. I showed her struggling, perspiring, and trembling as every day she worked up enough courage to descend five steps farther than she had the day before.

S: Stakes. Your protagonist must have a lot at stake during his venture. Ask yourself, "What would happen if my protagonist didn't meet his goal?" If your answer is, "Life would just go back to the way it was," your stakes aren't high enough. Your main character needs to burn some bridges so he can't go back unless he's victorious.

Remember me mentioning that I sent Aurora up to the rooftop in *The Awakening*? The story opens with her mother's funeral—Aurora has been her mother's nurse for the past ten years. And now that she is free to develop and enjoy a life of her own, she is imprisoned by her fears. So she goes up to the rooftop, fully intending to jump off, and is actually sitting on the ledge when she hears the voice from out of nowhere . . .

What is at stake? My reader knows that if Aurora doesn't meet her goals and conquer her agoraphobia, she's going to go back to the roof and finish what she started. Her life is riding on this venture.

What's at stake in nearly every James Bond film? The fate of the free world, of course. What's at stake in every story involving a kidnap victim? The victim's life. Sometimes a marriage or a detective's life are at risk, too. The more you put at stake, the better your story will be.

Using those four elements—WAGS—you can create a storyline in minutes. I'll pull some things from the top of my head, but you give it a try, too.

- W: different world: um . . . the world of fashion shoe design.
- A: active character: an ambitious young woman, fresh from fashion design school, wins the opportunity to intern at a famous Italian shoe design company.
- G: goal: when she discovers that someone has been leaking copies of the famous designer's shoes to an American competitor, she determines to find the culprit.
- S: stakes: as she snoops to discover the villain, she is discovered—and, depending upon the genre and age of the intended reader, either her reputation, her career, her life, or all three will be threatened.

See how it works? Now apply those four guidelines to your story and see how it measures up. Most stories fall short in the area of "high stakes"—we tend to shelter our protagonists and don't torture them nearly enough. Make sure your protagonist goes through the fire so at the end of the story he will either be worthy of his victory or sadder and much, much wiser.

Genres

Before you begin writing your novel, you should know which genre you're writing in. The number one mistake of beginning writers in this area is to not consider genre at all. Publishers have seasonal "lists" or catalogs to fill, and they may have room for two romances, three suspense novels, a western, and maybe one literary novel. Many genre readers are fanatically loyal—they'll read six or seven romances a month, or every mystery novel in a particular series. You should want your book to fill one of those available genre slots.

If you're writing a general novel, know that it can be harder to place a book in this category. An editor may love it, but if the sales and marketing folks don't know where the bookstores are going to put it, they're not going to be encouraging. And yes, the sales and marketing people do have a voice is whether or not your book is contracted.

I'm going to attempt to list some of the commonly accepted genres here, though they do change and shift over time. See if you can determine which category would best suit your novel:

- Romance: a story in which the romantic plot is the primary plot. The man and woman *always* get together at the end. If they don't, it's not a genre romance.
- Historical Romance
- Military Romance
- Cowboy Romance
- Inspirational Romance (includes a strong faith element, almost always Christian)
- Romantic Suspense
- Supernatural Romance
- Fantasy (can include time-travel)
- Historical
- Military/Spy novels
- Westerns
- Contemporary
- Literary
- Horror
- Women's Fiction: features adult women, often married, dealing with contemporary issues
- Chick Lit: feature twenty-something heroines in search of love
- Science Fiction/Futuristic (includes Dystopian)
- Bonnet books: feature small Amish or Mennonite communities

- Faith Fiction or Christian fiction: Christian faith is an intrinsic part of the plot
- RomCom (romantic comedy). Think Meg Ryan and Tom Hanks.

Each genre has its own conventions, and you shouldn't knowingly violate them if you want to sell your manuscript. You wouldn't send a romantic story where the man and woman part ways to a romance editor, for instance, and you wouldn't send a story about a Buddhist to a publisher of Christian fiction. If you want to write within a specific genre, read several books in that genre so you can learn what the conventions are.

Some genres fade away over time. I included Chick Lit on the list because it was so popular a few years ago (pink and green covers, first person, present tense, young girl who loves shopping and the big city), but as of this writing the genre's popularity is fading. Bonnet books are huge right now, but I predict the genre will morph into "small town" books, because I believe what readers are seeking is escape into a small, friendly, non-threatening environment like Mayberry, R.F.D.

So do your research. Visit libraries and book stores to find out what is currently selling. What genres appear on your bookstore shelves? (If they shelve by genre—some smaller stores shelve by author's last name.) Make sure you have a clear idea of what genre your book will sell in, because that's the bottom line. Where will your book fit on that bookstore shelf?

Finding Time to Write

How do you eat a cow? One bite at a time.

Many people are overwhelmed by the mere idea of writing a book. But it's not difficult when you think of it as writing a page a day. If you began today, a year from now you'd have 365 pages, a fairly hefty novel. If even that seems overwhelming, ask yourself what you'll have a year from now if you *don't* do anything to begin your book.

A page a day is a simplistic idea, however, because you will need several days of research and preparation. You'll also have days where you're in the groove and you'll write five pages, or even ten. Or maybe you'll get one of those delicious three-day weekends and somehow get an entire day to yourself—you may write three chapters!

I'm like most of you—busy. I have a family with children and a grandchild, I have two puppies who can be demanding, I try to exercise consistently, I clean my own home, I attend my church, I lead a neighborhood book club, I travel frequently, and I volunteer at my community animal shelter every week. I know you have a busy schedule, too.

But over the years, I've learned an important principle: we find time to do the things we really want to do. And if you really want to write a book, you can find the time.

Here's how.

Go to your computer and open your calendar program. Print out copies of the next few months. With the printed pages before you, put a slash through all the days you know you absolutely cannot work on your book. (I routinely mark through travel days, Saturdays, and some holidays. And my birthday.)

Now look at the remaining days and ask yourself where you can find a block of two or three free hours. Week nights? Sunday afternoons? Saturday mornings?

I have one friend who got up an hour early every morning to write her first book. I'm not sure I could think at five a.m., but she knew she'd be able to get her book done while the rest of the household slept. Maybe that will be your productive time, too.

Look for your open blocks of time, and block them out. Consider them sacrosanct, appointments you have with your book. Now, on that printed calendar, give yourself a goal for each block of time. It can be as simple as "research colonial period" or "write five pages" or "edit pages 4-13." If you're just starting out, though, you'll want to pencil in days for plotting, character development, and research.

More on what you'll be writing later. But first let's talk about the work of preparation.

Research

Whether you are writing fiction or nonfiction, you will have to do some research. You will have to read a lot of material on your nonfiction topic, and if you're writing a novel set in a real town, you'd better learn some street names and a bit of history about that town. If an issue arises in your book, you will have to be well-read on the latest information about that topic.

I've written several books that were fairly research-intensive, and people always ask how long it took me to do the research. They always look surprised when I tell them it only took a week or two.

Research can be like quicksand. You can get caught in it. The amount of material available, combined with the primal fear of the blank screen, can entice you to postpone the actual writing of your book far longer than necessary. Research can fritter away weeks, even months, until you forget the material you read when you began the research work.

So I advise this: spend a few days gathering as much information as you can. Print out *trustworthy* information from the Internet (that rules out a lot of material on Wikipedia), buy or borrow books, clip articles, look for YouTube videos on the topic. Then compile this information into a notebook, or make notes of where the information can be found.

(Note: when I say "a few days" keep in mind that writing is a full-time job for me, so I'm talking about forty hours or so of research. If you write when you can find a couple of hours here and there, you may need more than a few days.)

Next, read enough to get the Big Picture of whatever it is you're researching—social customs in medieval times, prion diseases, foreign adoption, in vitro fertilization, Cuban groceries, whatever. If you're setting your novel in a real location, use Google earth to get a bird's eye view of the town and zoom in on the house where you think your character would live. Print out a photo and keep it in your notebook. Take about a week to do this "macro" round of research.

Once you have a good understanding of the subjects involved in your book, spend some hours researching your characters. Figure out their personality type and create a personality profile for them (more on this in *Creating Extraordinary Characters*.) If your protagonist will be employed in an occupation you don't know well, do some research on what would be involved in your character's daily work. Is he a trial lawyer? A brain surgeon? Find a brain surgeon or lawyer who might be willing to sit for an interview or look at your manuscript to check for anything implausible. Sometimes it's far easier to give your characters an occupation you know well—that's why so many literary lawyers write legal thrillers.

Once you have a good handle on your subject and your protagonist's occupation, take some time to research the setting. If this is a real town, you can visit it (and claim expenses as tax deductions if you sell your book) or learn as much as you can through online research. If you're creating a fictional town, you will still need to establish a few details: where is it located? What state? Will your plot require you to know any particular laws of that state? What are the signs of seasonal change?

As you research, don't spend too much time gathering details. You can always go back and find the missing detail you need, but it will be impossible to gather every detail up front because you won't really know what you need until you finish the first draft.

When I'm first drafting, I will do almost anything to avoid stopping the flow of words onto my computer screen. If my characters sit down to eat in medieval England, I'll write something like:

> All eyes focused on King Henry as he took his place at the center of the table. Four servants brought in a steaming tray of [find out what the king would eat at a banquet], and the guests burst into applause.

I'll talk more about those brackets later, but you get the idea. Press on. You can always look up details later.

Drafting

When you think you've allowed enough time for your research tasks, pick up your calendar and look at the next blocks of available time. You're nearly ready to begin writing.

Before you do, however, you might want to pick up a package of note cards. Many writers—including me—find it useful to use note cards to represent scenes (fiction) or chapters (nonfiction) in the book we're about to write. Working either from a plot skeleton (fiction) or an outline (nonfiction), we use the notecards to very briefly sketch out either what will happen in a scene or what topics we plan to hit in this chapter. The beauty of using notecards is that you can tape them to the wall and move them around as other ideas come to you.

So if you like the idea of notecards, pencil in a day or two to write up your notecards for your book. If you're writing a novel, you may need sixty or more scenes, so don't feel that you have to do them all at once. But at least try to sketch out your scenes for the first part of the book: in plot skeleton parlance, that means you'll sketch out scenes from the beginning through the inciting incident and the establishment of the goal.

If you've purchased colored note cards, you might want to use pink cards for your heroine and blue for her love interest. But do whatever suits you.

When you've done your note cards, you are ready to begin writing. Take a deep breath and don't let the Fear of the Blank Screen postpone your efforts one more day.

Pick up your printed calendar, look at your next available writing blocks, and give yourself a word count goal for each. I don't know how fast you write; you're going to have to figure this one out yourself. But remember—a first draft is not a polished draft, so these don't have to be beautiful or fancy words. They're just words on the page, that's all. When I'm first-drafting, in an eight hour day I can slap between five and seven thousand words onto the screen.

But I wouldn't want anyone to read them.

The secret to getting a first draft finished is *not* to go back and edit—or if you absolutely cannot control the urge, then only look at the material you wrote the day before. Some folks spend all their time editing the book they *could finish* if they didn't spend all their time editing.

I've always felt that producing a first draft was like birthing a baby. First-drafting is my least favorite part of writing because it's doggone hard work—you are pulling story from of thin air. The process involves a lot of pain and suffering and panting and grumbling and occasional yelling, but when that baby is on the table, you're done. It may be a bloody mess, but it's alive and squalling, and you've done the hard work.

Now all you have to do is clean it up—and that's what subsequent drafts are about.

Whenever I teach, people always ask about my drafting/revision system, so I'm happy to explain it here. I write in layers because the more time I spend with a book, the better I know my characters and the deeper I can take my story. At the end of my first draft—which might be only half the length of a finished book—I finally feel that I know what my story is about and who my characters are. The plot skeleton doesn't give me that—it only provides a framework for what my story might become. The first draft wraps that skeleton in flesh, and it's the subsequent drafts that fatten the story up, clothe it in mystery or magic or humor, and deepen the theme.

Between every draft, I take a day or two for what I once heard Sol Stein call "triage." First, I go back through the manuscript and search for [, the left bracket, because those are the spots where I know I need to look something up. I take the time to find out what King Henry would eat at his medieval dinner, I look up the name of a cemetery in Kennebunkport, etc. Whatever details I now know I'll need, I take the time to look them up.

I also fill in any obvious gaps. Suppose I realized in chapter

seventeen that Thomas has a twin brother. I can't suddenly introduce this brother in chapter seventeen; that's much too late. So I
need to include the brother in an early scene, perhaps at the family
reunion in chapter four. So I'll go back to chapter four and write in
the brother, give him a name and a charming disposition, and add
whatever else I need to add.

If you've done a plot skeleton, as I always do, you have plenty of
room for discovery along the journey. Trust me, you will discover
story developments that simply didn't occur to you when you first
began plotting. So this triage time is useful for making notes in the
margins (the "insert comment" command in Microsoft Word is good
for this) or whatever else you need to do.

When you are ready to begin your second draft, your story
should be in fairly good shape. You have a plot with a beginning,
middle, and (hopefully) an end. When you take out your calendar to
schedule work on your second draft, you can no longer gauge your
progress by word count, nor can you use the computer's page count
—it will change as soon as you begin to add new material. So you
should print out a copy of your first draft and be sure to number the
pages. As you work on your second draft, assign yourself a certain
number of pages to edit per work block. Again, the number of pages
you assign depends completely on how much time you have available
and how quickly you work.

At this point, I can't tell you how many drafts to do. Some
writers do over twenty drafts of some sections, others do three. I
usually do four or five, depending on how much I struggled with
making the story conform to what I imagined it to be. But with each
subsequent draft my focus shifts from being story-centered to being
detail-centered. My first drafts are all about shaping story; my later
drafts are more about cleaning up the language and listening to the
rhythm of the words.

So I'll tell you what I do, but you work according to the way
you're wired.

As I mentioned, my second draft is all about filling in gaps, doing
the detailed research, and making sure the story and characters are

complete. By the time it's finished, the manuscript may be about three-quarters of its final length.

During my third draft, I focus on creating "mood music." If a scene is suspenseful, I might change it from daytime to evening; I might clear everyone out of the house, I might have thunder rumbling in the distance—or write in a power outage. Whatever suits the scene. If a scene is "loud," I might rewrite it so that it's quiet and more intense. I want to be sure each scene is set in the best location, at the best time, and is suited for eliciting emotion from my reader.

From the third draft forward, I use the search/replace feature of my word processing program to search out and edit weasel words.

I have my computer read the manuscript to me during the fourth draft. Apple computers have speech built in; PC users can always download Adobe Reader and use it to have the computer read a selection to them. Your ear will pick up repeated words, flat dialogue, and missing words much better than your eye will. You could read the pages aloud, but your eye will probably skip over all the mistakes it didn't see when the pages were on your computer.

While the computer reads a scene to me, I hold the printed pages in my hand and mark it quickly so I don't fall behind. I circle words that don't work, I write "rep" next to repeated words that strike my ear, and I write FIX in the margin if a passage simply isn't working. After I've listened to each scene, I go back and make those changes on the computer.

I usually set the manuscript aside for a couple of days before beginning the final draft, and during those days I ask myself if I've developed the theme enough . . . if my protagonist is sympathetic enough . . . and if the reader will take away what I want them to take away. Then I read through the manuscript fairly quickly just to make sure I've done all I can do.

Honestly, by this point I am dizzy with the story and the process. I am so close to it that I can't tell if it's the best thing I've ever written or the worst. All I can do is make sure it's the best and cleanest I can make it, and then I send it off to my agent.

As you write, you will develop your own processes. Some of my methods may work for you, some may seem like a lot of fuss and bother. We're all different, and thank goodness we are.

But if you have struggled to produce a complete manuscript, if you have found it difficult to set aside time for writing, I hope some of these suggestions will help you.

Time Management

If you habitually struggle with finding time for anything, I have a few tips that might prove helpful—they've certainly helped me.

1. Realize that you don't have to answer the phone. If the call is important, the caller can leave a message. You pay for telephone service, so you are the boss.

2. Learn to say no. Scarlett O'Hara had a little speech memorized for occasions when men proposed to her. It went something like, "Kind sir, I am not unaware of the honor you have bestowed upon me by asking me to be your wife, but I cannot in good conscience accept your offer . . ." You should come up with a similar speech when you're asked to head a charity drive or take an extra week for carpool or bake four dozen cookies for the bake sale. If the request interferes with your writing time, you should say, "Dear friend, I am not unaware of the honor you have bestowed upon me by asking me to participate in your endeavor . . ." Well, you get the idea.

3. Tame the television. Trust me, even with 500 channels, television isn't so compelling that you must watch it every night. Pick out the shows you really enjoy and watch those, but turn the thing off for everything else.

4. Capture stolen moments. When you find yourself waiting at the doctor's office, sitting in the carpool line, or standing in the queue at Starbucks, pull out the book you're reading for research or pop in your ear buds to

listen to an audio book. Either option is a good way to redeem your lost time.

5. Have a particular place to write. You'll save time if you don't have to "set up" your desk, computer, dictionary, music, whatever you use to get in the flow.

6. Remember this principle: your life consists of a finite succession of moments. Wasting time is literally wasting your life.

7. Harness the power of the carrot. Yep, you're the toiling donkey, so what will you use to reward yourself at the end of your writing time? A cold Diet Coke? A nap? Playtime with the puppy?

8. Remember that multi-tasking is a myth. When most people say they are multi-tasking, they are actually switch-tasking, shifting from one task to another. This is not an effective way to do anything.

In the 1740s, Lord Chesterfield offered the following advice to his son: "There is time enough for everything in the course of the day if you do but one thing at once, but there is not time enough in the year if you will do two things at a time." So when you're writing, focus on the writing.

Critique, Anyone?

Though I have never been part of a writers' group, many people swear that they are wonderful, supportive, and helpful. Some participate in local groups; others find critique groups online. If you think the experience would be something you'd enjoy, call your local library to ask if they know of writers' groups in your community.

If you join a group, however, make sure the group is building you up, not tearing you down. I've heard horror stories about jealousy and destructive criticism that fatally injured fledgling writers just as they were about to fly.

Years ago I read an anecdote in *Reader's Digest* that I've never forgotten. Seems a young husband watched his wife cook a ham, but was mystified when she cut off both ends before placing it in the oven. When he asked why she did it, she said, "Because my mother always did."

So they called Mom, asked her the same question, and got the same answer: "Because *my* mother always did."

So the newlyweds called Grandma and asked why she cut off both ends of the ham before baking. "Simple," she said. "My baking dish was too small for the ham."

That story reminds me of tales I've heard about critique group experiences. Someone in the group—someone who may be unpublished or self-published—will say that something *must* be written in such-and-such an way, and everyone will believe that pronouncement whether or not it is true.

Critique groups have their own jargon. I've been around other writers who talk about RUE (resist the urge to explain) and SDT (show, don't tell) as casually as chefs talk about spices. I had to laugh at one conference when a teaching friend told me that someone in her class had asked when "STDs were appropriate." Maybe *never*?

I've met with far too many writers who have been henpecked by critique groups who obey rules that are like Grandma's undersized baking pan. Sometimes these groups can be adamant about what can and cannot be done, and often they are the blind leading the blind.

I've discovered a condition I call Critique Group Dependency. I've read manuscripts that could have sparkled with verve, but the writer's critique groups scrubbed all the sparkle away. I've talked to writers at conferences who hesitantly told me, "My critique group feels this is too ___ (insert adjective), but I think it's what I want to say." I've seen manuscripts where the author second-guessed every other line based on feedback from her critique group.

Let me assure you—a writer's voice must be confident. At some point you have to trust yourself and block out other critics. Writing is a craft and an art, and sometimes the art overrules the craft. Yes, there are rules, but sometimes they can and should be broken. If you have to break them, break them boldly and be able to explain the reason for your choices.

If your critique group offers a suggestion and you are persuaded by their logic, fine, they've been helpful. But if they offer a suggestion that goes against all your instincts, thank them and forget it. Those folks around the table are not editors, they're writers, and *no one* is more critical about writing than another writer.

Trust me, nothing substitutes for experience. Listen to those who have been published many times; read books by editors and writers who know the ropes. Take all other advice lightly.

Another subtle danger lurks in critique groups—the danger of over-exposing the book that's dear to your heart. You can talk the magic and enthusiasm right out of your work if you're not careful. Or others could pick it to death and leave your darling looking like a Persian cat left out in the rain.

So be careful. If you think you might like to join a critique group, attend the first meeting and listen. See if the comments made about submitted work is constructive or destructive. What is the experience level of the other writers? Are they committed to helping each other, or are they primarily looking out for themselves?

I know wonderful critique groups exist. If you find a good one, count yourself fortunate and enjoy the feedback that should help you write a better book. I frequently use test readers, and their feedback is always valuable.

But I also know how criticism can sting. Most of us can read twenty wonderful comments and one negative, and it's the negative one that keeps us awake at night. So develop a thick skin, brace yourself, and make sure your manuscript is as polished as possible before you send it out into the world.

Writing is an act of bravery, after all.

Traditional or Self-Publishing

I didn't feel this book would be complete without discussing traditional and self-publishing. Writers today have more choices than ever, but you need to be fully informed in order to make the best choice possible.

Traditional publishing has a lot to recommend it. Writers become traditionally published when they submit a manuscript either directly to the publisher or to an agent who submits it to the traditional publishing house (many large houses won't accept unagented manuscripts). Manuscripts accepted by traditional publishing are usually the crème de la crème—acquisitions editors look for books that are well written and should sell to a large number of people. After acquiring the book, an editor at the publishing house will go through the manuscript and advise the writer about how to do a rewrite—yes, another draft. When that is complete, usually the same editor will do a line edit: he or she will go through the manuscript line by line, checking every word. After that, a copy editor will go through the work checking every fact, every spelling, and every punctuation mark. (Surprising, isn't it, that some typos still get through?) No wonder traditional publishing is still the ultimate dream for most writers.

Perhaps the most important consideration to a writer is that a traditional publishing house typically *pays the author an advance*, depending upon the projected sales of the book in the first year. The author pays nothing. The advance is supposed to give the writer money to live on while he's polishing the book and working on his next one.

After the book is completely edited, it will be professionally designed and typeset, then sent to the printer. During this process, a sales and marketing team will discuss the book and make plans for how they can best sell it. Years ago, virtually all marketing and publicity was handled by the publishing house (not surprising, since they don't want to lose the money they've invested in the project.) Today, however, most publishers expect the author to bear a large part of the marketing burden. Authors are expected to maintain audiences on Facebook, Twitter, and Pinterest. They are also expected to send regular newsletters to keep readers interested in their books.

The traditional publishers definitely have the upper hand when it comes to distribution. They have staff who handle the major sales channels—bookstore chains, large bookstores, Wal-Mart, Costco, Amazon, etc. These connections are already in place, so bookstores are told that new releases are coming, and many sales outlets place pre-orders in anticipation of a book's release date. Naturally, large pre-orders means lots of interest, and that is welcome news for the publisher and the author.

When the book is finally released—usually anywhere from eight months to a year after it is submitted—it is distributed to major bookstores and online retailers and placed on sale. The author hopes his earned royalties exceed the amount of the advance he was given —if it does, he will earn more royalties for as long as the book remains for sale. If it does not, the publisher will take the loss, and they will probably not be as eager to spend as much for the author's *second* book.

The advent of the ebook has drastically changed the publishing world. Even large publishers now are finding it difficult to stay afloat, and they are becoming far pickier about the books they choose to publish. Furthermore, the number of publishers is shrinking as more publishing houses merge.

Years ago, any writer who wanted to publish his own book had to spend thousands of dollars and find a place to store thousands of books (the more you ordered, the lower the price per book). "Vanity presses" abounded, and editors at these presses were not picky. They would print about anything that came to them, and very little real editing was done. The writer paid for everything, and though the subsidy publisher promised to market and distribute the book, very often this amounted to a mention in the company catalog and/or a listing at Amazon.com (do you realize how many books are listed on Amazon.com?).

Technology has dramatically changed self-publishing. The rise of the POD press (print on demand) has made it possible for writers to upload a book online, place it for sale on Amazon.com and other websites, and collect a steady trickle of royalties without any major upfront costs. Different POD programs offer different options, and many of them charge plenty for their editorial services, but theoretically a writer could self-publish cheaply.

The only problem is that most of these books are awful. They are written by people who have never studied the craft, they are not well edited, and the covers often look homemade. The books make it onto Amazon, true, and a few of the writer's friends and family may leave glowing reviews, but those reviews don't improve the quality of the book.

I'm not writing this to condemn self-publishing—the book you're reading now was self-published. But if you are interested in self-publishing, *please* do all you can to produce a quality product. If you want to sell more than one title, and especially if you hope to have any kind of career as a writer, learn how to write well, hire an editor, have a professional design your cover, and run your material by some test readers before you submit it.

Also be aware that you alone will be responsible for promoting, marketing, and distributing your book. You may not have to warehouse books in your garage, but you'll have to partner with a POD printer who is willing to print and ship books for you. It's a lot of work, and just because a book is on Amazon.com doesn't mean it will sell itself.

I have nothing against self-publishing. A lawyer friend of mine wrote a book on Florida law and self-published it successfully because he knew no traditional publisher would want to publish a book that would only be of interest to residents of the Sunshine State. I self-published this series of writing lessons because I wanted to try the *a la carte* approach and knew no traditional publisher would be interested in publishing a series of booklets. I've also self-published some of my traditionally-published books that have gone out of print—a situation that probably won't occur any more because digital and print on demand books can stay "in print" forever.

Yet too many people are publishing books without spending a

single hour studying the craft of writing. They're writing books without studying the "blueprints" of their genre. People call themselves *author* without investing an ounce of blood, sweat, or tears—just a few dollars.

They don't know what they're missing.

I'll wrap up this little section with a story: in his book *The Genius In All of Us: New Insights Into Genetics, Talent, and IQ*, David Shenk cites Stanford psychologist Walter Mischel's study of a particular group of four year olds. In the 1970s, he gathered them together and offered the children a choice: they could have one marshmallow immediately or wait a little while (while Mischel "ran an errand") for two marshmallows. The results:

- one-third of the kids immediately took the single marshmallow.
- one-third waited a few minutes but then gave in and settled for the single marshmallow.
- one-third patiently waited fifteen minutes for two marshmallows.

After fourteen years, Mischel checked in with the same subjects again. He compared the SAT scores of the original nonwaiting group to the waiting group and found the latter scored an average of 210 points higher.

Those with an early capacity for self-discipline and delayed gratification had gone on to much higher academic success. The delayed-gratification kids were also rated as much better able to cope with social and personal problems.

Why am I telling stories about children and marshmallows? Because the chief problem with self-published books is that they were published *too soon*. The writer hasn't taken the time to hone his skills, nor had he tested his material with a critique group, an early reader, or an acquisitions editor. When you hear an editor say, "I would love to publish this, but simply don't have a place for it in my list," then you know you're ready to publish in any venue.

The notion of *deliberate practice*, also explored by Shenk, says that aspiring performers concentrate on improving their work by engaging in practice activities designed to change and refine particular mechanisms. In other words, clarifies Shenk, "it is practice that doesn't take no for an answer; practice that perseveres; the type of practice where the individual keeps raising the bar of what he or she considers success."

How can you engage in deliberate practice? You find a writers group and endure solid critique without flinching. You read books on the craft of writing—and by reading this book, you're already doing that. You attend writing workshops and conferences. You enter your work into legitimate contests. (My first book was published because it won a contest.) You submit your work to magazines, online sites, and book publishers. You listen to feedback and work specifically on the areas where you have weaknesses.

Don't think that everything you do has to be centered on the one book you're working on. When I started, for the first five years I wrote anything anyone asked me to write—radio copy, catalog copy, articles, reports, interviews, personality profiles—and then I saw an ad about a children's picture book contest. Before I even thought about what sort of book I would write, I went to the library and borrowed a book on how to write children's picture books—and believe me, there's a blueprint. I learned that picture books are usually thirty-two pages and under 1,000 words, so that's what I wrote. And that story became my first published book.

When you're told that your novel has too much backstory, or that your nonfiction book is confusing, don't get defensive, just thank the person who was brave enough to offer their comments and look at your work with a critical eye. Were the comments justified? If so, how can you cut the backstory or clarify your material?

How can you make your work shine so that it stands out amid other manuscripts in the slush pile or sparkles amid the flood of self-published books on Amazon?

Publishers and editors want you to succeed because they need good books to publish. *I* want you to succeed because I need good books to read. But success often means that you're going to have to wait and work a while before you can have those two marshmallows.

So what are you waiting for? Start writing!

PLANS AND PROCESSES EXERCISES

1. Go to your computer and print out the calendar, one month per sheet, for as long as you think it will take you to produce your book. (Do not print more than 12 months—you can definitely write a book in a year!) Next, decide how many drafts you want to do. I do five (and I have given a detailed outline for my process in the writing lesson *The Art of Revision*, but you may work differently. In any case, divide your number of months by your number of drafts. If you printed 12 months and you want to do three drafts, you are allowing yourself four months per draft, right?)

2. Now cross out any dates on your calendar that you are NOT free to write—busy work days, travel days (unless you can write in a car or airport), holidays. Once that's done, divide the number of available days by the number of words you expect to be in your first draft. If you usually end up cutting, aim for a large number of words. If, like me, you write little and add as you go, aim for a lower number of words.

An average full-size novel can be anywhere from 70-95,000 words. Use that as your measuring stick.

Divide your number of words by available days assigned to that first draft. How many words must you produce every day? Pencil in those numbers on your calendar.

3. In subsequent drafts, you won't be counting words, but editing pages. You should print out a copy of your first draft and use the page total as your guide. How many available days do you have for editing this second (or third, fourth, or fifth) draft? Divide the number of pages by the number of days, and you'll have your daily goal. Don't pencil those goals on your calendar until after you've completed that first draft (because page numbers are constantly changing.)

4. Repeat the process for each draft, and by the time you reach the end of your calendar pages, you should have a completed book! Note: I gave you a brief description of the drafting process in this book, but *The Art of Revision* will give you a detailed guide of how to self-edit, particularly if you're writing fiction. I highly recommend that you read it when you're approaching your third draft.

5. Don't forget to answer this question, whether you're writing fiction or nonfiction: *My reader will receive* _____ *from reading my book.*

Chapter Seven

TENSION ON THE LINE

ARE YOU A FISHERMAN? MY DAD TOOK ME FISHING A COUPLE OF times when I was a kid, then years passed before I went fishing again. As it happens, the last time I went fishing I was in a dugout canoe on the Amazon River, fishing for piranha with a length of fishing line tied to a hook. Our guide could catch fish easily, as could Gaynel, my intrepid traveling companion. But no matter how hard I tried, I couldn't seem to manage the trick of hooking one of the little devils. The technique seemed simple: you dropped the baited hook and line over the side of the canoe, you let it dangle lazily in the water, and when you felt something tug at the bait, you set the hook with a jerk and then hauled up your catch. I felt lots of tugs during our afternoon of fishing, but I was never able to bring up a fish.

Of course you can always SPEAR a fish . . . but using a hook is easier, if you know the secret.

Maybe my subconscious didn't really *want* to catch a piranha. I watched with amazement as our native guide caught needle-toothed fish after fish and tossed them in a bucket. My amazement turned to fascination when after half an hour, he pulled a piranha from the bucket and put the tail of another fish near its mouth—the piranha, even after spending half an hour out of the water, greedily began to gobble up the food our guide offered.

Shudder. But I digress.

Though it looks easy, there is an art to hooking a piranha—you have to know when to keep the line relaxed and when to set the hook. And then, once your fish is hooked, you have to maintain constant tension on the line in order to pull in your prize.

The same principles apply to writing, and tension is all-important on the printed page. I've sat in workshops under New York agent Don Maass, a wonderful teacher, and heard him advise writers to make sure there's "tension on every page." He's absolutely right.

In this little booklet, the seventh in the *Lessons from the Writing Front* series, I will illustrate and explain several ways you can put tension on the page and keep your reader reading. Trust me—this lesson will pay off in a much more engrossing story.

It's the tension on the line that hooks—and keeps—a reader.

How Not to Create Tension

A lot of beginning writers assume that creating tension is easy—ha!--just like piranha fishing. They'll write something like:

CREAK!

Samantha cowered in the corner as the front door knob turned slowly. Earlier she had noticed a man standing outside on the sidewalk and doing nothing, just watching the house. Now she was home alone while Grandma played bingo down at the church. She was used to being alone at night, because she'd been living with her grandmother ever since her parents died in the same mysterious car crash that killed Grandpa.

Her heart pounded, her palms perspired, and her kneecaps jimmied up and down. She could run out the back door, but Grandma had probably already set the deadlock, and that required a key! Where was it? Grandma had gone through a litany of security measures when Samantha first moved in, but Sam had thought them all silly at the time. They didn't seem silly now!

CLICK!

Grandma kept her key hidden on a nail next to the door that led to the basement. She'd kept a keyed deadbolt on the back door ever since the teenage boys next door tried to break in and steal Molly, Grandma's pit bull. Molly had called to her at the animal shelter, Grandma always said, and she was nothing but a cuddle bug. But the boys next door saw Molly and thought of nothing but what they could make in a dog fighting ring with a dog of their own. Fortunately, Molly had lived a long and happy life after the attempted dognapping.

Her attention flew back to the door when it opened, and through the gloom Samantha saw the stranger clearly. He wore a rain-splattered trench coat, a hat, and galoshes. His face was long, with a sinister look about the eyes and the hawked nose. A long scar ran across his cheek and ended at his nose. Oddly enough, the chain from a pocket watch dangled from his coat pocket and glittered in the dim overhead light.

Samantha's heart skipped a beat when she saw what the man carried—a brown box with a tangle of wires protruding from the partially opened box.

Was that a BOMB?! Of course—Grandpa had been working at that top-secret lab doing work for the government, so he must have made someone very angry—angry enough to kill. But Grandpa was already dead, so why blow up the house now?

Because of Grandpa's research. He hadn't been studying atomic robots, as little Sally, Sam's niece, had said, but nanorobotics. Tiny little robots that could travel through a human's bloodstream and repair their DNA . . . or damage it. A science that had been quietly pursued for years, but had been largely relegated to horror films and literary thrillers until a few months ago.

A chill climbed the ladder of Samantha's spine. Of course— Grandpa the scientist had hidden some kind of evidence, some secret file or laptop or something in the house. She and Grandma might not even know what it was, but apparently someone wanted that evidence destroyed. That's why this man was carrying a bomb!

She needed to calm down. As long as the lights stayed dim, as long as she remained quiet, she might be able to remain hidden in this shadowed corner. The man might never even see her.

Still, her pounding heart nearly drowned out the ticking of the hall clock as the stranger kept coming and made his way to the dining room! Why on earth?

She closed her eyes and thought. Of course—the dining room

was the center of the house. If he left a bomb in that room, the ensuing blast would level the entire building.

What on earth was she going to do?

Okay . . . in that brief scene we have a frightened young woman and a stranger carrying a bomb—or at least we're told it's a bomb. The girl is home alone, Grandma is at the church playing bingo, and the family dog, a former pound puppy, has passed away. Grandpa was a scientist, he's now dead, and he'd been working on nanorobotics, a field with plenty of room for criminal mischief. We know the stranger is wearing a trench coat, a hat, and he has a scar across his sinister-looking face. We also know, oddly enough, that a gold watch chain is dangling from his coat pocket (though I can't imagine how Samantha knows the chain is attached to a watch, because the watch would be hidden inside the pocket.)

We know it's raining outside.

We know this is a bad man because he's entering the house without permission—and because he looks sinister.

We know Samantha is frightened because her pulse is pounding, her kneecaps are jerking, and her palms are sweaty.

We know the boys next door are thugs who think nothing of breaking and entering, stealing, and dog fighting.

We know Grandma is a kindly soul and animal lover.

We know Samantha is living with Grandma and has been for a while . . . and that she doesn't take danger very seriously, at least not until now.

We know Sam's parents are dead, killed in the same automobile accident that killed Grandpa.

We know the accident was mysterious.

We know the stranger hasn't seen Samantha yet.

We know she will be safe as long as she remains still and quiet.

We know he's going to the dining room because a bomb placed there will level the entire house.

After reading that scene, we know everything we need to know and then some. At the end of the scene, we have only one question, one delivered by Samantha herself: what is she going to do next?

That sample scene needs a lot of editing, but here's the chief problem: all the tension has been diffused because the writer told us *too much*. There's very little tension because we readers have only one unanswered question—and we may not care enough to read on for the answer.

The writer's job is *not* to answer every question in the reader's mind. The writer's job is to toss out hooks, laden with bait, and wait for them to snag the reader's interest and curiosity.

My novel *Magdalene* opens with these paragraphs:

> Silence, as heavy as doom, wraps itself around me as two guards lead me into the lower-level judgment hall. When I fold my hands, the *chink* of my chains disturbs the quiet.
>
> My judge, Flavius Gemellus, senior centurion of the *Cohors Secunda Italica Civum Romanorum*, looks up from the rolls of parchment on his desk, his eyes narrow. I don't blame him for being annoyed. I am not a Roman citizen, so I have no right to a trial. Besides, I have confessed and am ready to die.

When I teach this material in person, I read the above passage and ask my students to quickly lift their hands when I've read something that raises a question in their minds. Let's look at these paragraphs again, and I'll mark the places where I usually see a flutter of hands:

> Silence, as heavy as doom, wraps itself around me as two guards lead me into the lower-level judgment hall. *[Where is she?]* When I fold my hands, the *chink* of my chains disturbs the quiet. *[Why is she in chains?]*
>
> My judge, Flavius Gemellus, senior centurion of the *Cohors Secunda Italica Civum Romanorum*, looks up from the rolls of parchment on his desk, his eyes narrow. I don't blame him for being annoyed. I am not a Roman citizen, so I have no right to a trial.

[Why is she on trial?] Besides, I have confessed and am ready to die. *[Why would anyone confess, and why is she ready to die?]*

Do you see how it's done? As a storyteller, your task is to raise questions in the reader's mind, not to reveal everything up front. Respect your reader's intelligence enough to let them figure things out, and don't reveal anything the reader doesn't absolutely need to know.

Be careful, though--hooking the reader is not the same thing as leaving your reader in confusion. The reader isn't confused after reading the above passage; he's only asking questions. If the reader is confused because he can't figure out where or when or with whom the scene is anchored, he's likely to put your work down and not pick it up again. Those paragraphs from *Magdalene* paint a clear picture of a woman (we presume it's Mary Magdalene, because the reader almost always expects the first scene to be from the protagonist's point of view) in chains, standing before a busy Roman judge in a dank judgment hall. From just two paragraphs, we can safely assume the *where*, the *who*, and the *when*. We don't need a length introduction to set the stage of a prison in ancient Rome.

Many editors use the acronym RUE when editing manuscripts: *Resist the Urge to Explain.* Don't weigh down your prose with explanations, paragraphs of description, and backstory. All three do nothing to advance the plot and they dilute tension. If you have tied weights onto the top of your fishing line, you're going to lose your fish.

This is our mantra for this lesson: *Tension exists while the reader is waiting for an answer.*

Three Tension Killers

1. Explanations

In our sample scene, I've bold-faced all the places where an editor would rightly write RUE in the margin:

CREAK!

Samantha cowered in the corner as the front door knob turned slowly. Earlier she had noticed a man standing outside on the sidewalk and doing nothing, just watching the house. **Now she was home alone while Grandma played bingo down at the church. She was used to being alone at night, because she'd been living with her grandmother ever since her parents died in the same mysterious car crash that killed Grandpa.**

Her heart pounded, her palms perspired, and her kneecaps jimmied up and down. She could run out the back door, but Grandma had probably already set the deadlock, and that required a key and Samantha couldn't remember where it was. Grandma had gone through a litany of security measures when Samantha first moved in, but Sam had thought them all silly at the time. They didn't seem silly now!

CLICK!

Grandma kept her key hidden on a nail next to the door that led to the basement. **She'd kept a keyed deadbolt on that back door ever since the teenage boys next door tried to break in and steal Molly, Grandma's pit bull. Molly had called to her at the animal shelter, Grandma always said, and she was nothing but a cuddle bug.** But the boys next-door saw Molly and thought of nothing but what they could make in a dog fighting ring with a dog of their own. Fortunately, Molly had lived a long and happy life after the attempted dognapping.

Her attention flew back to the door when it opened, and through the gloom Samantha saw the stranger clearly. He wore a rain-splattered trench coat, a hat, and galoshes. His face was long, with a sinister look about the eyes and the hawked nose. A long scar ran across his cheek and ended at his nose. Oddly enough, the chain from a pocket watch dangled from his coat pocket and glittered in the dim overhead light.

Samantha's heart skipped a beat when she saw what the man carried—a brown box with a tangle of wires protruding from the partially opened box.

Was that a BOMB?! Of course—**Grandpa had been working**

at that top-secret lab doing work for the government, so he must have made someone very angry—angry enough to kill. But Grandpa was already dead, so why blow up the house now?

Because of Grandpa's research. He hadn't been studying atomic robots, as little Sally, Sam's niece, had said, but nanorobotics. Tiny little robots that could travel through a human's bloodstream and repair their DNA . . . or damage it. A science that had been quietly pursued for years, but had been largely relegated to horror films and literary thrillers until a few months ago.

A chill climbed the ladder of Samantha's spine. **Of course—Grandpa the scientist had hidden some kind of evidence, some secret file or laptop or something in the house. She and Grandma might not even know what it was, but apparently someone wanted that evidence destroyed. That's why this man was carrying a bomb!**

She needed to calm down. As long as the lights stayed dim, as long as she remained quiet, she might be able to remain hidden in this shadowed corner. The man might never even see her.

Still, her pounding heart nearly drowned out the ticking of the hall clock as the stranger kept coming and made his way to the dining room! Why on earth?

She closed her eyes and thought. **Of course—the dining room was the center of the house. If he left a bomb in that room, the ensuing blast would level the entire building.**

What on earth was she going to do?

That's a lot of explaining, and absolutely none of it is necessary to the scene. All it does is detract from the immediacy and danger our character is feeling. Read the scene aloud and omit the bolded sentences. Not great, but better, isn't it?

You've probably heard dozens of writing teachers admonish writers to "show, don't tell." Notice that nearly every bit of explanation is *telling*—even though it's disguised in the form of thoughts, the writer is trying hard to make sure you understand the situation fully.

But all that telling does nothing to increase tension. It only stuffs your reader with information he doesn't really need—or even want.

Remember: *tell your reader only what he absolutely needs to know when he absolutely needs to know it.*

2. Paragraphs of description

"Block descriptions" used to be in vogue, but most writers avoid them today because we are children of a video generation and we like action. So the preferred technique today is to put description in the action as the story moves forward. We only have one paragraph of block description in this scene (thank goodness!):

> Her attention flew back to the door when it opened, and through the gloom Samantha saw the stranger clearly. He wore a rain-splattered trench coat, a hat, and galoshes. His face was long, with a sinister look about the eyes and the hawked nose. A long scar ran across his cheek and ended at his nose. Oddly enough, the chain from a pocket watch dangled from his coat pocket and glittered in the dim overhead light.

So let's fix this—and let's also get rid of some assumptions Samantha makes that she really shouldn't be making.

> Her gaze flew back to the door when it opened, and through the dim light of the foyer lamp she saw the trench-coated stranger clearly. A scar marked his long face, traversing pocked cheeks and ending at his hawked nose. He crept forward, his wet galoshes leaving puddles on the polished wood floor, and paused to shift a box from one hip to the other. Samantha blinked when something glittered in the lamplight—a chain dangling from his coat pocket. Was it attached to a watch? Or to a garrote?

Much better! Now the action continues to move forward as the stranger comes into the house and Samantha reacts. And you may notice another important technique in raising tension—since you want your reader to ask questions, why not have your character ask them? By doing so, our character is gently hooking the reader herself.

Maybe that glittering item is a watch chain. But your reader is worried that it's a garrote, and she will keep reading to see if our heroine will be violently strangled before the scene is over.

A common writer's adage, usually attributed to Chekhov, says "if there's a rifle hanging over the mantle in the first act, it must be fired by the third." In other words, don't mention any unusual detail unless it will later be significant. In this situation, we could have the shiny chain attached to garrote, but I'm thinking it should be attached to a key or a vial or to some scientific gizmo that will help our intruder find an electronically tagged flash drive . . .

But if you're going to highlight an unusual object, it needs to have a purpose in the story even if the purpose is benign.

One caution: make sure your introduction of any significant object, scar, or characteristic is logical. Once I was reading a murder mystery by a best-selling mystery writer. She's old school, so there were lots of blocks of description, but in one description of a gardener she happened to write that he was left-handed.

That little tidbit was so out of place in the list of his physical attributes that I groaned. "That's it," I muttered. "He's the murderer, and they're going to prove it by saying the stab wound could only have been inflicted by a left-handed person."

Because I didn't want to waste several hours of my life reading a book in which the ending had been given away, I flipped to the back to check my theory. Yep, the gardener did it. I put the book down and never picked it up again—except maybe to sell it on eBay.

3. Backstory

There is a proper place for backstory: at the back of the story. But not up front, where your primary goal is to hook the reader and get him fully invested in your characters and story line. Backstory should also be avoided in fast-paced scenes of confrontation, battle, tragedy, or action. If your character is running for his life, it's not reasonable that he'd stop to remember the summer he spent with his Uncle Bart.

What is backstory? Any story bits that take place before the current scene's story time.

I've bold-faced all the bits of backstory in our sample scene. You'll notice that much of the backstory also qualifies as explanation —often they are one and the same.

CREAK!

Samantha cowered in the corner as the front door knob turned slowly. **Earlier she had noticed a man standing outside on the sidewalk and doing nothing, just watching the house.** Now she was home alone while Grandma played bingo down at the church. She was used to being alone at night, because **she'd been living with her grandmother ever since her parents died in the same mysterious car crash that killed Grandpa.**

Her heart pounded, her palms perspired, and her kneecaps jimmied up and down. She could run out the back door, but Grandma had probably already set the deadlock, and that required a key! Where was it? **Grandma had gone through a litany of security measures when Samantha first moved in, but Sam had thought them all silly at the time.** They didn't seem silly now!

CLICK!

Grandma kept her key hidden on a nail next to the door that led to the basement. **She'd kept a keyed deadbolt on that back door ever since the teenage boys next door tried to break in and steal Molly, Grandma's pit bull. Molly had called to her at the animal shelter, Grandma always said, and she was nothing but a cuddle bug. But the boys next-door saw Molly and thought of nothing but what they could make in a dog fighting ring with a dog of their own. Fortunately, Molly had lived a long and happy life after the attempted dognapping.**

Her attention flew back to the door when it opened, and through the gloom Samantha saw the stranger clearly. He wore a rain-splattered trench coat, a hat, and galoshes. His face was long, with a sinister look about the eyes and the hawked nose. A long scar ran across his cheek and ended at his nose. Oddly enough, the chain from a pocket watch dangled from his coat pocket and glittered in the dim overhead light.

Samantha's heart skipped a beat when she saw what the man carried—a brown box with a tangle of wires protruding from the partially opened box.

Was that a BOMB?! **Of course—Grandpa had been working at that top-secret lab doing work for the government,** so he must have made someone very angry—angry enough to kill. But Grandpa was already dead, so why blow up the house now?

Because of Grandpa's research. **He hadn't been studying atomic robots, as little Sally, Sam's niece, had said, but nanorobotics. Tiny little robots that could travel through a human's bloodstream and repair their DNA . . . or damage it. A science that had been quietly pursued for years, but had been largely relegated to horror films and literary thrillers until a few months ago.**

A chill climbed the ladder of Samantha's spine. **Of course— Grandpa the scientist had hidden some kind of evidence, some secret file or laptop or something in the house.** She and Grandma might not even know what it was, but apparently someone wanted that evidence destroyed. That's why this man was carrying a bomb!

She needed to calm down. As long as the lights stayed dim, as long as she remained quiet, she might be able to remain hidden in this shadowed corner. The man might never even see her.

Still, her pounding heart nearly drowned out the ticking of the hall clock as the stranger kept coming and made his way to the dining room! Why on earth?

She closed her eyes and thought. Of course—the dining room

was the center of the house. If he left a bomb in that room, the ensuing blast would level the entire building.

What on earth was she going to do?

Lots of backstory bits in our scene, and those paragraphs would be much improved without them. You may notice that all the backstory lines are introduced with the word "had"—because we use "had" to move us back and forth in story time. So when you're searching for backstory bits in your own story, use your word processing program's search feature to search for "had" or its contractions (like *hadn't*) and replace them with the same word, but in all capital letters. Then you'll easily be able to find the places where you might have slipped out of the immediacy of a scene and diluted your tension.

Now—please understand that backstory *can* serve an important function. In a slow, reflective scene, you may insert a recollection or a flashback to enlighten the reader about situations that have made your character the way she is in present story time. You may want to depict a scene from her childhood, or an episode that shaped her character. Backstory can be useful to explain why a character is distrustful, calculating, guarded, unusually kind and generous. But make sure these trips through time are in the proper place—not in an action scene, and not in the first thirty to fifty pages of your book. Your objective in both of those situations is to give your reader a breathless forward experience, to toss out hooks that create questions in your reader's mind, and keep your reader glued to the page.

Here's my attempt. You'll notice that I moved the scene forward a few moments to get rid of the backstory explanation about why Samantha was alone in the house. Also notice the lines where I included a few details without explanation: those are the hooks I'm tossing out to the reader. I've added the resulting questions in italics.

Samantha was strolling through the foyer when she glimpsed a heavy shadow through the stained glass door. *(Who's there?)* Someone stood just on the other side, but who? Not Nana, who'd just left for her bingo game. Not Robert, either, because Wednesday was his poker night. *(Who's Robert?)*

She frowned and hesitated, but the figure did not move to ring the doorbell or knock, neither did he look up. Instead he seemed to fumble with something in his hands, *(What's in his hand?)* then she heard a metallic scratch at the lock. *(Is he trying to jimmy the lock?)*

Her mouth went dry as her mind raced with possibilities: drunken neighbor? Thief? Serial killer? *(Which of the three is it?)*

She froze, torn between running toward the safety of her bedroom and remaining near the foyer so she could keep an eye on the intruder's progress. As the scratching continued, she moved away until she felt the wall at her back.

She crouched, trusting the heavy oak table to partly conceal her. *(Will it?)*

She cowered in the corner as the front door knob turned. Her heart pounded as she considered other options: she could run out the back door, but Nana always set the keyed deadlock before leaving and Samantha didn't remember where her grandmother kept the key. *(Why such a secure lock? Was it an unsafe neighborhood? Had she been threatened?)*

The door creaked, and Samantha's blood ran cold as it opened. Through the dim light of the foyer lamp she saw the trench-coated stranger clearly. A scar marked his long face, traversing pocked cheeks and ending at his hawked nose. He crept forward, his wet galoshes leaving puddles on the polished wood floor, and paused to shift a box from one hip to the other. *(What's in the box?)*

She blinked when something glittered in the lamplight—a chain dangling from his coat pocket. Was it attached to a watch? Or to a garrote? *(Ack! Which is it?)*

Her attention shifted when the man glanced at the cardboard box he carried. Sam could see nothing but a tangle of wires protruding from the top. *(What's inside?)*

Wires . . . could that be a bomb? *(Could it?)* Who would want to bomb her grandmother's house? *(Who?)* She was the nicest woman on the block, a sweet, church-going widow . . . *(So why would anyone want to hurt this woman? Or is Samantha worked up over nothing?)*

Samantha reminded herself to stay calm. As long as she remained quiet and the man kept his focus on his box, she might be able to remain hidden in the shadowed corner. *(Just maybe? Why doesn't she run?)*

As long as she could repress the frenzied scream clawing at the back of her throat. *(Is she going to be able to hold it together?)*

The reworked paragraph is still only a second draft, but it's much more tense. Look at all the little hooks tossed out to hook the reader. She will keep reading because she wants to know if this stranger was intent on doing the family harm, or if he's is a long-lost cousin returning an antique lamp.

The Dramatic Question

If you have done a good job of plotting your story (see *The Plot Skeleton,* book one of this series) you know the big dramatic question of your story is involved with the character's goal: Will Dorothy make it back to Kansas? Will Maria succeed at being a good nanny to the Von Trap family's children? Will James Bond be able to stop the evil villain from destroying the world?

But as you write your scenes, you will want to dangle other story questions as well. Those questions are what will keep your reader reading well past bedtime.

I can't tell you how many times I've had the TV on only as background noise, yet I can't leave the room because I've inadvertently been following a plotline and I can't rest until I find out if Sophia got over her laryngitis or if Jessica ever raised enough money for a prom dress. Do I care about those characters? Not really. Do I like those shows? Most of the time I don't even know the name of the program. But the story question hooks me, and something in me cannot move on until I discover the answer.

Tension exists while the reader is waiting for an answer.

We tossed out many story questions in our sample scene, but probably the primary question is either "what is the stranger doing in the house?" or "will Samantha survive her encounter with this intruder?", depending on where the story goes from this point. That question can remain unanswered for some time, and your reader will be hooked for as long as you prolong the suspense by withholding the answer. The period between story question and its answer can be called a "story arc." It's not the primary story arc spanning your entire story, but a mini-arc that can span two or scenes.

I'll confess I'm a huge fan of Masterpiece's *Downton Abbey*. There's a prevailing story arc that spans the entire series, and that is "Can this family preserve Downton's way of life and successfully hand it over to the next generation?" Robert, Lord of the Manor, raised that question in the first season when he declared that he was not the owner of the vast estate, but the caretaker for future generations. Other characters have reminded us of that story arc in subsequent episodes.

Yet each major character has a primary story arc, too—and many mini-arcs. We wonder if Daisy will ever find true love. Will Lady Edith ever get married? Will Mary step forward and become a modern woman, or will she cling to the traditions that separate the aristocrats from the commoners? Will the scheming Thomas ever get his comeuppance? Will Mrs. Patmore ever embrace electric appliances?

Along with those major questions, each episode tosses out a dozen smaller story hooks to keep viewers questioning, and that's why *Downton Abbey fascinates* millions of people across the world.

How can you plan, work with, and organize these story questions? Simple: chart them out.

When I used to write in Microsoft Word, I used an Excel chart to keep track of my scenes, timeline, details, and story arcs. Each row represented a scene, and I used *columns* for the details I wanted to track: point of view characters, time and date, major action, weather, mood, story details, story question asked, and story question answered.

POV Character	Scene action	Time/date	Story question asked	Story question answered
Samantha	She sees stranger in house	Wed, July 1, 8 p.m.	Who is the man in the house?	
Grandma	She's playing bingo	Wed, July 1, 8:30 p.m.	She has a premonition—what does it mean?	

This chart could be made in MS Word or in Excel.

See how it works? You can have as many columns and rows as you like, and use them to keep track of all kinds of details. When I wrote a series set in a mortuary, I needed columns to keep track of which random townspeople were in the mortuary, and what stage they were in—embalming, viewing, or funeral.

Now that I write in Scrivener (the amazing writing program found at www.literatureandlatte.com), I keep track of the same information, but I do it on the program's notecards instead of an Excel chart. Same system, different medium.

Whatever program you use, a system like this is quite useful for keeping track of when you present a story question and at what point you decide to answer it. Just remember to ask a different story question before you answer the first one so you always have a hook "in the water," so to speak.

Keep in mind that your major story question—will your character accomplish his goal?—needs to arc over the entire story and be resolved at the ending.

While we're on the subject, yes, a series of books can have a story question arcing over the entire series. Though it does require preplanning, it's a great way to keep readers interested in the characters and tie the books in a series together.

Down to Brass Tacks: Techniques for Increasing Tension

I demonstrated a couple of basic techniques and principles in the first part of this book (have your character present the story questions, keep the action moving forward), but there are other, larger techniques you can use to ratchet up the tension in your story. Without further ado, here they are:

Put your characters in **a crucible**: a confining space or situation they cannot escape. I did it in *The Elevator* and *Uncharted*. We are all capable of going a little crazy when we find ourselves in a situation we cannot escape or control, so whether it's three women trapped in an elevator or five friends trapped on a mysterious island, a crucible is enough to make characters crazy, too. In other stories, people have been stranded in space, trapped in mental institutions, unjustly sent to prison, trapped in spirit worlds, and many other situations. The rules of civilized society become skewed in these crucibles, and tension is almost inescapable.

Add a **ticking clock** to your story. If you're writing about a woman trying to raise money for a dramatic production of *Romeo and Juliet*, you might struggle to add tension until you add a deadline. And then raise the stakes: if she doesn't raise the money by June first, the drama club won't be able to perform their play. That's not so terrible, so the stakes aren't high enough. Add new layers: If the students can't perform, the school won't have enough money to refurbish the auditorium, and the school board will demolish the building, destroying the hopes and dreams of future thespians, including our brave young heroine, whose only ticket out of a horrible neighborhood is the theater. Better, huh?

No matter what your story, adding a deadline or a literal ticking clock (strapped to an explosive device?) will increase the stakes and raise the level of tension.

Get rid of the protagonist's best friend . . . or have him betray the protagonist with good intentions. We see this a lot in movies—the protagonist has one person whom he trusts, be it wife or best friend or mentor—and that person is either killed, kidnapped, or felled by some mysterious ailment. The protagonist loses a precious ally when his friend is removed or becomes untrustworthy. When your protagonist is hurt by this development, the tension level rises.

Equally as effective and perhaps even more poignant is when the protagonist's good friend betrays him due to a misunderstanding or because he thinks he knows what's best for the main character. That development not only raises tension, it makes the reader wince with sympathy.

Make a key piece of equipment or technology fail. Hey, it happens. The air conditioning goes out on the hottest day of the year, the launch button doesn't launch the rocket, the air hose springs a leak, or the brakes don't work. No matter what your genre, your protagonist will face a new and tension-raising complication when Murphy's Law kicks in and what could happen *does* happen . . . at the worst possible moment.

Introduce a mysterious stranger. It's been said that most plots are a variation of either a stranger coming to town or the protagonist leaving town, but those comings and goings can work wonders for your story's tension level, too. An unknown person enters your story world, and your protagonist doesn't know what to make of him or her. Will he be a friend? Is she a threat? Where did he come from?

Just remember not to give this character any point of view scenes. You don't want him Explaining All after his arrival in the story . . . unless he's lying. If you put us in his head, we'll know his thoughts and plans so the mystery (and the tension) will evaporate. *Tension exists when the reader waiting for an answer*: who is this man and what is his agenda?

Give your protagonist **a physical weakness**—and have it come in to play at a pivotal moment. Is she prone to migraines? Does she suffer from epilepsy? Hay fever? Claustrophobia? Fear of heights? Agoraphobia?

I'll never forget the masterful use of asthma in the movie *Signs*. The protagonist's son suffers from asthma, and sure enough, he has a severe asthma attack as aliens are entering the house and the family is barricaded in the basement. But at the end of the movie (spoiler ahead!), it's *because* the boy had asthma that he doesn't breathe deeply of the alien poison that would have killed him.

If your protagonist suffers from a fear of spiders, mention it early and then have a tarantula lurking beneath her bed at a moment when she needs to crawl beneath it to hide from the villain. (I know it's harsh, but our job is to torture our characters.)

Could he break his leg as the villain is chasing him? Could she turn an ankle running in her trademark high-heeled shoes?

Don't forget about the physical conditions that present themselves as we grow older. Consider the age of your protagonist—if she's a fifty-year-old woman, she could suffer from hot flashes at inconvenient times—and add a spark of humor to your story. Maybe he's a Jack Ryan type, but he's foiled at a crucial moment because he can't read the small print on a ticking bomb. Maybe she's off to meet the man of her dreams, but she can't remember where she put her car keys.

Physical weaknesses elicit sympathy from the reader because we all have them—and sympathy raises the level of tension as we wonder if the character is going to successfully cope with his weaknesses.

Dystopian novels are currently all the rage in young adult fiction, and the tension in those novels frequently rises from the protagonist's clashes with **social forces**: the government, war, rebellion, or a prevailing philosophy. But you don't have to set your novel in the future to employ social forces to raise tension. George Orwell did it in *Animal Farm* and *1984*. Harriet Beecher Stowe did it in *Uncle Tom's Cabin*.

What prevailing social attitudes drive you crazy? Whether it's political correctness run amuck or the devaluing of human life, take an issue, depict it at its extreme, and you're on your way to creating a novel with tension that derives from society itself.

Tension can often be escalated by **simple irritations**. A few days ago, a young husband who lived near me was texting his babysitter during the previews at a theater. The man behind him asked him to stop, the husband didn't, and a few minutes later the young husband lay dying on the floor, shot by the irritated moviegoer behind him.

In the 1993 movie *Falling Down*, Michael Douglas plays a down-on-his luck man who succumbs to road rage and embarks on a shotgun killing spree. Hurt people . . . hurt people, and if your protagonist is upset about something, his reactions to ordinary situations can be extremely out of proportion. Use the hurt in your protagonist's life to make your reader wonder what he or she will do next.

Give your protagonist **a special gift or ability**—the ability to fly, to see through walls, to sing, to run a mile in six seconds—then take that ability away at a crucial moment. He can be foiled by an enemy (Lex Luthor always managed to use kryptonite against Superman), develop a physical weakness, or simply not have the heart to use his special ability. The baseball player known for grand slams will face tremendous pressure if he falls into a batting slump. And that pumps up the tension as we root for the underdog and wonder if he will ever succeed again.

Don't forget the "big three" conflicts to increase tension: **man against man, man against nature, man against himself.** You may not have all three elements in your story, but these three never fail to increase the tension level.

Man against man may evoke images of war or criminal activity, but it could just as easily be two socialites sniping at each other over tea.

Man against nature could be depicted as a character surviving a blizzard, but it could just as easily be a woman surviving a rabid dog . . . or a child struggling to beat cancer.

And *man against himself* has to be one of the most powerful challenges of all. Maria would have been a perfectly fine governess at the Von Trapp family mansion if she hadn't fallen in love with the captain. She ran away after realizing she'd been betrayed . . . by her own rebellious heart.

The alcoholic struggling to defeat his demons and remain sober; the autistic woman trying to connect with the world outside herself; the broken-hearted widower reluctant to live without his wife—all of these storylines have the potential for poignant and powerful tension.

As millions of romance novels have illustrated, **sexual attraction** is a sure-fire source of tension. Hidden love can be a powerful motivator, and denied love can drive a character crazy. Even when love is encouraged and returned, a couple's desire for each other can send rational thought flying out the window.

So use that tension-trigger wisely. Allowing a couple to get together too soon may diffuse the sexual tension in a story even if it is not a genre romance, in which the couple typically resolves their differences and come together only at the end.

As you consider how to use sexual tension, ask yourself if your protagonist could:

- neglect his duty because he was spending the afternoon with his love
- violate a vow by pursuing his love interest
- cause others to suffer because he can't get his loved one out of his mind
- make a terrible decision because he's swayed by his scheming lover's opinion

A character's choices in love can have severe repercussions, giving you a great opportunity to explore them and increase tension. When your protagonist makes a wrong decision, your reader will be screaming, "No! Don't fall for her!" and that's delicious.

Subtext in dialogue is a wonderful way to raise tension. Many beginning writers create "on the nose" dialogue in which each character answers the other precisely as expected, creating a ping-pong effect. Good dialogue has unexpected beats and responses, keeping the reader slightly off balance. Subtext in dialogue—in which the characters speak more loudly through their actions and attitudes than through their words—is a wonderful source of tension.

If you have a moment, do an Internet search for "Hills Like White Elephants" by Ernest Hemingway. This is a simple short story, ostensibly about a man and a woman drinking beer at an outdoor café in Spain.

They chat about the hills, about the beer, and then the conversation takes a turn:

> 'It's really an awfully simple operation, Jig,' the man said. 'It's not really an operation at all.'
>
> The girl looked at the ground the table legs rested on.
>
> 'I know you wouldn't mind it, Jig. It's really not anything. It's just to let the air in.'
>
> The girl did not say anything.
>
> 'I'll go with you and I'll stay with you all the time. They just let the air in and then it's all perfectly natural.'
>
> 'Then what will we do afterwards?'
>
> 'We'll be fine afterwards. Just like we were before.'

Reading between the lines, a savvy reader understands that the woman is pregnant and the man is talking about an abortion. The word *abortion* is never used, neither are the words *baby* or *fetus*. But at this point the tension begins to rise, because the reader wonders why the man wants her to have an abortion and what decision the woman will make. Another question rises farther down the page—what did the woman ever see in this man?

The conversation continues, and we realize that the man is completely selfish, not wanting to have to share the woman with anyone else, not even a child. She finally begs him to stop talking.

And at the story's end, after the man has taken their bags to the train and spent a little time drinking at the bar, he returns to the woman.

> 'Do you feel better?' he asked.
>
> 'I feel fine,' she said. 'There's nothing wrong with me. I feel fine.'

In an ever-so-subtle line, Hemingway lets us know the woman

will keep the baby. She doesn't need an operation, and she won't have one. The reader's questions are finally answered.

After you've complete a first draft of your manuscript, print it out, stack the pages neatly, and then pull a page at random from the pile. Read what you've written with a marker in your hand, and highlight any line or passage that raises a question in the reader's mind. If you've written a page of pleasant description or genial conversation and you find nothing to highlight, it's time to rewrite.

Tension doesn't require bombs and bullets, arguments or spooky encounters. Now you know what it requires: questions without immediate answers.

"But I'm writing narrative," you may be whispering under your breath. "I'm writing a simple scene to move my character from one place to another. There's no confrontation, no real drama. Do I really need tension here?"

You do . . . unless you want your reader to skip those pages or put your book down. So how are you supposed to insert tension into a simple narrative?

From Donald Maass I learned four ways to insert tension into scenes—all kinds of scenes. Let's explore:

Action scenes: you might think an action scene—a fight, for instance, between the villain and the protagonist—wouldn't require any special emphasis on tension. After all, even thought the villain is mighty, our protagonist is the star of the book and he is imbued with the power of his convictions, right? So of course he has to win!

And therein lies the problem. If the reader assumes the protagonist will win, your fight scene will be utterly devoid of tension.

My husband loves action movies, and I like some of them, but I usually watch them with a book in hand because I don't care about the fight and chase sequences. I know who's going to win the fights and I know the good guys are going to get away. Never any doubt. So when people start fighting or chasing, I start reading my book.

So to keep your readers from skimming or skipping ahead, you need to create honest doubt in the reader's mind. How do you do that? *By creating doubt in your protagonist.*

Think of the first few Rocky movies—maybe all of them, but I can't remember the last few. Rocky movies usually open with a contented Rocky in his ordinary world, then he accepts a fight and gets trounced. He gets beaten so badly he's not sure if he can win again. And in his doubt lies the tension.

Your protagonist may be the star of the story, but he won't feel invincible if:

- he's emotionally upset about something that deeply affects him
- his love interest doesn't support him
- he is deathly ill.
- he has lost his special powers
- he has lost his mentor
- he hasn't eaten in three days
- or if he sparred with someone else and lost the fight.

The above list is far from exhaustive, so put on your thinking cap and see if you can invent unique situations that will cause your protagonist to question his abilities, his gifts, even his destiny. If your protagonist doubts himself, your reader will doubt him, too. All that doubt will raise questions about your protagonist's ability to be victorious, especially if the villain has the upper hand during the first three-quarters of the fight.

Dialog: to create tension in dialogue, make sure it exists between the conversing people and is not necessarily part of their topic. Two people may converse about a political opinion they share, but if they don't like each other, sparks can fly.

Example: Tom, Larry's boss, has ordered Larry to ask all the guys at the warehouse to contribute to the Fund for Orphans. Larry carries the donations to Tom's office and drops the container on his boss's desk.

Tom looked up, a spark of irritation in his eye. "What's this?"

Larry pressed his lips together. "You know. You asked me to

badger the guys for money; here it is. All sixty-seven dollars and twenty-three cents."

"That's all?"

"Money's tight now, at least for us working stiffs. The guys on the floor don't earn anywhere close to what you administrative fat cats get."

Tom sniffed, then lifted the rusty coffee can and set it on his open palm, as if weighing it. "For the record, I didn't ask you to badger anybody. And you should watch who you're calling a fat cat."

Larry ignored the warning, just as he'd ignored a dozen others. "Can I go?"

"You got some place to be?"

Larry wanted to answer that he'd rather be alone on the dark side of the moon with a severe rash on his privates than in this room with his former friend, but that response would get him a scowl and a fifteen-minute lecture intended to intimidate.

"Yeah," he finally said, sliding his hands into his pockets. "I got some place to be."

Tom lifted a brow as a wicked gleam entered his eye. "You old dog," he drawled, a lascivious smile crawling across his face. "Get out of here, then. Go get 'er, whoever she is."

Larry left the office, reflexively wiping his hands on his jeans. Every time he left that room, he felt like he needed a shower.

But he wouldn't have to suffer Tom much longer.

What questions did that scene raise in your mind? I found myself asking, "What happened between these two former friends? What event or circumstance accounts for the barely-tempered hostility between them?"

And at the mention of Larry ignoring yet another warning, I wanted to know if Tom would ever act on his not-so-subtle threats. And finally, "What's going to happen to Tom? Has Larry arranged a hit or something?" I'd read more to find out.

Exposition: "telling, not showing" does have its place, and sometimes you simply want to relay information to the reader as quickly, smoothly, and succinctly as possible. In those situations, you use exposition, so how do you inject tension into the facts and summary of narrative passages?

Maass advises writers to portray emotions in conflict and ideas at war with each other.

Let me whip up an example:

Greenhollow Hills lay just south of the intersection of the B&O Railroad line and Highway 19. The town's founders had chosen the spot because the central hill ascended to a point 400 feet above sea level, the perfect spot for a lookout tower. After a revival left the townsfolk convicted of sin and searching their Bibles, the population divided into two camps, each capable of ferocious fervor. The Arminian camp wanted to reinforce the lookout tower, because God would surely defend those with the will to defend themselves, while the Calvinists wanted to tear the tower down, confident that their fates had been predetermined and sealed since the beginning of time.

Every household proclaimed its theological stance on signs they hammered to their pristine picket fences. Women of the Tower Arminians wore red, the color of the Crusaders, and women of the Tower Calvinists favored white, the color worn by holy angels.

Versions of Shakespeare's saga of forbidden love played out in clandestine meetings as the daughters of Tower Arminians fell in love with the sons of Tower Calvinists and vice versa. Some claimed the nearby town of Runaway Junction owed its existence to these castoff and rebellious romantics.

Every year at the annual town meeting, each side sent its most eloquent speakers, who delivered impassioned speeches on the Advantages or the Uselessness of the Greenhollow Tower as viewed through the writings of Saint Paul. A vote was called, and each year the selectmen's votes resulted in a tie, prolonging the communal uncertainty and assuring each side that God had endorsed their position.

But in 1895, the unthinkable occurred: in the lonely hours of a windless June night, under cover of darkness, someone splashed the base of the old tower with kerosene. Within half an hour, the tower crumbled into ashes, and the townspeople crumpled in silence. Who would do such a terrible thing?

But more important—with the tower gone and its religious significance moot, what would give their lives meaning?

From this opening, I might follow with a scene in Miranda's point of view. She'd be one of the bereft Tower Calvinists, and her daughter a closet Tower Arminian in love with a boy from the other side of the debate.

This is a silly story, but it could be taken seriously if I wanted to stress how petty religious arguments can escalate into tragic separations. But I used simple exposition—which is "telling" in either the narrator's or a character's voice—to introduce a note of tension by introducing at least two questions: who set fire to the tower, and how will the townspeople cope now that the focus of their lives is gone? Will they rebuild it so they can continue their debate? Or will they move on to more important issues?

Description/Travel: If you must stop the action to write lengthy description, especially if your character is traveling (and it might be appropriate after an active scene if you want to vary the pacing of your story), then make sure to inject tension into the passage. How? By giving us the thoughts and conflicted feelings of the observer as he describes the view. You can do this no matter which point of view you choose—first, second, or third, but we need to have access to the character's thoughts.

Delia leaned against the cushions of the carriage as the horse slowed to a trot. She could see the vague outline of the grand brick house at the end of the carriageway, but the early morning fog prevented a clear view.

Her breathing quickened. Amazing how the mere sight of the house could arouse a feeling of panic within her. She was no longer a child, no longer the poor cousin tolerated only out of a sense of pity.

No one would scold her on this visit; no nanny would stand beside the door with a ruler to slap her wrist.

Everything had changed since Belmair. And everyone who had ever harmed her was dead.

Short and sweet, but it does the job. The reader is left with three big questions: what is Belmair, what happened there, and what happened to all those people who had harmed her?

The reader is much more interested in Delia than in the grand house or the foggy morning, so focus on her.

You could delete the sentences about Delia's childhood as the poor cousin and harsh nanny, but I let them stay because I wanted to give a little context in present story time.

If you wanted to write this scene in first person, you'd simply change the "she's" to "I's" and so forth.

Notice, please, that when you are writing in close third person point of view, you do not put thoughts into italics, nor do you need the words "she thought." Because we are solidly in Delia's head, the reader assumes the words on the page are Delia's thoughts. Simple. If this technique confuses you, please read book number three in this series, *Point of View*.

And finally: *It was a dark and stormy night*. Weather.

To increase the tension in your story, whip up a storm, a blizzard, or the hottest summer on record. We're constantly surrounded by weather, so why not use it? *Cujo* would not be the tension-filled story it is if Stephen King had set it in wintertime. If the weather had been cold, the woman and her son would have wanted to stay *in* the car, not escape it. But King set the story in a sweltering summer, and the heroine desperately needed to get out of the car to get water for her son, who was dehydrated almost to the point of death. But a rabid Saint Bernard lurked just outside . . .

So if your heroine is about to be attacked by a madman who breaks into the house, set the scene at night. During a storm. Arrange a power outage. The house is creaking. Her nerves are strung tight. Throw in a red herring, when the strange noise turns out to be a clumsy cat. And then, to prevent this scene from becoming a complete cliché, have the lights come back on. She relaxes, puts the butcher knife back in the drawer, and, smiling, turns around to find—

The madman.

Lights out again.

Clichés are clichés for a reason—they creep us out. So *do* use them if they work, but be sure to add a couple of unexpected twists so we are as caught by surprise as your heroine is.

Won't the reader think of a weather development as a convenient coincidence? Not if it works to your protagonist's *disadvantage*. As long as weather developments are making life more difficult for your characters, readers will hang on to read what happens next.

And, come to think of it, King's *Cujo* employs a crucible as well.

Chapter Breaks: you can increase the tension of your story with strategic chapter breaks. For instance, if I were writing a scene about the heroine and the madman in her house, I'd write this:

Charisa smiled as the kitchen lights blazed, revealing her aunt's charming red-and-white gingham kitchen. She lowered the butcher knife to the table and wiped her damp palm against her jeans.

The kitchen was exactly what it appeared to be—the warm heart of this home. The black cat above the stove still clicked in its steady rhythm, but now the sound was barely audible above the hum of the refrigerator. The sticky notes on the refrigerator fluttered, lifted by the steady stream of heat from the floor vent, and the dishwasher's blue light gleamed, reminding her that she needed to put the clean dishes away.

How silly she'd been, spooked by the darkness and unfamiliar surroundings. For the first time she felt grateful to be alone, so no one had seen her creeping around the house, knife raised like a scared teenager who'd witnessed too many horror films . . .

Chuckling, she opened a drawer and dropped the knife into it, taking comfort in the metallic clang of utensils. She slammed the drawer and began to hum, eager to get back to her book. She turned—

There he stood, his bloody hands reaching for her throat.

NEXT CHAPTER.

When readers say they've lost sleep over one of my books, I know I've done a good job of chapter placement. Many people read at night as they settle into bed, and most people will tell themselves, "One more chapter and I'll turn out the light."

But if your chapter ends like the example above, they're not going to turn out the light any time soon. They're going to keep reading until they hit another chapter, and how well you end *that* chapter may well determine if your reader *ever* gets to sleep.

In summary, how do we create tension? Tension exists when the reader is waiting for an answer, so be sure to use all the techniques we've explored to create scenes that leave the reader desperate to know what happens next.

The following story may be apocryphal, but I love it. Apparently two thespians were arguing about who was the better actor until the older man said, "I could upstage you without even being onstage."

The younger man snorted. "I'd like to see you try."

That night they performed their play and nothing seemed amiss until the older actor walked to a table, picked up a glass of water, and took a sip. He then lowered it, balancing it half-on, half-off the table, then he left the stage.

The younger actor continued with his dramatic monologue, but no one in the audience paid him any attention. They were fixated on the glass, each of them wondering if—when—it would fall and shatter.

The older man won the argument because he *did* upstage the younger actor. How? By creating a question in the minds of his audience. He created tension that mesmerized even the ushers in the theater.

You can do the same thing with your writing. Practice, practice, and begin to notice how other writers use these techniques to keep readers glued to their pages. After all, hooking readers is a lot easier than fishing for piranha.

Now, go write something that will keep me turning pages!

TENSION EXERCISES

1. GO BACK TO THE SCENE WITH SAMANTHA AND REWRITE IT . . . with all the tension killers removed and some new elements added. Ready? Write!

2. Okay, if you've done your homework, I imagine that you did one of three things. You either followed the example scene way too closely, feeling that you were somehow bound to the first draft. Good news! We are never bound to our first drafts; they are our scratch pads. Give yourself permission to break free and write what works.

Or maybe you went completely off the rails and wrote all kinds of things, inadvertently using backstory and more explanation and description. Sometimes, you know, creative freedom craves the restraint of craft.

Or maybe you did what I attempted to do: find the best way to write the scene in present story time without any unnecessary explanations, gimmicks (like using all caps), exclamation marks, overlong description, or backstory.

3. Look at your current work in progress. What are some elements you can add to amp up the tension? Especially look at any

scenes where a character is traveling, drinking coffee, or taking a shower. Readers know how to do all those things, so what can you write into your character's thoughts—or in action—to make this scene tense and unexpected?

4. Rewrite one of your scenes and add in either a ticking clock or a storm. Or give your character a migraine. How does that increase the tension?

5. Now that you've rewritten that scene, bring down the tension a bit by making the disturbance *quiet*. Give your character that migraine, but don't let him reveal that his head is splitting. Or have her rush away an unexpected guest without letting on that the kidnapper's deadline is approaching. How does changing that simple element increase the tension?

Chapter Eight

WRITING HISTORICAL FICTION

I'VE ALWAYS LOVED HISTORICAL FICTION. WHILE I WAS STILL IN elementary school I discovered a box of old abandoned books in our rental house, and I loved those books so much I carried them with me when my husband and I moved into a house of our own. Inside the corrugated walls of that box I found copies of *Jane Eyre*, *The Nun's Story*, and *Gone with the Wind* . . . and in reading those historical novels, I fell in love with other worlds and other eras.

I still have a couple of those old books, and I've read them many times over the years. That's a beautiful thing about historical fiction —it's timeless.

I don't know if an "official" definition exists for this genre, but you might say that historical fiction *is a novel set during a distinct period in history*. This time period might or might not be before the author's time. For instance, *The Nun's Story*, set in the years of World War II, wasn't considered historical fiction when it was published in 1956, but it qualifies today. I wouldn't apply a historical fiction label to *The Pearl*, my 2003 novel about cloning, but my grandchildren might.

Historical fiction is a broad genre encompassing a host of subgenres: romance, thrillers, the "history mystery," biblical novels, fantasy, "alternative history" (e.g. what if the Confederacy had won the Civil War?), science fiction, westerns, time travel, and many more. If you can imagine a story set in the past, you can research the setting for a historical novel and write it for juveniles or adults.

Who reads historical novels? Lots of people, but not everyone. I have observed a certain prejudice against historical novels among some readers, particularly if the novels seem daunting in plot, "history lessons," or language ("too many thee's and thou's," reported one reader). I am personally chagrinned whenever I open a book and find a chart of the protagonist's extended family on the fourth page. I can't help feeling that if I need a diagram to keep up, how could the book be a relaxing, entertaining read?

But not all historical novels are hard or difficult to read—the best ones are as entertaining as their contemporary versions. And they offer something contemporary novels don't—a detailed look into a world gone by, an age when people much like ourselves lived and loved and struggled against overwhelming odds.

The best historical novels entertain us by providing a cast of memorable, fascinating characters. When we become glued to the story because we can't wait to see what Scarlett or Pip will do next, the historical aspect seems almost incidental.

For most readers, historical novels offer more than an entertaining story—they also provide the reader with an enjoyable learning experience. As readers travel through the historical story world with the characters, they live through the vicarious experiences of living in another time, eating unusual foods, and observing unusual customs. A skillful historical novelist will populate her novel with lots of sensory details to enliven and enlarge the experience.

When I asked my blog readers to chime in with reasons why they liked to read historical fiction, I received several interesting answers:

From Linda: "I love historical fiction because it fascinates me to learn how people dealt with the challenges of daily life in those times, yet the interpersonal issues are timeless. It's easy to romanticize life 'way back when,' but daily life was hard--and yet people still loved, laughed, cried, hurt. [Historical fiction] gives me a greater appreciation for what we have today."

Kara wrote that she and a friend "like historical fiction because the time period is different than today. We live life today; we know what it's like. Historical fiction transports us to another time where life was not necessarily simpler, but different." She adds that contemporary fiction often "hits too close to home" in its subject matter, but the same subject in historical fiction allows for a certain emotional distance.

Holly likes historical fiction because "I learn about how people lived during various times in history--from traveling across the country in a wagon to sailing across the sea to life in communist Russia (all things I have never experienced). It teaches me something new. Also, I am transported to view another place and time, which thrills me!"

Margaret wrote that she enjoys historical fiction "because it is about events that really happened. Since those things occurred in the past, we can trace the outcome of those events. When we gain a deeper understanding of the beliefs and motivations of people in history and how these played out in the results of their actions, we gain important insights that help us make better decisions in the present."

Indeed. As George Santayana said, "Those who cannot remember the past are condemned to repeat it."

Pick a Time, Any Time!

What time periods are open to an author considering historical fiction? Nearly all of them! No period of time is too early to explore. Jean Auel's prehistoric novels are best-sellers. Tosca Lee's novel, *Havah*, is about Eve, the first woman on the planet.

Some historical periods have been explored more than others (the Civil War comes to mind), so the writer considering one of these eras had better come up with a unique twist on her story. You're more likely to pique an editor's interest if you're writing in a time period that hasn't been over-represented in your chosen market. So visit your local bookstore, make a note of what's on the shelves, and then *choose something else.* Why set out to be similar when you could be strikingly original?

Notice that I said *nearly* all time periods are open to the historical novelist. You can go back as far as you like, but be careful when considering more recent history. When I started writing, World War II books weren't considered historical, but now they are. The boundary line is always shifting, so if you want to write a book set in the disco world of the 1980s, better check with an editor to see if your book would be considered historical. Here's a tip—if you know lots of people who lived through the period you're considering, it's probably not unfamiliar enough to be deemed "historical."

My agent believes that a good rule of thumb is to *go back fifty years from the present.* Fifty years is long enough for a decade to be considered "historical."

Historical Settings

Where should you set your historical novel? The answer depends on the size of your story canvas. Is your story broad, with a cast of many characters and involving incidents of war, disease, or major national calamity? Then set your story in the midst of the action and feature the people who faced the most significant changes. For instance, if you want to write a heroic adventure novel focused on the 1986 Challenger explosion, you should set it at Cape Kennedy or Houston.

But if your story is smaller, if you plan on writing about the effects of the Challenger disaster on an astronaut's estranged wife, then you could set it in a small town in Alabama, where the woman hears about her husband's death and wonders why the people around her continue with life-as-usual while for her time is standing still.

Wherever you set your novel, remember that for the story to be effective, you must shrink any major event down to a size that will greatly affect your protagonist. "When writing about war," the old writing adage goes, "write about one man's war."

On September 11, 2001, I was in Springfield, Missouri, with my friend Lori Copeland. We had just finished writing one of our Heavenly Daze novels, and that morning I was getting ready to go to the airport. I had the television on, and watched as a second jet tore through the second tower at the World Trade Center.

I called upstairs to Lori and her husband, and together we huddled before the television and watched the horrific events unfold. We saw the disasters at the Pentagon and in Pennsylvania; we stared as the New York towers crumbled to the ground and dust-coated people ran screaming through the streets. As I watched, the writer part of my brain kept thinking, *How could I write about this? I can't. It's too big. Too horrible. Too big.*

Many novelists, of course, have written stories about what happened on that terrible September 11th, but each of them narrowed the spotlight until it shone only on one or two people. My book club recently read *Extremely Loud and Incredibly Close*, by Jonathan Safran Foer, and I was impressed at how skillfully the author wrapped that huge event around a young autistic boy who lost his father when the towers fell.

So if you want to write about the Vietnam War, the fall of Jericho, the exodus from Egypt, or the first moon landing, wrap your world event around one extremely interesting protagonist. Let us experience the events of that time through his or her eyes, and your reader will experience the situation for himself. Take the event that is "too big" to handle, and shrink it to a mallet that smacks your protagonist's ordinary world and sends it spinning out of control.

Now you're ready to proceed.

Wait—what about your plot? Don't you need a plot before you begin researching?

Not necessarily. You may have a vague idea about your story's focus and direction, but keep an open mind as you dig into the research. You may discover little nuggets of information that will greatly enrich your plot and add key complications to your story.

When I set out to write my first adult novel, I talked with the editor for whom I'd written several juvenile novels. He'd asked me to consider adult fiction, and I was happy to expand my horizons. Our conversation went something like this:

"So," I began, "what would you like me to submit? A contemporary novel or historical?"

"Historicals seem to be selling best right now."

"Okay. What about the time period? Any preference?"

"The Civil War has been done to death . . . and so has life on the prairie."

"Okay . . . hmm. I can't think of any Christian novels set in medieval times. What about that era?"

"Go for it."

So I did.

I went to my office and began to research medieval times—and I learned that those years were called the Dark Ages for good reasons. Most people were illiterate, the Catholic church was the only established church in Europe, and people tended to be either very wealthy or desperately poor.

I sketched out a plot about the beautiful daughter of a poor villein (the English version of a serf) who grows up in a castle as a playmate to the nobleman's daughter. When the noble family has no more use for her—especially when it becomes clear that she has fallen in love with the nobleman's oldest son—they marry her off to the village brute.

My poor protagonist would be abused and unloved, but she would conquer her foes and find true love and happiness at the end of the story.

But . . . what about the middle of the book? What sorts of complications could I create that would forge a will of iron in my gentle protagonist?

As I researched medieval society and common beliefs of the period, I learned that during the Middle Ages people believed that twins were the result of a woman's union with two different men. Ah! Perfect.

My protagonist's brutish husband had been cruel enough, but after giving birth to one child, when she shrieks and prepares to give birth to yet another, the man flies into a rage and is determined to kill her for her adultery.

Research provided a perfectly logical and fascinating development to move my story forward and turn my gentle heroine into a steely-eyed woman bent on revenge.

First, We Create Characters

In *Creating Extraordinary Characters*, the second lesson in the Writing Lessons series, I give tips on how to create characters that are larger than life. Those lessons still apply when you're writing historical fiction, because without characters, plot is only stage direction.

If your characters seem a bit blank when you're just starting out, don't worry. As you research and fine-tune your plot, you'll begin to understand what your characters must be in order to carry off the story. I never feel that I know my characters until I've finished the first draft. We're like strangers mingling at a party, sharing a few whispers and hinting at buried secrets. By the time I finish the second or third draft, however, I could tell you what my characters like to eat for dinner.

Here's a useful tip on naming historical characters. If you're writing an American character who was born sometime after 1880, be sure to visit Social Security's baby name database: http://www.ssa.gov/oact/babynames/decades/

This site lists the most popular 100 baby names by year and decade, and even though "John" and "Mary" ruled the lists for years, you can find some memorable and appropriate-for-the-time names in those long lists.

If you're naming characters who lived well before the nineteenth century, skim through the original sources you've used for research. The people mentioned within those pages are likely to have names common to the time.

I also heartily recommend Writer's Digest's *Character Naming Sourcebook* by Sherrilyn Kenyon. Along with several interesting articles about the importance of character names, this book offers lists of names grouped by geographic and/or historical categories. So you can find names for your Arthurian knight, your Greek fisherman, your Native American trapper (listed by tribe!), and your Welsh poet. A wonderful tool now available in print and e-book editions.

Next, We Research

No matter when or where you set your historical novel, you should pay attention to a key convention of the genre: get your history right. Though some authors do exercise artistic license and take liberties with recorded history, I'd advise against it. Unless you're writing a novel of alternative history ("Imagine a world in which Hitler completely conquered Europe"), historical readers want to trust that you've done your homework.

We've all seen notes from the author at the back of a novel explaining why he moved the Battle of Shrewsbury from Monday to Thursday. If you absolutely *have* to change recorded history, be sure to mention it in an afterword or other commentary. If you don't, some sharp-eyed historian will take you to task in an email, write a horrible review on Amazon.com, and generally let it be known that you are a novelist who does not research properly.

(Sometimes they do those things even if you *do* research properly. If your version contradicts the sappy Hollywood version of an historic event, you will be branded as a heretic even though you are correct and Hollywood is wrong. That's when you take a deep breath and repeat: "Life is too short to waste time with critics.")

For years now, I have listed my sources and references in the back of my historical novels. First, I think it's fair and a nice gesture to acknowledge the authors whose work helped me write a story. Second, it's a subtle way to show the reader that you have done your homework. Finally, some readers become fascinated with a story or historical era, and a list of references sends them off to learn more about your chosen time period.

A bibliographic list is certainly not a necessity, but I think the

advantages of including such a list far outweigh the option of not
including one.

Though I could spend an entire day exploring rabbit trails, I
force myself to remember that the first phase of research is the
Macro Phase. I need to learn about "big picture" concepts and
issues; I do not yet need to learn about trivial details.

So here's a checklist of general areas we need to research as we
begin our novels:

- Society: What were the prevailing attitudes of society?
  How did society treat men, women, children, and slaves?
  Were most people educated and if so, how? What were
  the jobs of ordinary people? What were the prevailing
  attitudes toward racial differences?
- Housing: Where did most people live? How were homes
  constructed? How did the homes of the wealthy differ
  from those of the poor? Did wealthy and poor neighbors
  ever mix? Did they ever intermarry?
- Religion: What was the prevailing religion, and how did it
  influence the common man's daily life? Who were the
  religious authorities of that time and place? What sort of
  power did they have—ecclesiastical or governmental or
  both? What sort of religious education did the common
  man receive, and how did he receive it? What did the
  Church, temple, or sacred place mean to him? Was his
  relationship with his god personal or prescribed?
- (Incidentally, I've had occasional Amazon reviewers chide
  me for "inserting" my "Christian beliefs" into a historical
  story when all I did was paint a realistic picture of an era
  in which evangelism and the Christian religion were high
  priorities. Unfortunately, the average modern reader has
  no idea that the practice of religion and discussion of
  religious topics was woven into the fabric of historical
  cultures and societies. Frankly, I would be suspicious if I
  read a historical novel in which characters did not place a

high value on religion and man's relationship with God. Secularism did not begin to pervade Western society until after the nineteenth century rise of Darwinism.)

- Government: Who was king or prime minister or president in your protagonist's nation? What sort of government was in place, and how did its work, taxes, and wars affect the people of your story? Did governmental authorities keep their distance, or did they meddle in the daily lives of your characters?

- Daily life: What did your characters eat and how did they obtain their food? How was food preserved, served, and obtained? How much time was spent in the preparing and storage of food? Was the food supply seasonal? If so, how did the seasons of scarcity and plenty affect your characters?

- How did the common man travel from place to place? How would your protagonist transport goods? (A great many Christmas movies and nativity stories were ruined for me when I researched the novella, *The Nativity Story*. I learned that donkeys were used to carry water jars, bedding, and supplies when people traveled from one city to another. So Mary probably didn't ride that donkey on her journey to Bethlehem, she walked. Which makes me respect her all the more.)

- What language(s) did your protagonist speak? What sort of music could he hear, and when did he hear it? What did your characters do for recreation?

- Clothing: what did people wear to work? To church? How did garments for the wealthy differ from the clothing of the poor? What about underwear? How did mothers dress their children? Did they diaper their babies? How long did it take a woman to get dressed—and would she require help from a servant? How did men wear their hair—and how did it differ from women's hairstyles? What might you find in a typical character's closet or trunk?

- I have several books about clothing on my shelf, the most useful of which is *Costume 1066-1966*, by John Peacock (Thames and Hudson, 1986, 2006). I'm sure there are newer versions of books like this, but this one has always given me clothing for men and women by regnal year. It's been invaluable.)
- Weather/climate: How did the weather and climate of your story setting affect your characters? (Florida, for instance, wasn't densely settled until the invention of air conditioning.) How did technology—or the lack of it—shape your story world? How will it affect your characters over the course of the novel? Will the climate and/or setting greatly affect your characters' health?
- Medicine: What illnesses were prevalent during this era? Any prevalent plagues? Did people understand the concept of germs and contamination? How did they dispose of the dead? How did women endure childbirth? How did superstition and/or religion affect medical practice? Who were the medical experts—doctors, witch doctors, or religious leaders? Where did the sick go for treatment? How was surgery, if any, accomplished? What was used to alleviate pain? What was the average lifespan? How high was the infant mortality rate?
- The world: what was known about creation in your story era? About the origin of man? What scientific discoveries were made during this time period? What countries were born, and what kingdoms overthrown? What technology existed as your story begins, and what new technologies could have arrived during the course of your novel?

The questions I've asked are not meant to be exhaustive—in fact, I've only scratched the surface of the overall concepts we need to investigate before beginning a historical novel.

. . .

Make the Information Accessible

So . . . how do we conduct all this research? And how do we remember everything we will need to know?

First, we read. Find books on your time period and begin to skim through them, absorbing concepts, big picture ideas, and miscellaneous information. Don't worry about memorizing details, but set up some kind of note taking system so you'll know where to find the details when you need them.

When I first began to write historical novels, I devised a system of notecards. I limited the notecards to one topic each, and I jotted the name of the source in a corner so I could always go directly to the book to read further.

All the note-taking in the world won't help you if you can't find a specific note when you need it. Once I became familiar with computer databases, I did the same thing on "virtual" notecards, jotting down little bits of information on small cards and mentioning the name of the source. I used to use an expensive database called *Ask Sam*, and it was invaluable because I could simply type in a word —"donkey"—and immediately find the book where I'd read that women did not ride donkeys in ancient Palestine.

These days I write in Scrivener, an easy to use writing program that lets me keep my research in the same file as my manuscript. My notes are still computer-searchable, so I can find the quote or information I need with a few keystrokes. And now that so much trustworthy information is found online, I can highlight a section of text on a website, click a key, and have it immediately pasted into my research notes. Technology is wonderful . . . when it works.

When the information you need is not on the Internet (or if what's on the Internet isn't trustworthy), buy books and mark useful pages with highlighting and sticky tabs. If your budget doesn't allow you to buy many books, go to the library and make copious notes on note cards or your laptop.

A caveat: read novels set in your chosen time period at your own risk. I never allow myself to trust the accuracy of other novelists, especially since I heard one writer say that if she didn't know something, she simply "made something up!" Even the most careful of writers has to invent *some* facts, and how can a reader know which facts were researched and which were invented?

If you shouldn't rely on novels, what sorts of books should you read for research? Anything and everything else. Children's nonfiction books can be helpful because they tend to boil topics down to the important highlights. Children's paper doll books can give great insight as to the clothing and hairstyles of an era. Textbooks, biographies, and nonfiction books of all types may prove useful.

Once I was browsing in an antique store and spotted an old scrapbook, filled with clippings from nineteenth century newspapers. I quickly paid five dollars to buy the book, then took it home, amazed by the clippings from the Civil War era newspapers. The papers printed detailed obituaries, prayers, religious lessons . . . amazing. You never know what you'll find if you keep your eyes open.

Most useful of all are books written in the era you've chosen for your story. Yes, you can find ancient writings. I used several translated ancient Egyptian texts in my "Joseph" novels, and I used the sixteenth-century diaries of John White to write my novel on the lost colony of Roanoke. Original sources are invaluable to a historical novelist.

Speaking of John White . . . After *Roanoke* was published, someone wrote to my publisher and complained that I had made a mistake in the book because I mentioned idols. She insisted that the original native Americans did not participate in idol worship.

When my publisher quizzed me about it, I flipped through the book and found the disputed paragraph:

"The Indians are truly capable of Christian love," her uncle had once written her father, "for they naturally share all things in common and know neither jealousy, selfishness, or ambition. They believe that one god created the world, and another restored it after the great flood. They have part of the truth and part of the nature of Christ, but they worship idols, fallen spirits, and can be most cruel to their enemies. We have a most urgent responsibility to bring them to the truth of the Gospel of Jesus Christ."

Once I found and identified the reference to idols, I was happy to report that *I* hadn't said the natives worshipped idols—John White did, for the words I used came directly from one of his letters. Granted, White assumed the Indians' carved images were idols while we would probably call them *totems*. Still, what was a sixteenth-century Englishman to think? Allowing historical characters to speak for themselves is a wonderful way to steep your story in authenticity.

In the macro research phase, you goal is to gather information to help you understand the overall world of your characters. As you begin to ingest this information, you will discover interesting facts that you can use to flesh out your plot ideas. If you discover something surprising, grab onto that nugget and record it where you'll be sure to have access to it. Anything that surprises you will probably surprise your reader as well. And that's a huge part of what makes reading so rewarding and entertaining.

At Some Point, Stop

Someone recently asked me, "Is it possible to research too much?" In a word, yes. Some writers, myself included, suffer from the Fear of the Blank Screen. If you enjoy research (and people who suffer from Blank Screen Phobia find almost *anything* more enjoyable than beginning the dreaded first draft), you can be tempted to research for months when a week would suffice.

Step 2: Sketch Out Your Plot Skeleton

The first Writing Lesson from the Front book, *The Plot Skeleton*, thoroughly discusses how to construct and plan a plot, so I won't rehash that material here. (If you haven't read that book, you probably should. A historical novel does not work without a structurally sound plot.)

Take what you've learned from your research, place your protagonist in your nascent story world, and begin to sketch out scenes that fit your story skeleton. I use notecards, either paper cards or the virtual cards in Scrivener, and on each I simply write a sentence or two about what will happen in each scene:

> This is where Jocelyn goes to dinner with the brothers and their mother.

Once you have a stack of scene cards (I tend to divide the plot into thirds and tackle each third separately), you're ready to begin writing your first draft scenes. Remember: the goal of a first draft is not to create something beautiful, **it's to get the story down.**

When you find that you've written

> Jocelyn shoved her voluminous skirt aside and sat down to a plate of
> –

If you have no idea what Jocelyn would be eating at the Duke's palace, insert brackets and something like this:

> [find out what's on the menu at Duke's!]

and keep writing.

I'm a *huge* believer in getting the story down before you do any backtracking or editing. Too many writers get sidetracked trying to fill in the blanks, and they never finish that first draft.

Pushing that first draft out is just like birthing a baby. You sweat and groan and find the process a painful ordeal, but when that squalling mess arrives on your desk, you're elated. You can always clean up a mess. Your book exists. You've done it. You've written (the first draft of) a book.

After an hour or a day or a week of celebration, take time for a day of triage—you need to fix the manuscript where it's bleeding. Search for brackets, and when you spot your note about finding out what they were eating at the Duke's, now you have to time to do *micro* research, getting all the details right.

After you've filled in all your bracket queries, go back and make sure you haven't contradicted any recorded history. You'll find it helpful to create a timeline (you can design a simple one in Microsoft Excel), and make sure that the historic Battle of Waterloo, which occurred on Sunday, June 18th, 1815, doesn't occur on Friday in your story. If George met Martha for the first time in Vicksburg, you can't have them meeting in Richmond.

How do you do this? Simple. On the Excel spreadsheet, assign each scene to a row. Use the columns to keep track of whatever information you need—I use Point of View (who is the POV character in each scene), date, time, action, weather, dramatic question raised, dramatic question answered, and anything else I need for the story.

By assigning each scene to a date, I can see where I need to insert phrases like "Four weeks later, George went to Vicksburg . . ." or "Later that afternoon . . ."

Not only do timelines help you keep track of important historical dates, but they help a novelist remember that characters do move through weeks and holidays. Many times I have written about people going to work day after day, but a timeline helped me realize that I forgot to mention weekends. Or I've had characters go through December without ever mentioning Christmas—a huge event for every family, every year. Keeping a good timeline will help anchor your novel to the real world, past or present.

When Historical Sources Disagree

What do you do when the historical experts don't agree on times, dates, or places? You're more likely to run into this problem when you write about ancient eras—eighteenth dynasty Egypt, for instance, or almost any period of Old Testament history. In this situation, a novelist is forced to gather as many expert opinions as possible and then make an informed choice. Choose the option that best fits with the other facts you've learned about the period.

And if you're writing about any ancient culture mentioned in the Bible, do not be afraid to trust its original text (Greek or Hebrew). Some translations use euphemisms that can lead you astray. Time after time, the Bible's veracity has been verified by archeological discoveries. I would trust it above any other source.

Speaking of the Bible—some people assume that "biblical fiction" and "historical fiction about Bible characters" are the same thing, but to me they are quite different. I doubt if many other people share my opinion, but to me the key difference lies in how the book is written.

A novelist may take a Bible story and flesh it out, drawing mostly on religious books and commentaries.

Or a novelist may take biblical characters and flesh them out, drawing on religious books and historical documents and ancient texts.

While both methods are certainly legitimate, I enjoy the latter approach, and in examining other records from the time of biblical characters, I have discovered logical complications and plot developments not even hinted at in the Bible. Because so much of the novel is based on extra-biblical material, I consider it more historical fiction than purely biblical.

In writing historical novels featuring Joseph, Moses, Esther, Mary Magdalene, and the nativity, I've found fascinating facts in Jewish texts, agnostic accounts, and even books written from an Islamic perspective. I don't agree with everything I read, of course, but learning to see historical events from other perspectives helps me sharpen my own.

For instance, as I began to develop my novel on Esther, I knew I had to come up with story elements no one had used before. Nearly everyone—Christians and Jews—knows the story of the brave, beautiful girl who courageously confronted a king and saved her people, so how could I tell the story in a unique way?

In search of an answer, I studied every book I could find on ancient Persia. I studied the government, the historical figures, the architecture, the palaces. I studied biographies of Xerxes, the king; Darius, his father; and Artaxerxes, his son. I read accounts of the Persians' treaties with neighboring nations, including Israel. I even found a book on the women of ancient Persia.

After reading all those accounts, I had a rich tapestry of information to deepen my novel.

How Contemporary Readers Relate to Historical Characters

How can you make sure a story of the past appeals to people of the present? Simple. Don't major on the historical events, but center the story on your characters and their *unchanging human frailties.* People are people, no matter when they live. They love, they suffer, they go to war, they raise children, they seek meaning and honor in their lives . . . or not. No matter when they lived, some people strive to be good; some people choose to do evil, but each man justifies his actions according to his individual moral code.

Basic human emotional needs do not change. We have them in common with our forefathers, and they are the key to helping your modern reader bond with your historical characters.

Focus on your characters as they strive and grow through difficult tasks, and your contemporary readers will relate because we face the same sorts of challenges. Give your historical characters universal flaws—greed, jealousy, rivalry, lack, bitterness, a desire for revenge, a yearning for love—and set them in their unique time and place.

Don't spend most of your time writing about historical events— write about people moving *through* historical events, resisting change, struggling to survive, striving to protect the ideals and the people they love—and you'll create a gripping story.

I'm often asked if we're "allowed" to use real people in historical novels. Of course! Just be aware that relatively contemporary people have traceable histories, and the more famous that person, the more material already exists on him or her. If you unwittingly get something wrong, you may rouse the ire of historians.

In several of his novels, Caleb Carr has used historical people as peripheral characters. These "real" people add a note of authenticity to his story without forcing him to become an expert on that famous person's history.

Describing the Unfamiliar

The historical novelist shares a problem with fantasy and science fiction writers: how can we avoid stopping the action and yet show our character using or wearing or eating something a modern reader won't immediately understand? If you stop to explain, for instance, what a *trebuchet* is or how it works, an editor is likely to scrawl RUE (resist the urge to explain) in the margin.

So—how do you avoid static paragraphs of explanation? You *show the object at work or in use.* Like this:

Rulf hoisted the basket of stones to his shoulder and stared at the massive trebuchet making slow progress up the hill. A dozen of the king's men strained at its side, sweat runneling down their backs as they pushed at the groaning timber frame.

Finally the foreman called a halt. The men braced the wheels and pulled the ropes that lowered the bucket to the platform, then one of them looked up and motioned to Rulf and the others who perspired beneath their heavy loads.

Rulf lumbered forward and scanned the city wall for the glint of bronze-tipped spears. Behind the crenellations, a pair of enemy archers peered through an opening and eyed his progress. With any luck, they wouldn't waste an arrow on him, a mere beast of burden.

Grunting, he tipped his basket into the wooden bucket, then backed away. When loaded with stones and boiling oil, the trebuchet might inflict some damage after the first launch, but he was willing to bet that he'd be climbing this hill many more times before sunset. A wall like that wouldn't crumble easily.

After reading the above paragraphs, you still may not know the dictionary definition of *trebuchet*, but I'll bet you're visualizing one of those medieval machines that flings a bucketful of rocks and/or boiling oil on and over a city wall. That's all you need to know—and active description is much more effective than stopping the story action to insert a dictionary entry.

The same holds true for historical events. Don't halt the action to relate a history lesson, detail a genealogy, or explain backstory. If you've made us care about your characters, don't cheat us of a minute with them.

Underline this: don't write any paragraphs your reader is going to skim.

In *Stein on Writing*, Sol Stein says: "In fiction, when information obtrudes the experience of the story pauses. Raw information comes across as an interruption, the author filling in. The fiction writer must avoid anything that distracts from the experience even momentarily. A failure to understand this . . . is a major reason for the rejection of novels."

You are There

How can you write a scene that makes your reader feel as if they are standing in the same room as your protagonist? You do it by invoking sensory details. Don't be so caught up in relating dialogue and action that you forget to make your reader's senses tingle. Help him not only see and hear the event of the scene, but smell, taste, touch, and intuit details, too.

Notice the sensory details in this brief bit from my novel about Esther. I've bolded words that evoke something to hear, see, taste, touch, or smell.

> As girls, Parysatis and I had often remarked about the discernible difference in the city's atmosphere when the king was away from his palace. We had **groaned** about how boring and dull Susa was without him, but that difference was magnified a hundredfold when one lived in the royal fortress. When I'd entered the palace, the harem **buzzed** with activity and **every slave walked with a brisk** step, never lingering for more than a moment in any one spot. But once the king and his household departed, an air of somnolence descended over the place.
>
> Those of us who had been gathered into the complex reserved for virgins grew sluggish and **lazy in the heat**. We were still fed **choice foods** (Artystone claimed the eunuchs were fattening us like lambs for the slaughter) and given our beauty treatments: each morning we bathed in waters **laced with myrrh,** and each evening our handmaids **massaged perfumed** oils into our skin. I had already begun to notice the difference—when I removed my tunic each night, the fabric **smelled of sweet flowers.**

By sprinkling your prose with words that evoke sensory details, you are placing your reader in the scene. Some words and phrases are more loaded than others—for instance, if I write "the sag-bellied rat skittered across the prison's stone floor," you can almost hear the chink of chains, see the damp wetness of the rocks, and smell the odor of filth and disease.

. . .

Historical Dialogue

We might as well admit it—people of yesteryear spoke differently than we do today. Not only were their accents unlike ours, but their language was more formal—or less formal, depending upon whether you're writing about cavemen or the founding fathers.

If you insist on writing dialogue that sounds exactly like your characters would speak it, you may lose readers because few people have the patience to sift through dense, boring dialogue. Never forget that we are a video generation. We have grown up with television and movies; we are used to stories that flow past our eyes. Consequentially, we don't have a lot of patience.

Dialogue is not and should not be exact spoken speech. Exact speech is dull, even if you're writing the conversations of twenty-first century Americans. So much of what we say is senseless filler.

"Hey."

"Hey yourself."

"Where ya been?"

"Nowheres."

"Jeet?"

"Had a burger 'n fries."

"Yeah, well. Henry's coming over."

Dull, dull, and hard to read besides. Learn how to condense your character's dialogue so that it includes only important information plus a sprinkling of color.

Len greeted Chip with the usual greeting, then informed him that his dead uncle Henry was on his way over.

See? Sometimes you don't need dialogue at all. Or you can introduce it with narrative and *then* let it take off.

Since dialog is not real speech, don't be tempted to write phonetically despite what you've read in *Gone with the Wind*. Writing like this—*luheek thuh suhoond uh doomzdeh*—is too hard to read. (Translation: "like the sound of doomsday" written in an Irish dialect.)

Instead of foisting strange spellings on your reader, indicate a dialect by word choice: "Sure, and don't I know you're goin' with me?" (Still speaking like an Irish woman, but without the impossible spellings.)

A single dropped "g" and appropriate word choice can effectively convey a dialect and not distract your reader from the story.

I enjoy traveling to places where I set my books, and on my trips I always carry a little notebook. In it I jot any unusual (to me) word choices that I might be able to use in a book. For instance, in the United States a sign on a stony hillside would say, "Watch for Falling Rocks." In Ireland, a similar sign said, "Mind Your Windscreen."

At Disney World, as you step off the monorail you hear, "Watch your step." In London, as you step out of the subway you hear "Mind the gap."

In Ireland, I picked up little phrases like these:

> I tried to ring him
>> He was a lovely man
>> He was all of a dither
>> He's a lovely little fella
>> The cheek of him!
>> He was obviously having me on
>> He was chancin' his arm.

Having access to little conversation fillers like these can give your dialog loads of color. In the same way, as you read original documents from your chosen historical period, keep a list of phrases you might be able to employ in your dialog. Here are a few from my notes on the Elizabethan period:

> I do beg and pray you
>> Mind your manners, varlet
>> Hold, sirrah

Mark me

Is aught amiss?

I trow you could

Pray do not tell

Nothing of import

Beshrew this

A pox on him!

In the same vein, be aware of your readers' sensibilities. Profanity is repulsive to many readers, and you can often create the same effect by writing some variation of "He cursed" instead of using profanity. Words that were powerful oaths in Shakespeare's day (Zounds!) don't usually offend most contemporary readers because we're unfamiliar with the word's meaning and connotation (God's wounds—swearing by Christ's wounds). On the other hand, some words that offend today wouldn't have offended a previous generation . . . yet you are writing for contemporary readers.

Historical novelist Stephanie Grace Whitson says, "I do not have my white people calling my black people what white people called black people back then. I do not have my white people thinking about my Lakota people what white people thought about Lakota people back then. And I certainly do not have my people (except the bad ones) *smell* like they smelled back then."

Novels are never completely realistic (and neither is TV. Have you ever wondered when Jack Bauer finds time to go to the restroom?) And no matter how much research we do, we who have been molded by twenty-first century events and culture may never fully understand the mindsets of previous generations. I don't suppose a novelist can ever write a novel that is totally accurate and true to the period. We aim for verisimilitude, we strive to never contradict historical fact, but we must acknowledge that we write for modern readers.

I cringe every time I watch "I Love Lucy" and see Ricky spanking his wife. That TV show, which aired its final episode around the time I was born, presents a mindset in which it's okay for men to strike their wives. Few people flinched in the 1950s; some people probably thought Ricky was being funny. But cultural perspectives change, sometimes drastically.

If you want your novel to reach the emotional core of your present-day reader, you need to keep her perceptions and attitudes in mind so she won't be ripped out of the story you're trying to tell.

Historical fiction pairs story with a rich tapestry of sights, sounds, tastes, aromas, textures, and challenges. Historical novelists strive to be true to their chosen historical period; but they must keep their modern readers in mind—after all, the story is written for them.

When written well, contemporary readers come away feeling that they've not only had a moving emotional experience, but they've lived and learned in a fascinating era far removed from the twenty-first century.

Writing a historical novel may be more involved than writing a contemporary story, but the rewards and the experience are worth the extra work.

Now . . . what era are *you* eager to write about?

HISTORICAL EXERCISES

1. ONE OF THE BIGGEST CHALLENGES FACING THE HISTORICAL novelist is describing objects or tools with which the reader will be unfamiliar. You don't want to insert a paragraph of explanation (which would stop the forward motion), nor do you want to include a glossary at the back of the book (which would stop the reader's reading). So how do you do it? You show the object in use.

So let's do the opposite. Let's say your reader is a reader from Victorian England. How would you write a scene in which your protagonist uses a smart phone to check the weather? Give it a try now!

2. Have you decided on the time period for your novel? Write a scene in which your protagonist goes shopping for food. Where does he or she go? What is available? How are the items purchased? How is the food kept from spoiling? How is it transported home? Make sure everything you write makes sense to a modern reader without stopping the action to explain.

3. In time past, most marriages were arranged—it's only in relatively recent history that men and women are given the free choice to choose their mates. Modern readers love a love story, but most marriages were not love matches, but arrangements made for financial or social reasons. Will your protagonist be married? How can

you legitimately arrange a marriage and create a story modern readers will love?

4. In years past, religion played a huge role in people's everyday lives. Many people today care little for religion, or exhibit only a form of worship, and most governments are decidedly secular. How can you create the spiritual world of your historical characters? Do your characters pray? Make sacrifices? Does their god speak to them? Who were the religious leaders and what kind of power did they wield? How can you show how important a god or gods were to this historical society?

Chapter Nine

THE FICTION WRITER'S BOOK OF CHECKLISTS

THE LIST IS YOUR FRIEND

I freely confess: I love lists. In Myers-Briggs parlance I am a "judger," which means I love organization and schedules. I *adore* lists. Sometimes I will create a list after I've completed tasks just for the simple pleasure of checking things off.

I realize that not everyone loves lists. People who are "perceivers" in Myers-Briggs language are more spontaneous. They are naturally averse to lists, and would rather go with the flow than be accountable to a piece of paper with jottings on it.

This book is for both groups. If you are a "J" like me, mostly left-brained, you'll take to this book like a kid to a snow cone on a sweltering summer day. If you are a "P" like my husband, you may sigh and groan or even break out in hives, but trust me—this book could well become your best writing friend.

Many of the items on these lists will use language and lessons thoroughly explained in the other **Writing Lessons from the Front** books. If you have read the previous lessons, particularly the volumes on plotting, weasel words, maintaining tension, and creating characters, you should have no trouble understanding and implementing the items on these lists.

And oh, the joy of checking things off . . .

I've purchased many a writing workbook over the years, and found many of them helpful. But I've always yearned for a book that would walk me through the process step-by-step, making sure I don't overlook anything and reminding me of all the things I've learned about writing.

That's why I put this book together. It refers to many of the other booklets in the **Writing Lessons** series, but mostly it is intended to be a guide, a mentor, that will walk you through from the idea to publication.

I am sure this book will evolve as time passes. You will think of things you want to add to your personal checklist, and I will think of things I want to add to this book.

For your additions, I've left room at the end of each chapter for notes.

For my additions, it might be a good idea to invest in an electronic copy of this book. If you buy a Kindle book, you can click "update" in the "manage my Kindle" section of Amazon, and the latest version will always be installed on your Kindle reader. Plus, the hyperlinks will be live for you.

One final note: You may photocopy these pages and use the lists **for your own personal use.** If you want to share the material with a friend or a class, point others to an online bookstore and this writer and the international copyright authorities will thank you. To share these pages otherwise would be a violation of copyright law.

And now—to the lists!

PREWRITING

PREWRITING CHECKLIST

Make no mistake, a writer should do a lot of work before he or she ever begins to write a short story or novel. In movies and on television, writers simply sit down and begin to type, but you don't believe everything you see in films, do you?

If you don't do your prewriting tasks first, you'll end up doing them later. Trust me, it's easier to do them beforehand.

So here are the items, large and small, that should be on your prewriting checklist. You don't have to do these in order, but the order is a logical progression.

The Puzzle Pieces

When writers get the initial idea for a story, they usually have only a few pieces of the puzzle. For a novel or short story, they may have the plot concept, a setting, a character, a theme, or any combination of those things. What pieces of the puzzle do you have? What pieces have you not figured out yet?

Write out what you know. Don't worry about what you don't know—the missing pieces will come to you as you work on the book.

☐ My plot concept—and what makes it unique:

My protagonist—and what makes him/her unique and not the average person on the street:

My setting and what makes it unique:

My theme—and why it's important to people everywhere:

PREWRITING RESEARCH

If you've filled out at least three of those four concepts, you're well on your way to fleshing out your story. Before you begin writing, you will also need to do some research. You don't have to research every single little detail, because you won't know what details you need until you're well into your story. But you will need the "big picture" details about your setting, your protagonist's profession and background, and your plot's unique elements. As to theme, it might be helpful to explore other works written with the same theme, or grab a book of quotations and see what famous people have said about your theme.

Examples: You want to write about a medical researcher who goes to the rain forest canopy to find a cure for Fatal Familial Insomnia, a genetic disease that has begun to afflict her and will one day afflict her daughter. Those were the elements I cobbled together when I began to write *The Canopy*. I didn't know my theme at first, but after a couple of drafts, I realized the story was about the nature of faith.

My protagonist was a medical researcher with FFI, so I had to establish a believable medical background for my character, plus I had to learn about the causes and symptoms of FFI, an actual disease.

Setting: the rain forest canopy. I had read an article in the *New York Times* Sunday magazine about the rain forest canopy, and about how it has a completely different ecosystem from the world below. An astounding number of pharmaceuticals and products come from the rain forest canopy, so researchers spend a lot of time among the trees.

The plot: I had to figure out how a woman could get to the rain forest, why she was desperate to get to the rain forest, and why she was so desperate to find a cure for her disease (it wasn't enough that she needed to cure herself. The stakes were greatly increased once I added in the daughter who likely would inherit the same disease).

☐ What are the areas you need to research?

What do you need to know about your setting, fictional or actual?

What do you need to know about topics that figure into your plot?

What do you need to research about elements of your chosen time period?

What do you need to research about your protagonist's occupation?

Can you think of any other particular areas in which you'll need to do at least cursory research?

YOUR STORY IDEA

Before you actually do the research, let's check the foundation of your story idea. A good story idea must have these four elements represented by WAGS (a wonderful acronym I learned from the late Gary Provost).

The story must offer the reader:

W: a different **world**. The story may begin in the ordinary world, but it must transport the reader to a place that's *unusual for the typical reader*. It could be the world of high finance, the world of mortuary science, or the world of the rain forest. It may be an actual world (Neptune, anyone?) or a metaphorical world (the world of canine beauty pageants). But it should be something that the typical reader will find interesting.

☐ Where does your story take the reader? From where to where?
☐ Are you sure the "different world" will be interesting and unique to an ordinary reader?

A: Your story must have **active** characters. Your character must set out on a journey to win something or someone or to do something. He can't simply sit at home and observe life as it marches by. He has to be in the game.

□ How is your character **active**? He doesn't have to be an athlete, but he can't be a person who sits around and lets everyone else do the work. Is he personally and actively involved in the story? What is he reaching for?

G: His **Goal**. What is your character's goal? Is it filmable? Is it something long term, something that can't easily be achieved in one or two chapters?

The goal needs to be something that's visual, filmable. It can't be something as subjective as "I want to be a better person." The goal also needs to be large enough, challenging enough, that the protagonist *works throughout the entire story* to achieve it. If your character sets out to win a neighborhood skating contest and he does it in chapter two, he either needs a bigger goal—the world cup in skating —or he needs a major handicap—he's blind.

Better yet, write the bigger goal *and* the handicap into your story.

□ Your character's goal:

S: Your story needs high **stakes**. It's not enough to win or do something purely for personal satisfaction; your story will be stronger if a larger issue is involved:

He wins the skating contest to prove to his girlfriend that he can take care of her if they get married.

James Bond always captures the villain (the goal) to save the world (the high stakes).

My medical researcher wanted to find a cure for FFI (the goal) in order to save her daughter's life (the high stakes).

What happens if your protagonist doesn't achieve her goal? If you answer is, "Well, life just goes back to normal," your stakes are not high enough. Find a way to put life, love, or survival on the line. Increase the stakes and you'll vastly improve your story.

□ What's at stake in your story? What is your protagonist risking?

What happens if he doesn't achieve his goal?

PRE-PLOTTING

Now that you've checked out your idea and figured out what you'll need to research, put this book down and start digging. Go online, read books, talk to experts. Research can be an ongoing process (and for me, it usually is), but it's important to get the details right from the start in order to save yourself plot problems later.

During first draft of my novel *The Elevator,* I wrote a couple of important scenes where the characters crawl out of the elevator through a hatch on the top and then climb a ladder inside the elevator shaft. I waited until the third draft, until I consulted an elevator expert, and then I learned that despite all the movies and TV shows I'd seen with these elements, 1) elevator hatches cannot be opened from the inside and 2) elevator shafts do not have ladders.

I strive to get the details right, so I had to go back and make some major plot changes. Fortunately, having my rescuer climb around in the elevator shaft *without* a ladder proved to be much more exciting and dangerous.

So get started on your research now, and be aware that you will need to keep researching as you write.

Prewriting Plot

Some writers say they write "by the seat of the pants" and others like to outline. I prefer a hybrid approach because writing without an outline would cause me to chase every little thought that came into my mind and I'd write tons and tons of pages that would end up on the cutting room floor.

If I write a complete outline, however, I always find that I've lost the joy of the story. I feel as though I've already written it, and who wants to be confined to an outline, anyway? I never know who my characters are or what's going to happen to them until I finish the second or third draft.

So how do we start writing without choosing one approach or the other? I do a plot skeleton.

If you haven't read the lesson in book one, *The Plot Skeleton,* this is where you need to pick up a copy and read it because I'm not going to repeat everything here. It's a quick read and may be the most helpful plotting book you've ever read, as it boils plot down to the, um, bare bones.

Now it's time to sketch out enough of a plot that you know where you are going. But since this plot is only bare bones, you still have room for discovery, and the skeleton is flexible enough that you can change and add without any problem. If you stick to the plot skeleton, you'll have a great story with all the right pieces in place, but you can love the writing as you learn who your characters are and what they want.

The plot skeleton begins with:

☐ The head: the protagonist. Who is the ONE (primary) protagonist of your story? You may have an ensemble cast, but the book is one person's story. Who is this person?

This person needs three things, and you should illustrate them in the first 20-25 percent of your story. Do you have these "bones" in place?

1. An obvious problem. Start the story off with action—not the main story problem, but an interesting problem in the character's ordinary world.

2. A hidden need. This character is missing some quality in his life, and you must illustrate this without being obvious about it. Often this is a wound the character received in his or her childhood.

3. Admirable qualities. Show us something likeable about this character, even if he's a bad guy. After all, Don Corleone killed people, but his crime family had a moral code—they didn't sell drugs. Dexter Morgan is a psychopathic serial killer, but he only kills murderers.

Show us your character's sense of humor. Make him or her good on the job. Can you show your protagonist's vulnerabilities? Does he adore his little girl? Is she kind to her neighbors? Does he swoon over his dog? Don't tell us these things about your protagonist; illustrate these qualities in scenes that reveal character as he interacts with neighbors, coworkers, friends, and enemies.

☐ How can you demonstrate admirable qualities? Jot down some scene ideas:

The next element in the plot skeleton is the inciting incident. This should occur at about 20-25 percent of the way into your story—why? Because if the cancer diagnosis or the kidnapping or the bomb happens to your protagonist on page one, we don't know enough about him to care very much. Once we have emotionally invested in your character, *then* give us that life-changing incident, the thing that moves your protagonist from his ordinary world to the unique story world.

Dorothy moves from Kansas to Oz via a tornado.

Luke Skywalker moves from that blah planet to the world of Jedi knights.

Clarice Starling moves from the FBI Academy to the real world of serial killers, both on the loose and in prison.

Rapunzel moves from her secluded tower to the world of freedom and danger.

□ What is your inciting incident, and how do you make it happen? Many times the inciting incident is ushered in through a phone call or an invitation—the character is literally invited to join an expedition or a group or a study. What is your plan?

Almost immediately after (or right before) the inciting incident, your protagonist sets a goal—and he or she will strive to reach this goal throughout the entire story.

Dorothy steps out in Oz and declares "I want to go home!"

In Disney's *Tangled*, Rapunzel wants to see the floating lights that appear on her birthday each year.

Clarice wants to find the serial killer.

Luke Skywalker wants to help defeat the Death Star.

James Bond *always* wants to save the world.

□ What is your protagonist's goal? He or she may have other subgoals along the way (Dorothy has to follow a yellow brick road, get a broomstick, and kill a witch before she can go home), but there should be an overarching goal for the story.

You considered this when we were testing your story idea, but test it again—does your protagonist have a visual, film-able goal that will last the entire story? Write it down, and as you write, remind yourself of what your character wants. Your protagonist's desire is the engine that will keep your story moving forward.

□ What does your protagonist desperately want?

Now that your character is in the story world with a goal, you need to set up a series of complications that stand in the way of his/her reaching that goal. Make a list, and try to order them from least troublesome to most troublesome.

How many complications do you need? Enough to fill the length of your story (and by all means, if you need to list them on a separate sheet of paper, please do). If you're writing a short story, you need far fewer complications than you would need for a novel. But you always need at least three. I write children's picture books, and even those spare stories need at least three complications. Two just doesn't' work.

If you're having trouble coming up with complications, don't forget about antagonists. An antagonist is not necessarily a villain—some stories don't have actual villains, though thrillers and murder mysteries do. An antagonist is anyone who stands in the way of your protagonist's effort to reach her goal, so sometimes a best friend can be an antagonist. Or a mother. Or a lover. That best friend can be an antagonist in chapter ten, and back off in chapter fifteen, so the title is transferable.

☐ What other characters in your story can, at some point, serve as an antagonist and add complications?

Your list of complications will be growing and evolving as you write your book, so if you've come up with several good ideas, that's fine for now. Let's move on.

You should save the worst, most horrible, most disastrous complication for last—because it will result in another plot point, the *bleakest moment*. The bleakest moment occurs when your protagonist has no more hope—that last complication was so terrible that he can't see a way to move forward. He is broken, lost, and ready to call it quits.

What is the bleakest moment in your story? Be careful—most writers' first attempt results in a situation that isn't nearly bleak enough. Always remember—your goal is to TORTURE your protagonist. Don't have mercy on him, especially not at this point. If you made him sick, make his illness worse. If his best friend has turned his back on your protagonist, think about killing the best friend instead. Make the bleakest moment as desperate and hopeless as you can.

☐ Is your bleakest moment as bleak as you can make it? How can you make it bleaker?

Now that your main character is at this terrible, horrible, no good, very bad point, you need to send in the cavalry. Your protagonist needs some help, and it will come from outside himself. The helper will not—should not—solve the protagonist's problem, but he or she will give your protagonist a solid push in the right direction.

After Dorothy sees the wizard take off in the balloon, she's stuck, without hope, and in her bleakest moment. But here comes Glenda the good witch to remind Dorothy that she's wearing the powerful ruby slippers.

In practically every episode of *Home Improvement,* Tim the "Tool Man" Taylor gets himself into trouble with his wife or his kids and ends up outside, groaning about his troubles. Wilson, the ever-present helper, always pops up from behind the fence to give Tim some advice and help him on his way.

Maria, governess to the Von Trapp children in *The Sound of Music,* realizes that she's fallen in love with the captain, her employer. That's hopeless, so she runs back to the convent, where the Reverend Mother Emmanuel reminds her that she can't run from her problems, she has to "climb every mountain" and get out there and find her dream.

□ At your character's bleakest moment, he can't help himself. (If he could, it wouldn't be a very bleak moment.) So who is going to come along to give your desperate and depressed protagonist a much-needed shove in the right direction? Who is it, and what are they going to say or do?

After the helper dispenses that helpful advice or encouragement, your protagonist will pick himself up and brush himself off because he has learned a lesson.

Dorothy learns there's no place like home.

Maria learns she can't run from her problems.

Through Mary Poppins, Mr. Banks learns how to be a good father.

□ What does your character learn?

Now that your character has learned a lesson, he or she must put it to good use. She will make a decision to do something that will wrap up the end of the story and show us how this character has changed. This decision will answer the "hidden need" you established in the first part of your story.

At the beginning of *The Wizard of Oz*, Dorothy is living on her aunt and uncle's farm, but she's not happy about it. Without being told, we know that something happened to her parents and she's having trouble accepting that her home is now with her aunt and uncle.

But at the end of the story, after Glenda tells her about the ruby slippers, Dorothy learns there's no place like home and makes the decision to use the power of the ruby slippers to return to Kansas. She wakes up in her own bed, surrounded by her aunt and uncle and all the farm hands, and she's delighted to be there.

Lesson—decision—hidden need met and illustrated.

Now that your character has learned an important lesson, what does he decide to do—and make sure this is something that he couldn't have done at the beginning of the story.

□ What does your character do, and how does this illustrate that he's been changed? That his hidden need has been met?

This is the spot where I must remind you that writing a good story is not easy. If it were, everybody could do it. Hidden needs are tricky because, well, they're hidden. And coming up with a universal human need that will resonate with nearly every reader can be difficult—but if you excel in this area, your story will reach into your reader's heart and yank on those emotional strings that bind the human race together. And that's what stories are supposed to do—affect the emotions.

The last "bone" in the plot skeleton is the resolution, and it's fairly simple: write a scene or two that shows us that your character has returned to his ordinary world as a different person. He's been changed for the better, and he is either going to live happily ever after or be sadder, but wiser.

□ What do you envision as the ending for your story? Does it clearly show that your protagonist has changed? How has this changed enriched his world and his relationships?

CREATING YOUR CHARACTERS

Only one more major area to tackle in the prewriting stage: characters.

In my lesson *Creating Extraordinary Characters,* I explain how to use the Myers-Briggs personality profile to quickly create realistic characters, so I won't repeat all that information here. But you should follow that plan or something like it, and sketch out brief profiles of your major characters before you write. You don't have to journal their thoughts for a month (though some writers find that helpful) or create pictures of their home (also helpful for some), but you can do those things if you want to.

For our purposes, let's sketch out the major characters—and only you know how many characters you're going to need. Here's a fact to keep in mind: try not to populate your story with more characters than you need. The more people you put on your pages, the more people your reader have to keep in their heads—and readers get tired of keeping track of lost of characters. Consider populating your book with story *types* (protagonist, antagonist, mentor, best friend, etc.), and you'll have a more manageable cast.

Most important character to define in detail: your protagonist, the person who is either telling this story or whose story this is.

☐ What is your protagonist's full name?
    Personality type?
    Chief personality characteristics?
    Birthdate and age when story begins?
    Physical appearance:
    Married?
    Children?
    What are his/her secrets?
    Education?
    Goals in life?
    How would he/she describe himself/herself?
    Occupation:
    Dreams:
    Other notes:

The story's chief or sometimes antagonist:
    What is his/her full name?
    Personality type?
    Chief personality characteristics?
    Birthdate and age when story begins?
    Physical appearance:
    Married?
    Children?
    What are his/her secrets?
    Education?
    Goals in life?
    How would he/she describe himself/herself?
    Occupation:
    Dreams:
    Other notes:

The protagonist's confidante or best friend:
    What is this character's full name?
    Personality type?
    Chief personality characteristics?

Birthdate and age when story begins?
Physical appearance:
Married?
Children?
What are his/her secrets?
Education?
Goals in life?
How would he/she describe himself/herself?
Occupation:
Dreams:
Other notes:

Does your protagonist have a mentor or hero?
What is this character's full name?
Personality type?
Chief personality characteristics?
Birthdate and age when story begins?
Physical appearance:
Married?
Children?
What are his/her secrets?
Education?
Goals in life?
How would he/she describe himsclf/herself?
Occupation:
Dreams:
Other notes on other characters:

You get the idea. Figure out how many characters you need to tell your story, and fill out a brief profile for each one. As you write, you may find that you need other characters, or you may find that you don't need as many as you thought. Adjust your cast, and flesh out their profiles as needed. You don't need a complete history of a character that appears only briefly and doesn't play a major role in the story.

One more tip: I often go online to a stock photo website to get pictures of my characters. I don't publish those photos, and I don't care if they are watermarked, but I find that just looking at my character's face helps me remember who he is—people's faces, after all, reflect their personalities.

So I might go to a site like www.tonystone.com and type "man single thirties" to find photos of thirty-year-old men. I'll scroll through them until I spot my character (they tend to jump out at me) and then I'll right-click and save to my computer or print the photo and tape it to the shelf above my desk. Either way, I have a quick reminder of exactly who my character is and what he looks like. This little trick can also help you make sure all your characters don't end up looking the same.

Point of View Characters

A point of view character is a character who helps tell the story. If you're not familiar with point of view, you should read the *Point of View* writing lesson (Book 3), but know this: with each point of view character you add to your story, you lessen the reader's emotional attachment to all your characters.

Twilight is written in first person point of view, and Bella is the only point of view character in the book—and that's why teenage girls (and grown women) identified with her so easily. Stephenie Meyer wrote another manuscript, *Rising Sun,* which tells the same story as *Twilight* except the book is from Edward's point of view. She could have written *Twilight* from Edward's and Bella's alternating points of view, but I'm guessing she didn't want to dilute the reader's identification with Bella. Smart move.

In *The Fine Art of Insincerity*, I wrote about three sisters, and I let each sister have her own point of view in first person. One of the sisters was the protagonist, but the other sisters got plenty of "face time." After the book came out, I was reading Amazon reviews and noticed a common theme: "I identified with one sister, but not the other two" and "I couldn't identify with any of the sisters."

Ah—lesson learned. I needed three point of view characters in order to tell the story, but if the plot hadn't required it, I could have increased my readers' identification and sympathy if I'd used only one point of view character.

☐ How many point of view characters are you planning to use? Is it possible for you to decrease that number in order to increase reader identification?

Have you determined which point of view (first person, third person, second person, omniscient) will work best for the way you want to tell your story? Again, if you aren't familiar with point of view, you need to read book three in these writing lessons. It's a crucial tool, and your POV choice needs to be nailed down fairly early—unless you want to spend a later draft changing all your "I"s to "he"s, etc.

Moving Forward

Deep breath. You've tested your story idea, done preliminary research, sketched out your plot skeleton, determined your point of view, and created brief profiles of your main characters.

As you tackle the prewriting, be careful—if you spend too much time prewriting, you may find that you are suffering from Dread of the Blank Screen. It's okay, all writers are afflicted with that from time to time, but eventually you will reach a point where you must begin writing.

Methinks you are ready to begin a first draft.

Your Personal Prewriting Checklist

Because I know that my lists won't necessarily be *your* lists, I'm leaving a blank page at the end of each chapter so you can add lists of tasks you'd like to complete at this stage. So be my guest and create some check boxes of your own.

FIRST DRAFT CHECKLIST

Before I jump into the first draft checklist, I want to share what may prove to be one of the best tips you'll ever receive: Scrivener.

Scrivener is a handy dandy writing program that does everything a writer needs a program to do. It holds all your research, saves automatically, allows you to create note cards for scenes and move them around, reads a manuscript back to you, and will store photos of your characters. You can download it at www.literatureandlatte.com and try it for thirty days before deciding to buy. Best of all, you can purchase it for under fifty bucks.

Before I discovered Scrivener, I used to write in Word, keep my notes in OneNote, manage a timeline in Excel, and kept a notebook filled with cluttered pages. Now that I write in Scrivener, I don't need any of those other programs and my notes and manuscript are kept in a single file. (Back in my early days, word processors weren't as reliable, so I saved every chapter in a different file. If a file got corrupted, I would only lose a chapter, not the entire book.)

Editors still want you to submit a Word document so you won't be completely rid of Microsoft, but you can write your book in Scrivener, do a compile and export it to Word, and then send it off to your publisher or editor. You could also compile it as a .mobi file for Kindle, an epub file for iBooks, or as html for a website. Scrivener is the best thing since the typewriter, and you should definitely try it. When you open the program, you'll immediately see the interactive tutorial, and the learning curve isn't extreme. You'll be up and writing in no time.

And no, I don't own stock in the company, nor am I paid for endorsements. I just couldn't imagine writing a novel or a nonfiction book in anything else.

Your Goal as a First-Drafter

Get the story down. That's all you need to do. (And isn't that enough?)

Don't stop to edit, don't go back and rethink, don't rephrase, rehash, or rerun. Just get the story into the computer.

You might find it helpful to pull out your plot skeleton and create "scene cards" with a brief synopsis of the action of each scene on the card. You can do this with real paper notecards (I used to do this), or you can simply use the virtual notecards in Scrivener.

No matter what method you chose, you can color code your cards by POV, change their order, or arrange them by plot/subplot. With paper cards you can plaster your rooms or toss them in the air when you hit a blank wall. They are yours to command.

In Scrivener, whatever you write on the top of the card becomes a "headline" that will show up when you choose "outline view." If you reserve the second line of the card for time and date, choosing "outline view" will give you an instant story timeline—important for editors when they're trying to make sure you haven't jumbled your story events. You can use the rest of the front of your card for whatever you like—I usually write a brief synopsis of the action that should take place in that scene.

So my scene card, whether virtual or real, will look something like this:

Bathsheba goes in to see David.
Friday morning, March 13, 996 B.C.

Bathsheba goes in to remind David that he promised to make Solomon his heir.

If you're using real cards, when you sit down to write, simply choose a card and write that scene in your word processor. If you're using Scrivener, a click in the upper left corner will take you to what I think of as the virtual "back" of the card, which is the blank manuscript screen. Write away, not stopping until you have finished the scene.

Scrivener, by the way, has another feature I love. To the right, there's an optional box in which you can make notes—either on the scene in front of you, or on the document as a whole. For instance, if I were writing the Bathsheba scene, in the "notes" frame I might type: *Make sure you've written a romantic scene in which David makes this promise.* I will see this note later, then go back and write the scene I was missing.

If you're writing in Microsoft Word, you can create notes to yourself with the "comments" feature. Just click on "insert" in the menu bar and choose "new comment." You can type, "this sounds horrible, so fix it later" or "you need to create a new character to plan the heist" or "this might be a good place to insert a thematic emblem."

As you're writing scenes in your first draft, if you realize you're missing some information—for instance, if your character sits down to dinner in a medieval castle and you have no idea what would be on the menu—have your character sit down, and then type [BE SURE TO LOOK UP WHAT THEY ATE AT FEASTS] and keep going. If you stop to look things up, you'll lose your forward momentum, and that's a big loss. You'll stop to look something up online, then you'll be distracted by email, then you'll see a fascinating notice about celebrities with bad plastic surgery, then the phone will ring, then you'll remember the wet laundry . . . see what I mean?

You can always go back—and you will, later—to look up what you need to know, but don't stop during your first draft. Press on, friend, press on.

First draft checklists:

☐ Check out Scrivener. If you like it, use it.

☐ Write your scene cards.

☐ Write those scenes. They don't have to be pretty and no one expects them to be perfect, but they need to exist before you can move on. So write!

P.S. One feature I love in Scrivener is the "goals" target. You can set a manuscript goal of so many words, and a daily goal of so many words to write each day. I always open this box and drag it to a lower corner of my computer screen. At a glance I can tell how I'm progressing with the entire manuscript and with my daily goal. And when I reach my daily goal, I push away from the desk and quit. Why?

To be a writer, you need to have a life, for it's your life that imparts the understanding and personal experiences you need to craft a good story.

What makes a good story? The truths I learn, translated into fictional characters' lives, reaches out to the reader and resonates with what they've experienced and learned. That's human connection, and it's indispensable.

☐ If you're writing in Word, when you finish that first draft, save your document as "YourTitledraft1." You may never need to open this file again, but disaster strikes you'll have a copy.

If you're writing in Scrivener, you don't need to change your Scrivener file. But go to the menu, choose File, then Compile, and let Scrivener export your document as a Word or other text file. Name that file "YourTitledraft1," and you'll have a good copy if you ever need it.

Now that you've finished that first draft, pat yourself on the back. Thousands of people sit down to write a novel and never get this far. Why? Because they don't know how to construct a plot, because they keep going back to revise, or because they simply run out of steam. By working carefully, completing your pre-writing, constructing a plot skeleton, and pressing forward, you've reached the all-important first draft goal.

Now that your book exists, you can flesh it out, clean it up, and make it everything it should be. So be encouraged, and let's move forward!

Your Personal First Draft Checklists:

SECOND DRAFT CHECKLIST

From Sol Stein, I learned to take a couple of days between drafts for "triage." You may be familiar with the concept of triage—in the medical field, it means looking over all the patients who need treatment and deciding who needs it most urgently.

In writing, "triage" is the day or two or three you take between drafts to patch the places that are bleeding. Remember all those brackets you placed in the first draft when you realized you needed to do a bit more research? Triage is where you search for the brackets (use your word processor's search feature) and then fill in the space with whatever information you need.

Triage is also where you look over the notes you've made to yourself—whether you made them in the Scrivener sidebar or with the "comments" feature in Word—and go back and fix what needs fixing.

You may be wondering if there's an advantage to inserting bracketed notes into the text instead of using comments in a sidebar. Not really. You can make notes however you please. I tend to use the brackets for material I actually have to look up and sidebar notes for more thematic issues, or things that are going to require a new scene or a new character. But you can make notations any way you like—as long as you make notations instead of backtracking and trying to fix things as you go.

□ Take a few days to do triage on your manuscript and fix any problems that immediately come to mind. Don't worry about the things that don't come to mind—you'll find them later.

□ If you're writing in Word, the first step in actually going through your second draft is to take that .doc file you saved as "Your-Titledraft1" and now save it as "YourTitledraft2." Keep "YourTitle-draft1" for posterity, but now you'll be saving all your changes on the second file.

If you're writing in Scrivener, don't change anything, just open your file and head back to the first scene. But do be sure you have done a compile and saved that first draft as a Word document. You will probably never need it, but at least you'll have it.

The Second Draft

The first draft is about getting the story down. The second draft is about filling in the gaps, deepening the characters, and making the story as solid as possible.

□ If you haven't already done so, create a title page for your story, complete with your name and address (or your agent's), the title of the book, and your byline. Just seeing that page helps you feel more professional, doesn't it?

Below your byline, write a one-sentence synopsis of your story. Imagine that you're in an elevator with an editor or agent, and you have only thirty seconds to explain what your story is about:

Magic and danger await Dorothy Gale, a young orphan, when a tornado picks her up in Kansas and drops her in a mysterious land called Oz.

A police chief with a deadly fear of water must overcome demanding tourists and a greedy mayor when a giant shark threatens the safety of his oceanfront town.

With a dangerous hurricane approaching, three women are trapped together in an elevator, never realizing that they have something in common: the dead man on the fortieth floor.

Why do we write this synopsis? Knowing exactly what your story is about might help you sell it to an editor or agent. But the chief benefit is that this exercise will help you *focus* on exactly what your story is about. Too many writers get bogged down in the details.

☐ Write a one-sentence synopsis of your story.

Now that you've condensed your story to a single sentence, back up a bit and write a paragraph that could serve as back cover copy for your printed story. In this copy, remember that you can't give away the ending. The purpose of this paragraph isn't to synopsize the story, it's to hook a reader's curiosity and reveal the genre and style of the story.

Don't worry about getting this paragraph exactly right on the first try—you will be editing it through each subsequent draft. But it's important to get your thoughts on paper.

Here's my back cover copy for one of my recent novels, *Passing Strangers:*

A train roars over the rails, carrying passengers on a trip that will change their lives. Among the many people aboard the 97 Silver Meteor are Andie Crystal, a lonely young woman hiding from her youth as a reality TV star; Matthew Scofield, a widower struggling to manage his responsibilities to his two young children; and Janette Turlington, a middle-aged mother running from a situation that has destroyed the peace in her home and marriage. These three form a makeshift family on an Amtrak tour through the Southern seaboard, a journey that just might heal their wounded hearts and restore them to the people to whom they matter most.

☐Now it's your turn. Write a paragraph of back cover copy that would hook a reader's interest as well as indicate the genre and style of your story.

Once you have written a paragraph of back cover copy, give some thought to an epigraph for your story. (An epigraph is a brief quotation from poetry or prose that is featured on a single page.) You don't have to use an epigraph, but I love them because they hint at the story's theme and tone. I daresay most readers read them and forget them, but why not use one?

To find a good epigraph, consider the theme or some other element of your story. Is your story about a journey? Sisters? Family? Finance?

Pull out a good book of quotations or go online and search for quotes that echo or state this theme. You might want to jot down several options and keep them in your notes—by the time you have finished and polished the book, one of the quotes will seem more perfect than the others. If you can't find the perfect quote, use one of your own—just make sure it's poetic and lovely and perfect for your book. I couldn't find a suitable quote for my novel *The Shadow Women,* so I wrote one myself and attributed it to my someday pen name, Darien Haynes.

☐Find the several good quotes that might work as an epigraph for your story. Write them down or put them in your Scrivener file. Later you can settle on the best one.

Why are we doing things that may seem superfluous? First, they aren't superfluous—you will need them eventually, so you might as well write them now. Second, writing these bits forces you to hone your thoughts and narrow the focus of your story. Too often I ask writers what their story-in-progress is about and hear, "Oh, it's about a woman who does this and then that happens and this happens and then . . ."

Narrow your focus to an ice pick's point. Being able to describe your story in one paragraph and one sentence is important.

The Second Draft

Now you are ready to begin the process of second-drafting your story. Start at the beginning and work through it, changing words as necessary. You should have already filled in most of the bracketed missing bits, so in this draft you are working to:

- --cut unnecessary rabbit trails and descriptions
- --add emotion where needed
- --move backstory to the back of the story.
- --fill in any missing scenes that are needed to clarify, add foreshadowing, introduce characters you didn't know you needed until you were first drafting, and anything else that seems obvious to you.

Remember, however, the faithful acronym RUE—resist the urge to explain. In previous lessons (especially *Tension on the Line*), I explained that the writer's job is to toss out hooks, not to answer all the reader's questions up front. You don't want to confuse the reader, but you do want to raise provocative questions so he keeps turning those pages.

Anything in your story that does not advance plot or deepen characterization shouldn't be in the story. It needs to be cut.

Before you groan, be aware that I know how painful cutting can be. So here's a trick to make it easier. If you're writing in word, open a new document and name it "Cut materials for Possible Later Use." If you're writing in Scrivener, simply make a new card and call it by the same name.

If you find that you've gone on and on about the beauty of the beach sunset, cut those paragraphs down to size by selecting, cutting, and pasting the material in your "cut materials" file or card. That way you haven't wasted your precious time, energy, and words, you've simply moved those words to another safe place. Do this as you work through the story, and I'm betting that you won't even miss those bits. But if you discover that you do need them, you'll still have them.

□ As you go through the manuscript this second time, cut anything that doesn't advance plot or deepen character and place it in a "cut materials" file.

Pumping up: you may not have this problem, but I often do. I am an emotional person, but I'm more of a thinker than a feeler. In my early days, I tended to write things like:

She stared at him. "I'm mad!"

Well, maybe I wasn't quite *that* on the nose, but my novels were long on thought and short on emotion. But why do people read fiction? To *feel*. If they want facts, they'll read nonfiction. People read novels because they want to feel and have a vicarious experience in your protagonist's skin.

So when Jane's husband leaves her, you can't leave Jane crying on the couch and cut to a scene break. You need to flesh out that scene and place us in Jane's head and heart so that we know what she's thinking and feel what she's feeling.

I explained how to do this in the *Evoking Emotion* lesson, so I won't repeat that information here. But if something horrific or wonderful or amazing or frightening has happened to your character, make sure the reader has the opportunity to feel all those emotions for herself. (Hint: don't show emotion through exclamation marks. We have to do it through words, images, and metaphors.)

□ As you go through your novel this second time, look at each scene as a detached unit and ask yourself if you're fully exploring the emotion in the scene. Not every scene has to involve major drama, and sometimes emotion is best expressed through understatement and subtext, but each major development in your story should evoke strong emotions from your characters. Make sure your reader has the opportunity to feel that emotion for herself.

☐ Remember that emotion is rarely pure—love, for instance, is comprised of jealousy, joy, sorrow, and happiness, just to name a few typical feelings. A grieving person moves through shock, denial, anger, bargaining, depression, and, finally, acceptance.

When something important happens in your story, your characters are likely to be feeling several emotions, many within minutes, so be sure your characters go through every emotion that suits their personalities.

☐ At every major event in your novel, do your characters experience and relate the appropriate emotion? Do your characters experience only one *note* of that emotion, or do you portray the true richness of an emotional experience?

Backstory is anything that happens in your story prior to current story time. It is usually introduced through entire scenes or through recollections.

If you're writing a contemporary novel and you want to reveal how the protagonist's parents met, you might write a separate scene that begins:

In the summer of 1972, a long-haired twenty-year-old nonconformist left home to hitchhike across the country because everyone else was doing it.

You would follow that opening sentence with an entire scene in which Dad met Mom.

If you don't want to give much attention to how your protagonist's parents met, you might write a recollection, which is a small flashback inserted within a present story scene:

John stared at his kids, who murdered and stabbed and exploded bombs without flinching, their fingers moving soundlessly over the game controller. He had grown up with simpler entertainments—Legos and toy fire trucks and a green rubber Gumby who survived everything but the microwave. But life was less technological in 1952, and so was childhood.

"Gotcha!" his son yelled, actually rising two inches off the floor in his excitement.

John shook his head. That was probably the most exercise his kid would get all day. He and Marge never thought their kids would turn out quite like this.

Do you see the recollection? An easy way to spot them is to look for the "had"—"had" almost always signals a step backward in story time.

Both recollections and complete scene flashbacks are perfectly fine, but they should occur after the first 20-25 percent of your story. Why? Because the modern reader has grown up in a video generation, and we are accustomed to forward movement. We don't want to be slowed by history, and we don't want to stop to enjoy your character's memories *until we are fully invested* in his situation. Exactly when that occurs probably varies from story to story and reader to reader, but if a person is at least 20 percent into the book, odds are that he's ready and willing to let a character pause for a few moments of backstory.

You will find tons of older books crammed with backstory at the beginning—but they were written for a different reader. You will find some current books that have lots of backstory in the beginning. Backstory up front is not a fatal flaw, but I can promise you this— your story will be stronger if you move that backstory backward a few chapters (or cut it entirely). Ask yourself—is it important that my reader know this *now*? If not, move it.

There's a little writing rule that's worth memorizing: **only tell**

your reader what he needs to know when he needs to know it. Not before.

☐ Go through the first 50 pages or so of your story and highlight any passages of backstory—look for the "hads" to help you spot it. Then cut that backstory, place it in your "cut materials" file, and pull it out only if and when you need it. If that material is important, you can probably make it much better and stronger by placing it back in the story at a point where your character is tormented, sad, reflective, or having his bleakest moment.

Above all, avoid the chapter two "backstory dump." Nothing marks a beginning writer faster than a ton of backstory in chapter two.

The Three Primary Plots

This section isn't about plotting your story; you've already done that. But since many novels sag in the middle, the place for complications and obstacles, this little tip might help you keep the action moving forward if you hit a roadblock.

All plots can be boiled down to one of these three: man against man, man against nature, or man against himself. One of these should dominate throughout your book. But if you're writing about a man who's trying to find his kidnapped daughter and you need a break from constant back-and-forth between villain and hero, consider a couple of scenes in one of the other plots. He's on his way to deliver the ransom money, but an unexpected tornado picks up his car and drops him ten miles away. Or one of his multiple personalities takes over and hops a jet for Vegas. You get the idea.

Character Considerations

Perfect people are perfectly boring. We want to root for a protagonist, but he or she needs to have some weakness or flaw to make him fully human. Even Superman has to deal with Kryptonite, right?

On the flip side, completely evil villains can come off as caricatures, so make sure to give your villain a touch of goodness. Hannibal Lecter is a twisted, sick psychopath, but we can't help admiring his intelligence, his brilliant deductions, and the fact that he won't harm Clarice, the protagonist of *The Silence of the Lambs*. So let your good guys have weaknesses and flaws; let your villains love something—the dog, his children, the American way.

Have you given your protagonist a weakness or flaw? What is it and how to you demonstrate it?

Have you given your villain or antagonist a virtue or two? How do you demonstrate those? (Note: "antagonist" can be a temporary role, assigned to one character for a while and another one later. Make sure these are real people, not merely props.)

In *Creating Extraordinary Characters*, I explain how to make sure you are pushing your character enough. Read it for more information on the subject.

☐ Agent and author Donald Maass says writers should always write down something our characters:

> *would never, ever think*
> *would never, ever say*
> *or would never, ever do.*

Then we must make sure our characters are pushed to a place where they will think, say, and do those things.

Take a moment to sketch out those possibilities for your protagonist and your villain, if your story has one:

Have you made certain your character is pushed to the point where we don't just see the outer person, but the person he or she is inside?

What do you get when you squeeze an orange? You don't necessarily get orange juice; you get whatever's inside that orange peel. In the same way, it's only when your character is extremely pushed and pressured that we see the deep and inner character that lives inside his skin.

☐ How have you pushed your character? Have you pushed him hard enough?

What do people think about your character when viewing this person in an ordinary situation?

What do they see when your character is pushed to his limits that they would *never* see in an ordinary situation?

Have you made your protagonist sufficiently sympathetic? Have you put him in a situation where he's embarrassed? Rebuffed? Humiliated? Readers bond with our characters when our characters suffer because we've all been in dark places.

☐ What have you done—in the first few pages of the book—to make your character sympathetic to your reader?

Have you made your protagonist sufficiently strong and admirable? Have we seen her exhibit a particular talent? Is she exceptionally good at what she does? Have we seen her do something kind or thoughtful? Does she love her kids? Her dog? Have we seen her refuse to do something, however small, against her personal code of honor?

Have you shown the reader all these traits up front, before the inciting incident? (You can keep demonstrating admirable characteristics, but it's important that we admire and sympathize with your character almost immediately.)

☐ In what ways have you made your character admirable?

As the story progresses, it's important to have *conflicted* characters. In *Twilight*, Edward loves Bella and wants to save her life, but he is also enticed by the smell of her blood and wants desperately to drink it. Can't get any more conflicted than that.

☐ As your story progresses, what strong *opposite* desires does your protagonist exhibit? He could, for instance, listen to the voice of reason more than the voice of passion, or vice versa. Is there a point at which he is tempted to change his mind and pursue the opposite inclination?

Most readers expect to meet the protagonist in the first scene. It's jarring to read a book's chapter two and realize that another character is the story protagonist. If you absolutely must open your story in the point of view of a character who is not your protagonist, can you move that scene to a prologue in order to provide some distance?

In many thrillers and murder mysteries, a prologue opens with a dead body or a murder victim, then in the first chapter we meet the protagonist or detective going about his ordinary work. He will then get a call to come investigate the dead body, or he will stumble over it on his way home.

☐ Would your story be more effective if you opened chapter one with a scene in the protagonist's point of view? If you are not already doing so, can you move whatever you have as the first scene into a prologue?

Many beginning writers open with a prologue for all the wrong reasons. Sometimes they are providing backstory that would be much more effective at the back of the story or on the cutting room floor. Sometimes, because writers can't think of an exciting, gripping beginning, they grab an exciting scene from the end of the book and call it a prologue.

Shaking head here. That's a cheap trick; please don't do it.

☐ If you have a prologue, do you have a legitimate reason for using it? A genre reason (such as the dead body in a mystery story) would qualify. An omniscient scene to set the tone might qualify. But a backstory dump or the "promotion" of a climactic scene should be nixed.

The Issues in Your Story

Closely aligned to the idea of high stakes in your story is the matter of larger than life issues. At its core, what is your story about?

Was *Breaking Bad* about a dying cancer patient trying to provide for his family or was it about how the fatal flaw of pride can destroy everything in a man's life, even the man himself? Walter White, chemistry teacher, tells himself that his decision to cook methamphetamine is to provide for his family, but when he reaches a point where his family is secure, he can't stop his criminal sideline—he doesn't want to. He's the best cook in the business, and pride drives him forward. When a man associated with the production of methamphetamine is killed and Walt's ATF agent brother-in-law says the dead guy must be the mythical genius for which the ATF has been searching, Walt can't resist saying something like, "Really? He couldn't have been that smart."

Walt becomes the living personification of how pride goes before a fall, yet he can't resist because hubris drives him to ruin.

☐ Look beyond what your character is doing on the page and ask yourself why he's doing it. What is his motivation? Is he only serving himself, or he is motivated by a desire to save the world? His family?

Is he risking everything he holds important in order to make a million bucks or because he loves his family?

Have your character ask himself why he has accepted the challenge presented by the inciting incident—is he motivated by love? Pride? Selflessness?

If you haven't nailed down the bigger picture, take some time to do so. Clarify your character's motivations, then write some scenes where he or she is forced to verbalize the truth.

If you hit a wall and need something to help you further define your character, try **putting your protagonist in a situation where he or she doesn't belong**. The "fish out of water" scenario creates great comedy and equally great drama.

In *The Proposal*, Sandra Bullock's urbanite tough-as-nails boss is completely thrown for a loop—and made vulnerable—when circumstances force her to go to Alaska with her co-worker for an arranged marriage.

In *Sons of Anarchy*, the writers placed a "good girl"—who went on to become a neonatal surgeon—inside an outlaw motorcycle club when she married the boy she loved in high school.

Comedy and drama abound in *Crocodile Dundee* when a New York reporter journeys to the Australian outback . . . and when the wilderness man she meets travels back to New York with her. Both of them have a turn at being "fish out of water," with lots of opportunities for comedy and drama.

□ Can you create comedy and/or conflict by placing your protagonist in a place or situation where he doesn't belong? How will you do that?

What complications will develop as a result of this character being in this place or situation?

What is your character's exit strategy? Will he conform to this new world, or return to his former world with new lessons and/or new relationships?

To introduce and **explain an unusual object or procedure, record its effect.** For instance, if my mad scientist has invented a gadget he calls a *zilm*, I would not take two paragraphs to explain what it is, though it would be simple to write a scene where he explains his invention to a colleague. But if no colleague is around, I could write something like this:

> Dr. Williams checked right and left to be sure no one was watching, then he stepped into the closet that held his safe. Carefully, as not to upset the delicate balance of the treasure inside, he punched in his digital code, then ever-so-gently slid the tray toward him.
>
> The zilm sat on top, glowing slightly in the dim overhead light. He exhaled, as awed as ever, and the metal zingblats vibrated, filling the air with a purring sound.
>
> "Very good," he crooned, swiveling in slow motion to avoid any sudden movement of air against the zingblats. "We must keep you in the subsonic range."
>
> He set the tray on the kitchen counter, then picked up his

harmonica. Pressing the metal edge against his lips, he blew a note at 276 megahertz. The zingblats pulsated and sang the note back to him as the zilm's liquid center expanded, rising and falling as it breathed in the music.

Williams shifted the harmonica and played a G; the zingblats quivered and repeated the sound. The zilm's blood red center shuddered and solidified like an egg yolk on the griddle, but when Williams stopped blowing, the zilm settled back to its natural aqueous state.

He smiled. His creation thrived on music, ate it up. How would it respond if he played Beethoven's Ninth?

He had no time to wonder. At that instant his assistant's teakettle shrieked from the stove, and the zilm responded with a mad shudder and a whimper. Then it exploded like a bloody eyeball, spattering his lab coat and fouling his glasses.

He sighed and wiped his face with a handkerchief. Tomorrow, without fail, he would make certain his assistant vanished forever.

How much more effective—and fun—is this than saying, "The zilm —four inches square, with a red yolk-like substance in the center, with serrated edges that tended to react to moving air—sat in the center of the tray."

You've heard it before: *show, don't tell*. This technique works beautifully in historical novels where you want to describe an ancient weapon or practice, and in specialized fields like medicine or technology. It's standard practice in science fiction. Show the character interacting with the practice or object that would be unfamiliar to the typical modern reader—and have fun with it.

☐ Go through your story and look for any titles, objects, practices, or creatures you've explained or described in block description. Highlight and cut those explanations and descriptions, and instead give us a scene where a character shows us how he or she relates to or interacts with whatever you're trying to illustrate.

Settings

Check the settings of your novel—it might be helpful to record the settings of each scene on your timeline or in your (temporary) chapter heading. Are you placing your characters in the same locations over and over again? Do they always have discussions at the kitchen table? Might it be more appropriate if you moved some of those talks to the bedroom? To the curb? As your characters walk the block in their neighborhood?

When deciding the setting for a scene, consider the emotional content of the scene and think about where that might be most poignant and effective. For instance, if a husband and wife want to talk about their son's death, it might be good to have them confront each other in his bedroom—or in *their* bedroom, where he was conceived.

☐ List all the locations where scenes in your novel take place, then count how many times each location is used.

Once you have a list, see if any one location is over-used without a good reason. Consider mixing them up, or finding new places where your characters can interact.

Timing.

To speed up story time, make your sentences short and clipped.

He glanced at his watch. She was late, as always. Ten minutes. Twenty. Thirty.

After wasting sixty minutes of his life, John stood, handed the velvet ring box to a homeless man, and said good-bye to Eleanor forever.

Twenty years passed. Milton would later realize that he changed very little with the passing of time, but Tia had bloomed like a rare, exquisite rosebud.

☐ Can you find places in your book where nothing happens for an extended stretch of time? Can you make those motionless moments pass more quickly by shortening your sentences and paragraphs? Search for them, and give this technique a try.

To slow down story time, make your sentences longer, run on, continuous, and never-ending. Almost.

Why would you want to slow down story time? Sometimes a crucial story event happens too quickly—a gunshot, a car crash, a lightning strike. When a quick event is important to the story and to your protagonist, you need to s-t-r-e-t-c-h that moment, and you do it by breaking every rule you've ever heard about run-on sentences.

He saw the gun, the muzzle flash, and felt the sharp pain at his gut before his ears rang with the sound, but what was it they told him in medical school, that bullets were supersonic, that they did more damage going in than most people realized, and that what we saw on TV was laughable, even a .30 caliber bullet would carve a hole in a man's middle before landing against his spine, or, worse yet, flying through him and gutting some poor innocent bystander who happened to be in the way or by the elevator or waiting for his pregnant wife to bring their first child into the world . . .

By writing something like the paragraph above, you have slowed the speed of a supersonic bullet to as long as it takes a reader to read that run-on sentence.

☐ Can you find crucial events in your novel that occur in a heartbeat? Or even in a moment or two? If so, use the technique above to slow down story time. Let us see and feel what the point of view character is thinking and feeling in that life-passing-before-the-eyes moment.

Genre Considerations

In your second draft, it's also important that you consider any particular elements that are expected in your genre: for instance, a romance where the hero and heroine do not get together is *not* a romance. It may be a fine story, but romance readers who pick it up expecting a romance will be peeved if your lovers aren't united at the ending.

In a mystery, the detective must reveal who the killer or criminal is at the end.

In a thriller, the protagonist and villain must have a confrontation before the ending.

To what genre would your novel or short story belong? Don't automatically say "general"—books classified as general fiction are harder to sell than genre books because no one knows what to expect of them. Readers love the familiar, so if you're starting out, or even if you have fewer than five published books to your credit, you'd do well to place your first five books in a specific genre.

My book *A Time to Mend* is a romance. Though there is an important medical subplot, the story's prime focus is the attraction between a doctor and a nurse and how they must overcome various obstacles—including her breast cancer-- that would keep them apart.

☐ What genre does your novel or short story fit? What are other best-selling books in this same genre? What elements do they have in common—and does your novel or short story have these same elements?

I've compiled a list of things you should consider about a few popular genres. This list is certainly not exhaustive, but will give you a head start in understanding what conventions you need to consider as you second-draft your book. If your genre is not listed here, read several books in your chosen genre and make a list of the elements these books have in common.

Romances

☐ Do your hero and heroine meet early in the book? Do they like what they see, but are put off by some perceived attribute of the other person?

If there are other strong subplots, does the romance remain the central story?

Review any scenes containing sexual tension. Have you implemented any complications or obstacles that will be impossible to overcome? (Wouldn't be wise to have your hero fall in love with a woman who turns out to be his sister.) Have you illustrated these scenes with lots of emotional description?

Miscommunication is a common complication used in romances, but it tends to make your characters look stupid and it frustrates your reader. (Why doesn't she just tell him the truth? Because there'd be no story if she did.) If one of your characters is believing a lie or suffering under a delusion, wrap up that complication fairly quickly, or you'll wear out your reader's welcome.

As you near the end of the story, make sure you have used beautiful, poetic language in the hero's declaration of love and commitment.

When your hero and heroine are declaring their love for one another, make sure you depict enough physical contact to emphasize their language. I'm not talking about rolling around on a mattress— I'm talking about affirming touches, kisses, and other signs of love suitable for the time and place.

Before the ending of the romantic novel, it's a good idea to have the hero and heroine summarize all the things that kept them apart —and realize how they've learned and grown to overcome those issues. They have not only changed, but now they have a better and more appreciative understanding of the other.

Mysteries/Thrillers

First, understand the difference between a mystery and a thriller. A mystery is a "who dun it" where a detective investigates a crime, uncovers clues and red herrings, and reveals the solution to the crime at the end of the novel. A mystery is a puzzle, and the fun of reading a mystery is trying to solve the crime along with the detective.

Because mysteries are a game, the reader should not have complete access to the detective's thoughts and deductions—that's why many mysteries are written in a detached third person point of view and/or narrated by a third party, such as Sherlock Holmes's Dr. Watson. This enables the reader to "see" the same clues Sherlock sees, but not know what he is thinking. We have to be as brilliant as Sherlock to sort out the real clues, toss out the red herrings, and come up with a solution. In a mystery, we rarely have access to the criminal's thoughts, if at all. If we do, his identity is disguised.

A thriller, however, is not a puzzle—it's a race and a competition between a heroic protagonist (who may or may not be a cop) and a dastardly villain. These stories may be written in first or third person, and will have scenes from both the hero's and the villain's point of view. The pace of a thriller increases as the hero and the villain get closer and closer to each other and the inevitable confrontation.

At the beginning of a thriller, the villain usually has far more resources than the hero. He may be wealthy, brilliant, good-looking, or all three. He may have a lofty reason for his crimes, but underneath it all, he may simply be cruel or psychopathic.

At the beginning of a thriller, the hero may be down on his luck, laid off, struggling financially, and in the midst of breaking up with his true love. He may have lost all confidence in his heroic abilities and wonder if he's ever done anything worthwhile.

Then a crime occurs and the hero becomes involved. He takes a personal interest in the situation, and as he moves closer to the villain, the villain takes a personal interest in the hero. They set their sites on each other.

Key point: The villain will win the early rounds, but as the story progresses, his madness or villainy or greed or pride will overcome his reason and the inherent goodness of the protagonist will begin to shift events in the hero's favor. And at the confrontation, you can bet the villain will land some painful blows—or kill the best friend, or the dog, or hurt the hero's daughter or wife or girlfriend—but the hero's virtue and nobility will give him the strength to rise up, steady himself, and win the day.

And we will cheer him all the way

☐ Is your story a mystery or a thriller?

If you're writing a mystery, have you taken care to hide the detective's reasoning via a third party narrator or through careful use of third person point of view? Have you also disguised the criminal so the reader isn't "spoiled" along the way?

At the end of the story, have you allowed the detective to reveal the criminal and receive confirmation? Did you account for all the clues and explain why the red herrings were not legitimate clues? Nothing drives a mystery reader crazier than an author who forgets to tie up some loose end.

If your story is a thriller, have you given us scenes in the hero's and the villain's point of view?

☐ Have you made certain that the villain is worthy of the hero's efforts? He must be a superlative villain—conquering a weakling isn't heroic. Your villain must have many resources at his disposal, far more than the hero.

☐ Make sure your villain makes an appalling moral choice—if he's going to be bad, let him consciously choose to be bad. Does he?

Have you made certain that the hero takes some serious hits during the story timeline? He must lose some battles and suffer some meaningful losses before he'll be sufficiently motivated to keep fighting. But don't destroy him completely—he needs a good reason to stay in the battle.

What serious losses does your protagonist suffer?

In the movie *Braveheart*, based on the true story of William Wallace, Wallace loses his wife to the enemy. That situation would decimate many heroes in contemporary thrillers, but Wallace fights on, not only for his late wife, but for his country and his people. He finds a higher goal, and remains in the struggle. (*Braveheart* is considered to be a historical story, but compare the movie's structure with the structure of a thriller as outlined above. Even though Wallace dies in the end, he is victorious in his cause. So maybe we could think of *Braveheart* as a historical thriller in kilts.)

Women's Fiction

Women's fiction usually features a female protagonist thirty or older, married or not, often with children. While this woman may have romance in her life, the primary plot is not a romance—it's a plot that involves the issues contemporary women face in their lives: dealing with children, family, aging parents, wayward husbands, and other family problems. She may or may not have a career, and she may be just like the woman who lives next door to you. But her problem is not ordinary, and neither is she. When put to the test, she will be stressed to the breaking point, she will suffer far more than your next-door-neighbor, and the lesson she will learn changes her life forever.

☐ Does the book you've been describing as women's fiction fit the above description?

Many women's fiction books are written in first person. If you're using first person—or even third—you should avoid excess introspection because it slows down the pace of your novel.

☐ Do you have scenes where your heroine is drinking coffee, taking a bath, or driving the car while she thinks? Try rewriting the scene so that she's thinking those thoughts—or some of them—while she's engaged in something active. Maybe even voicing those thoughts in a confrontation with her spouse or best friend. Conflict is always more interesting than coffee-drinking.

Juvenile fiction:

It may seem odd, but parents are rarely featured in juvenile fiction. Why? Because the child protagonist (you *do* have a child protagonist, right?) must be the active character in the story. He must be the one learning the lesson, making the decisions, accepting the challenges, and experiencing the bleakest moment. If a parental unit is always stepping in to solve the kid's problem, the story isn't going to work.

☐ Do you have a child protagonist who is a little bit older than the outside age of your target reader? If you're aiming for 8-10 year olds, have your protagonist be ten or eleven. Kids love to read about older kids, not younger, and while girls will happily read about boys, most boys do not like to read about girls.

Is the child protagonist in your book the center of the story? Is he the one who solves the problem and learns a lesson? Is he the one celebrating at the end?

Have you kept the adults at a safe distance? Don't let them do anything that the child character could do for himself.

☐ If you're writing a picture book, go through the manuscript and circle any adjectives. Now consider your illustrations. If the illustrations make your adjectives redundant (Billy wore a **blue** jacket—the picture will reveal that the jacket is blue), cut them.

For picture books, check your word count. Picture books are designed to be read by an adult to a child, and they should contain no more words than an adult can read in one comfortable sitting. I'd aim for 1200 words, tops. One thousand words would be better. Eight hundred words, better still.

Remember that the illustrations should carry half the weight of the story. If you're struggling to trim a word count, let the pictures do some of the work.

To write any kind of juvenile fiction successfully, read, read, read. Some of my favorite books were written for children, so delight yourself in classics like *Bridge to Terabithia* and *Mike Mulligan and his Steam Shovel* before sitting down to write.

Don't assume that children's books are easier to write—they're not. In some ways they are a unique challenge.

Other genres:

Genres fall in and out of favor (chick lit used to be hot, now it's not), so pay a visit to your local bookstore and ask a clerk what's selling well. Study the best-seller lists. Read the books on those lists.

Many genres employ specific point of view choices, tenses, even cover designs. For instance, when chick lit was popular, these books were usually written in first person, present tense, and featured pink and green covers. Publishing is all about "brand identification," and genre books are designed similarly so readers who pick up a book in any given genre will have a good idea of what to expect.

Your Personal Second Draft Checklist:

THIRD DRAFT CHECKLIST

Before beginning your third draft, take a couple of days for triage. Go through your manuscript and look for any notes you've made to yourself. Take care of the spots where your manuscript is bleeding, and then you'll be ready to move on.

In the third and subsequent drafts, you will be shifting from working primarily on the creative side of your brain to the "nuts and bolts" side of your brain. While you are free to write if you find you need another scene, the third draft is primarily about becoming your own best editor.

If you've not read the *Track Down the Weasel Words* lesson, this would be a good time to do that. Because the first thing we're going to do is track down and highlight those weasel words.

Everyone has his or her own list of overused or weak words, but here are some of mine: *was, were, that, really, suddenly, very, just, began to, started to, there were, there was, up, down, to her feet, etc.*

I use the search/replace feature in Scrivener or Word to search for the words on my weasel words list, then I tell the program to replace those words with the same word in all caps. For instance:

Search for _was_ (the underscore represents a space)
Replace with _WAS_.

Search for _brow
Replace with _BROW

When I have done that procedure for every word on my list, my
manuscript is dotted with lots of words in all caps. That's okay. The
simple act of going through the manuscript to replace those words
with proper capitalization will force me to evaluate: can I find a
better way to say this? A more active way? Can I replace this wimpy
verb with an active verb? Can I delete this word altogether?

THAT can often be deleted.

Anyone who sits DOWN can also sit.

VERY usually needs to disappear.

Ditto for SUDDENLY.

And remember—my favorite English teacher always told me that
we should pay ourselves a quarter for every word we can cut. Briefer
is better, so learn to write tight.

If you're brave—and I hope you are—you might want to do a
search for *ly* (no space before) and replace with LY. This will highlight all of your adverbs, and 90 percent of them need to go. Trust
me, you'll be grateful when they're all lying dead on the floor.

☐ Have you done a search for your weasel words? If you haven't yet
discovered your weasel words, have you done a search for the words
in my list? Most writers commonly overuse them.

Have you noticed that you have people smiling a lot? Frowning
frequently? Are their brows punctuating every sentence? Are your
characters nodding every other paragraph?

Check your speech attributions. "He said/she said" is always best. Do
not have people chortling, huffing, snarking, giggling, or yelling their
words. Also keep the adverbs out of your speech attributions: don't
write "he said angrily" when you can put that anger in what he says.

☐ Search for the word *of.* Some phrases require it ("The Tower of London"), but others need to be shortened: *he wore a sweater of dark blue* might be stronger if you wrote *he wore a dark blue sweater.*

On that note, search for every *it.* You can keep any *it* that clearly refers to something: *she wore a hat with flowers on it.* You know without thinking that *it* refers to the blue hat.

But if you've written *It's hard to get around the inevitable,* whoa! What is that *it* referring to? Unless that's in dialogue (people don't usually worry about grammatical preciseness in spoken speech), back up and ask yourself what you're trying to say. Perhaps you want to say, *Life happens no matter what you do.* Figure it out.

Beginnings and Endings

In this third draft, you'll want to spend extra time on the beginnings and endings of scenes. Scenes should end with a punchy line, something that seems to signal the end to a scene. Scenes should open with something interesting as well, some sentence that lets the reader know who the point of view character is.

All scenes should be anchored in a specific time and place. A scene may open with a bit of narrative, but by the end of that scene, the reader should feel as if he or she knows where the POV character is and when the scene is taking place.

☐ Check your scenes. Are all of them set in a certain time and place? You should be able to chart them on a timeline and give each scene a date, time, and location.

If you're writing narrative, which can cover a lot of time and many places, conclude the scene with a bit of action that can be anchored in a specific time and place.

Here's an example from *Bathsheba*, greatly condensed:

[Narrative] Nine years passed—years in which David, my lord and king and husband, grew old. From his wives and concubines he no longer sought pleasure, but warmth, yet we were growing old with him. To better care for the aging king, one of his servants suggested that the palace seek out a young woman, a virgin, who would become his handmaid. She would care for him, feed him, and sleep with him to keep him warm.

. . .

I spent hours praying over the situation, then one day an old friend came to visit. "The prophet Nathan," my servant told me, "waits for you in the palace garden."

. . .

I pulled my veil over my graying hair and hurried outside, then slipped up the stairs to the elevated garden. Nathan sat in a shady alcove, but he rose and bowed when he saw me.

☐ Check your scenes and look for narrative. By the end of the scene, have you anchored your POV character in a specific place and time?

Will the reader realize who the POV character is by the time he's read the first or second sentence in the scene? Some books use devices to handle this problem, especially if the book is written in first person so each character refers to himself as "I." The POV character's name may be a heading in each chapter, for instance, or the character scenes may be typeset in different fonts.

Check the ending of your scenes. Every scene doesn't have to end with a bang, but the last sentence should feel like a conclusion or a natural stopping place. The scene should not feel as though you ran out of things to say.

Check the last paragraph of the last scene in your book. This paragraph should have as much punch as the first line and first paragraph of your story. In the beginning, however, you were trying to hook the reader's interest. At the ending, you are trying to deliver an emotional punch that will resonate long after the reader puts the book down.

How do you do that? Consider echoing the theme of the story. What is your theme, and how can you restate or illustrate it in your ending?

Some of the most powerful endings bring the story full circle by repeating the beginning of the story. The character is either in the same place, thinking the same thoughts, or seeing the same view, but now he or she is deeply changed, so those thoughts, that view, are seen and felt from a different perspective.

☐ What is the theme of your story? Does your ending reflect or echo this theme?

☐ What is happening at the beginning of your story? Where is your protagonist? What is he thinking and/or viewing? Is there any way you can include some of these elements in your ending?

Example: my work-in-progress, *Bathsheba*, opens like this:

> According to family history, when my parents presented me to Samuel at the time of my mother's purification, the *Ruach HaKodesh* touched the ordinarily eloquent prophet in such a way that the torrent of words from his lips resembled nothing so much as a stream of gibberish. Though my parents strained to understand the prophet's words, they caught only a few. My father recalled hearing "mother to a great man" and "affect the future of Isra'el." My mother, on the other hand, caught only two words: "*tob* woman," a phrase that pleased her very much.
>
> At only eighty days old, I retained no memory of my encounter with the prophet, but in the years ahead I came to understand that a river of foretellings and curses had carved out the events of my life, a torrent of words with the power to rip me from people I loved and settle me on unexpected shores.

My novel closes like this:

> I am now an old woman of more than seventy years. I have known great sorrow, and I have known great joy. But throughout the winding length of my life, I have been pulled

and directed by words that sprang from prophets' lips after being breathed by the *Ruach HaKodesh*.

And I am content.

The same idea is present in both passages—we are powerless before prophecies from the Spirit of God.

☐ How can you incorporate the theme, the location, or the ideas from your beginning into your ending? Make some notes below, then see what you can do:

Mood Music

The third draft is a great time to insert what I call "mood music." If your point of view character is in a good mood, think Disney and write in some birds chirping—no, singing—outside her window. Don't overdo it, just put them in the scene.

If she's in a melancholy mood, write in some rain or dark clouds or a headache.

If she's alone in a big house and a madman is chasing her, change that rain to a thunderstorm.

If she's in an ancient prison, write in the drip of moisture from the stone walls and have a rat skitter away from a cone of lantern light.

If she's on a picnic with her true love, have them idly remark on a pair of foxes playing hide and seek in the tall grass.

See what I mean? Add some sensory details that contribute to the mood of the scene, but keep them subtle—mood music should remain in the background, not become part of the plot.

☐ Go through your major scenes (where decisions are made or new information is learned) and make sure you've written in mood music to heighten the emotion of that scene.

List your most important scenes:

Now, beside each scene description, note the mood of that scene.

Next, think of something you can use to elevate and heighten the mood in that scene. Be sure to keep these sensory details—something to see, hear, taste, touch, feel, or intuit—in the background.

The All-Important Beginning

In the third draft, spend some extra time on your beginning, especially your first sentence. Why? Because you only have a few seconds to hook your reader. People browsing in a bookstore see the spine first, then the cover, then they might flip the book over to skim the back cover copy. If all those things have piqued their interest, they will then open the book and read your first line—so it had better be the best line in the book.

Here's a hint: make sure your first sentence has a person (because we enjoy reading about people more than reading about weather, furniture, landscapes, or galaxies far, far away) and something that raises a provocative question.

When I teach, I have my students write their first sentences on a slip of paper, then pass them all forward. Under the cover of anonymity, I read each of the sentences aloud and ask the class to respond in one of three ways. If they were totally hooked and would keep reading, they are to raise their hands high. If they were interested and *might* keep reading, they raise their hands about shoulder height. And if the sentence didn't grab them, they don't raise their hands at all.

It's always a revealing exercise, as writers who thought they had a good opening realize it isn't as strong as they thought.

Even something like, "Oh no! He was going to kill her!" can be dull because 1) it feels cliché and 2) we don't know who's saying this, so we don't care. Unless a bit of opening dialogue is so clever that it has to be coming from an intelligent or interesting character, it can fall flat.

So change:

Julie Smith opened her eyes and knew she was in trouble.

to

Julie Smith opened her eyes into darkness and felt the slick satin of a cheap casket beneath her fingertips.

Yowsers! How'd she get in a casket? Did someone buy her alive? Does she sleep in a casket? Is she one of the undead? Has someone tried to kill her? Or is she the victim of an inexperienced doctor? She probably works with a mortuary, because she's quick to identify that "slick satin" with a "cheap casket."

See how a few details can raise several provocative questions in the reader's mind? That's what you want to do. That's how you keep people reading. You would not want to say:

Julie Smith opened her eyes and felt the slick satin of a cheap casket beneath her fingertips, then wailed because her evil step father had finally carried out his threats to kill her for the insurance money.

That sentence gives too much information. Your task in the first sentence—indeed, the first chapter—is to give enough information to arouse interest, not to explain every detail.

But be careful—I've read some manuscripts that gave so little information that I was confused. If your reader can't tell what's going on, they may put the book down. People read for entertainment, after all, and if a book is too much work, why not watch TV?

☐ Read your first sentence. Does it contain a person? (Not necessarily a named person, just a person). And does it give us details that raise a provocative question in the reader's mind? If your first sentence doesn't work, play around with it until it does. Or start over.

Write several variations of your opening line below, then try them out on impartial friends. Which one hooks their interest best?

Maintain the Tension

I have taken several writing workshops from the fabulous agent and teacher Donald Maass, and one thing he stresses is that a manuscript should have tension on every page. Literally. If you have scenes where nothing is happening—no doubts, no questions being raised in the reader's mind, no reason to wonder about the health and safety of your protagonist—then you need to do some tweaking.

By tension, I don't mean that you need a bomb going off on every page. Or a fist fight. Or an argument. But you need to have something that piques your reader's interest and causes him to wonder or worry about what's going to happen next.

The writing lesson *Tension on the Line* contains a full discussion and examples of how to insert tension, so I won't regurgitate everything here. But you do need to be aware that your manuscript needs tension . . . all over the place.

☐ Because we tend to get involved in our stories when we're reading straight through them, we have to look for tension in a more detached manner. So print out your manuscript and pull a page from the stack—any page. Now read the text on that page and highlight all the phrases or questions that will raise tension in the reader. Not finding any? Then you need to work on that scene.

Do this for at least twenty pages. Or, if you're adverse to printing stacks of paper, pull up your manuscript on the computer and scroll to a random page. Read that page only and look for tension. Highlight the things that raise questions in the reader's mind. If you can't find anything on a given page, rework the scene.

Keep a Timeline

Trust me, you'll be glad you did. When you keep a detailed timeline, not only will you make sure that your characters are aging properly, you can also guarantee that they won't get mail on Sunday and won't forget to observe or even mention Christmas during their December crisis.

There are myriad ways to keep timelines, ranging from using an actual calendar or maintaining a timeline in a computer document.

Previously I mentioned that I used to use Excel to keep my timelines. Each row was a scene, and the columns were the name of the POV character, the date of the scene, the time of the scene, the weather, the mood, the principal action, or whatever details you need to keep track of.

Now that I use Scrivener, I keep a timeline on the notecards. The first line of the notecard is the scene title, and if I place the day, time, and date on the second line, then my timeline becomes visible whenever I click "outline view." Very simple.

If you print out your timeline, in whatever form you keep it, and submit it with your manuscript, your editor will rise up and call you blessed.

So if you haven't been keeping a timeline in drafts one and two, this third draft—when all your story elements should be in place—is a great time to start.

☐ Create a timeline for your story in a format to your liking. Make certain every scene is represented on it, and use it to make sure your protagonist isn't 20 in 2002 and 25 in 2005. If your story or novel covers a timespan greater than a year, your character will need to experience birthdays, holidays, anniversaries, weekends, etc. By forcing yourself to make your story adhere to a calendar, you'll actually be giving yourself more fodder for the story engine. How does your character celebrate Christmas in the midst of turmoil? How does he feel about his birthday during his struggles?

☐ Jot down some "calendar conflicts" your protagonist needs to experience.

Create a Style Sheet

A style sheet is a page of notes that will be useful to the editor, and it's a good idea to create one. I usually include the names of all the characters with the correct spelling, also the names of any places, brands, schools, etc., mentioned in the story. It's also a good idea to note if these are actual characters and places or fictional characters and places.

For instance, if you place a White Castle burger restaurant in Newtown, Virginia, no one will care because Newtown, VA is fictional. But if you place a White Castle in Newtown, England, you might get letters from irate readers . . . because I doubt that city has a White Castle that sells burgers. (Then again, they might have an actual white castle . . .)

On my style sheet I also list any unusual words that I use so the proofreaders can check my spelling, and any foreign phrases with their meanings. I also list the main characters' ages at the beginning of the story, so the proofreader or copy editor will find it easier to track the age of each character as time passes in the story.

It's also a good idea to give a brief physical description of each character: Joe Smith, brown hair, blue eyes, medium build. You'd be surprised how often characters can change eye color in the course of a novel.

On a style sheet I would also mention whether or not I'm capitalizing pronouns that stand for God and other stylistic choices. Some publishing houses capitalize certain words, and others don't, so your choice isn't as important as *consistency*. If you capitalize the endearment *Honey* in one scene, you should do it throughout the story.

☐ As you move through your book on this next draft, start a style sheet and add to it whenever you come across a new character name, foreign phrase, location, etc. A style sheet's main purpose is to help copyeditors understand why you made the choices you made, so think like a copy editor as you compile your list.

Odds and Ends

Names: People rarely use each other's names in dialog. I hardly ever use my husband's name because if I have to call him, I say, "Honey?" But when we're talking, I don't say, "Honey, you need to call the doctor," or "I feel, honey, that you shouldn't do that." Occasionally for emphasis, yes. But routinely, no.

☐ So look through your manuscript and see if your characters are constantly using the other person's name in dialogue. Nine times out of ten, the name shouldn't be there.

☐ Don't use phonetic spellings in your dialogue except for the occasional dropped g in something like "dreamin' of a white Christmas." Far better to indicate someone's foreign or unusual speech by word choice.

   ☐ Do a search for things that will make you blush later, especially when body parts are involved.

> She threw up her hands.
>   *That's just gross.*
>   He sat and drank his coffee with a jerk.
>   *Who was the jerk?*
>   Her eyes darted across the room.
>   *I hope someone corralled those slippery things.*
>   She nodded her head.
>   *What else is she going to nod?*
>   She clapped her hands.
>   *What else is she going to clap, her flippers?*
>   His heart thumped in his chest.
>   *Where else is it going to thump?*
>   She rose to her feet.
>   *What else would she rise to?*
>   He caught her eye.
>   *Did she intend to throw it?* (Okay, that one is fairly colloquial, but still . . .)

When you're riding a wave of inspiration, it's easy to not pay attention to the words flowing out of your brain. Trust me—I've written some zingers before, but they were so bad I've wiped them out of my memory.

So turn on your inner editor and look at your words and phrases with a literal eye. Eyes don't dart, but gazes do. Hands can lift. People can sit.

And watch out for "she rolled her eyes." First, it's overused. Second, when I read that phrase, I see a girl rolling a couple of glass eyeballs like dice on a sidewalk.

☐ Check your chapter breaks. Big shifts of time and/or place deserve a chapter break. And so do readers. Depending on your story, insert a chapter break every 15-20 pages, just so the reader has a nice stopping place.

Sometimes do the opposite. Insert a chapter break at a tense moment to entice your reader to begin another chapter.

☐ Write in a "stream of consciousness"—when the reader gets every thought running through your POV character's mind—only when the character is sick, drunk, or otherwise indisposed. Avoid this technique at other times, as it can become wearying for your reader.

☐ Incidental characters such as the newspaper boy, the postal carrier, and the taxi driver do not need names unless they play an important role in the story. Readers don't like having to keep up with too many named characters.

☐ Show and tell: If the information is part of a longer list of information, tell it. If this information will cause a reaction in your protagonist, show it.

Example:

Glenda undid the lock and took inventory: The trunk contained a vintage dress, a package of faded love letters, and several packets of old Simplicity sewing patterns.

OR

Glenda shoved aside the vintage dress and the package of faded love letters, but her heart skipped a beat when she spied a packet of old sewing patterns, circa 1952. There it was, the dress. The one her mother had worn in the yellowed photograph. The one in which she'd been holding another baby, a baby who wasn't Glenda.

If an item or a situation will cause an emotional reaction in a character, show it in detail.

☐ Profanity. From reading reviews on Amazon.com, I've learned that lots of readers enjoy "a good, clean story" because it doesn't rattle their senses with offensive language.

You may think I'm being prudish, but rough language makes a *lot* of people uncomfortable. That statement is probably a little less true with every passing year, but anything that breaks the "fictive dream" for a reader weakens the story, and profanity is one of the things that can interrupt a reader's reading experience.

When I am writing characters who would and do use profanity, however, I will usually write something like "he turned the air blue with expletives" or "he cursed."

Writing dialogue with profanity is easy. Finding a way to impart that same flavor and information without profanity is a challenge.

If you don't want to avoid profanity completely, at least know that there are mildly offensive words and highly offensive words. And while most people don't mind reading the mildly offensive words, they can become extremely annoyed when a book for which they paid good money contains highly offensive words that make them want to toss the book in the trash. Just sayin'.

Sensory Details

One of my favorite compliments from a reader is, "I felt like I was there, right in the middle of the story!" How do you make a reader feel like they are right in the middle of the action? You do it by including lots of sensory details in your scenes.

You are probably familiar with the five senses: seeing, hearing, tasting, touching, smelling. I would add another: intuiting. Sometimes our characters can feel a sense of foreboding, something that makes gooseflesh appear on their arms.

Seeing is easy to incorporate because we often describe what our characters are seeing. Hearing is also easy because stories usually have lots of dialogue. But don't forget the sounds of the environment in your scene.

What about taste? Your characters don't have to be eating in every scene, but you can also taste blood, tears, and even fear.

Touch? Have your character feel surfaces beneath his palm, feel chills racing up her spine, or a pounding migraine.

Smell? People smell perfumes, sweat, burning fires, dogs, urine, rats, and flowers. Scientists tell us that familiar scents (or odors) are linked to our memories, and can quickly evoke a memory of a distant time when we breathed in the same scent.

And foreboding/intuition—people can sense when something's not right. Did you know that animals can sense approaching earthquakes? The human sense of intuition may not be quite so well developed, but it exists. Your character may shiver and joke that someone just walked across his grave, but he's experienced a feeling we all recognize. Déjà vu is a similar sort of feeling.

Enrich your scenes with at least two or three sensory details, and your reader will feel that he or she is experiencing the story along with your protagonist.

☐ Go through your scenes and highlight (or mark in the margin of a printed copy) any time you've said something that evokes one of the five senses. Aim to have at least two or three senses evoked in each scene (all five might result in sensory overload).

☐ Check your character descriptions. When describing a character, start with the larger picture and focus. Don't give us an entire paragraph of block description, but sprinkle the descriptive details through the character's actions.

This used to be the standard way to describe a character:

John Lee walked into the room, all six foot three inches of him, dressed in Levi's and a plaid cowboy shirt. Dolly felt her gaze rove over his broad chest and strong arms, then she focused on his chiseled face. That strong jaw, that classic nose were truly noteworthy, but those blue eyes were unforgettable.

The following is a better way to describe a character—it's more active. Notice though, that both descriptions begin with his overall impression—height—and focus on the most compelling aspect of this person, his eyes. Begin macro, finish micro.

John Lee strode into the room, dwarfing the knot of less-statuesque men huddled around the punch bowl. He walked over the guest register, his cowboy boots clunking on the wooden floor, and wiped his hands on his blue jeans before picking up a pen to sign the register.

Dolly felt her gaze rove over his broad shoulders, then her throat tightened when he looked up and caught her watching him. His classic nose crinkled when he smiled, and his unforgettable blue eyes sparked with interest . . .

☐ Check your dialog to be sure it corresponds with the age, rank, and social status of the speaker. I've read many a well-intentioned manuscript written by an older person about a child who doesn't speak like any kid I know. If you're going to write in a child's or teen's POV, it's imperative that you spend some time with children or teens of the appropriate age. Learn their language, but not too much of their slang. Slang changes quickly, and if you incorporate too much, your book will be dated in no time. Learn speech patterns. Study how children and teens think, and spent time talking to your own kids or the neighbors'. Then you'll be better prepared to write realistic dialogue.

Your personal third draft checklist:

FOURTH DRAFT CHECKLIST

Take a couple of days for triage after you've completed your third draft. If you've made notes to yourself in sidebars or comment balloons, go back and fix or incorporate whatever you feel needs to be done.

Then print out your manuscript, settle back in your easy chair, and grab a pen or marker with brightly colored ink. This fourth draft offers a delicious change of pace because you're going to use your ears.

When people read a book, they hear the words in their heads—or in their voice, if they're reading aloud. The way your words *sound*, therefore, is extremely important. You need to listen to your manuscript, and you can do that in several ways.

I have a friend who pays someone to come over and read the manuscript aloud. That's fine, but I don't do that because 1) I'm cheap, 2) my editing is done in snatches of time, and 3) it's likely that a reader would subconsciously correct typos I need to hear.

I've heard other people say that they read the manuscript aloud themselves. That's fine but 1) your eye will probably gloss over the typos you've been glossing over all along and 2) you are likely to read dramatically, inserting the emotion you felt as you wrote. A reader won't know what emotion you were feeling, so your *words* have to evoke that emotion, not your voice.

I prefer having the computer read to me. It's been years since I worked on a PC, but I believe you can install text-to-speech capabilities if you download the free program called Adobe Reader. Once it's installed and activated, you can highlight any portion of text (chapters or scenes) and then right click and Adobe Reader should read the text for you. Another choice might be Natural Reader (www.naturalreaders.com). I understand that Windows has a program called Narrator, but I don't believe it works within Microsoft Word.

If you're working on a Mac, a text-to-speech program is built in. To activate it, go to your system preferences, click on "dictation and speech," and choose your favorite voice. Select the checkbox that says "speak selected text when key is pressed." Then choose the key combination you'd like to use to activate the voice.

With that done, open your document, highlight the text you'd like to listen to, and then press your selected key combination. The computer will begin to read your text in a slightly robotic voice (the quality has greatly improved over the years). The nice thing about the robotic voice is that the emotion will not be in the voice. This should allow you to evaluate whether or not your words are carrying the emotional weight you intended.

The computer will read every word just as it is. I have a tendency to leave out little words, and the computer reading makes that obvious. As my selected voice reads, I turn my back to the computer so I won't be tempted to edit onscreen, and follow along on the printed page with pen in hand. Whenever I hear a mistake or something clunks on my ear, I make a quick mark on the page so I can go back and fix it.

The primary benefit of having the computer read a manuscript is that your ear will catch repeated words and sounds that your eye may miss. Something like "He stared at her as she went down the stairs" will sound awkward and clumsy, but it'll look fine on the page. I find that even sentences like "I planted roses by the graveside today because I'd never seen such a fine summer day" don't work when read aloud.

Whenever I hear this repetition or echo, I circle the repeated words and write "rep" in the margin. Sometimes I will realize that I've used the same word three times in one paragraph, so I'll circle all of them. The more distinctive the word, the more it will stand out.

Sometimes listening to your manuscript will help you realize that you've only given a couple of lines—only seconds in listening time—to explore a major character epiphany, or a realization that needs more than a few blink lines to develop. Or perhaps the opposite is true—your character may be musing over something, and they keep thinking and thinking and thinking while nothing of interest is happening on the page.

So use your fourth draft to listen to your manuscript. After you've gone through a chapter or a scene, turn back to your computer and enter your changes. If you've made major edits to a paragraph or scene, listen to it again to make sure it flows. There is a rhythm to language, and when it *sounds* right, it usually *is* right.

In this fourth draft, pay special attention to your plot strings. Many times I've been working on a later draft and I've decided to make a change in the plot. Maybe it's a small change and maybe it's a big change, but when making changes at this late stage, a writer must be very careful not to pull a string and unravel the entire book.

In *Bathsheba*, for instance, early on I decided that she would come to love King David after the death of their first son. From that point on, she would love him.

But in a later draft, I realized that I was missing a great opportunity for conflict if I did that—after all, the timespan of the book continues until after David's death. And Bathsheba had lots of reasons *not* to love David—he was an inattentive father, he surrendered seven of Saul's sons to the Gibeonites for execution, and he had forced himself on her when they first met. Oh, and he had her husband murdered. Plenty of reasons for her not to fall head over heels in love with the king, right?

So I made the change in one pivotal scene, then I had to go back through the entire book to check Bathsheba's thoughts and feelings about David. She needed an attitude shift, and she needed it in nearly all of her POV scenes.

So when you pull one string in your tightly constructed plot, you must go back and make sure that you haven't created inconsistencies in the rest of the story. Making changes at this late stage isn't easy, but it's certainly possible and often advisable.

To create the best possible book, sometimes it's necessary to make changes—so when your editor speaks, you shouldn't be defensive or lazy; you should listen.

☐ Have you made large or small changes in your story in a later draft? Have you gone back to examine all relevant previous scenes to make sure nothing contradicts the change you've made? Do that now.

Your personal fourth draft checklist:

FINAL DRAFT CHECKLIST

You have spent at least two drafts writing and fleshing out your story. You have spent at least two drafts self-editing your story. If you feel you need another draft or two to keep working on drafting or self-editing, by all means, keep working.

But when it's time for the final draft, these are the things you should to to add a bit of professional polish to your manuscript.

☐ Use the search/replace function of your word processor to search for [space, space] and replace with [space]. And because spaces are invisible, you should put your cursor in the search box and hit the space bar two times. Then put your cursor in the replace box and hit it once. Repeat as many times as needed until you have no double spaces in your manuscript.

When students regularly took typing classes, they were taught to separate sentences with two spaces, and that habit dies hard with a lot of folks—and sometimes extra spaces creep into our documents. Doing this search and replace will ferret them out.

☐ Search for any ellipses. Though some word processors are set to automatically replace . . . with [dot dot dot], the correct way to use them is [space dot space dot space dot.] You rarely need to use four dots in fiction because they pertain to quoted reference material.

You can use an ellipsis when someone takes a poignant pause in dialogue: "You know . . . I thought he loved me."

Or you can use them when someone trails off in thought: "I knew a lad like Billy once . . ."

Do not use ellipses when someone is interrupted in dialogue. That calls for an em dash (when you type hyphen hyphen, most word processors immediately replace them with a long dash—that's the em dash).

"Get out of here, you lazy—"
"Now Melly, let's not lose our tempers."

☐ Search for your exclamation points and delete almost all of them. Keep them only if someone is screaming for help . . . or on fire. Maybe.

Nothing marks an amateur manuscript faster than an overdose of exclamation marks.

☐ Consider adding a symbol to your story. What is an object that can represent something significant to your protagonist? Write it into at the beginning or middle of the story, then mention it again at the end of your story . . . and let the reader see how your changed protagonist views this symbol in a different way.

In my novel *Doesn't She Look Natural*, Jen is newly divorced, and she wants to reconcile with her husband. She keeps her wedding rings in a box in her bureau, and at least once in the story she pulls them out to try them on, praying that she'll be wearing them again soon.

Then her ex-husband shows up to tell her he's marrying his girl-friend, and the news devastates Jen. But as he's leaving, his car is involved in an auto accident and he's killed. Jen, who has heretofore hated all things funereal, goes to the mortuary to slip her wedding band onto her deceased husband's pinky finger. She's saying goodbye to him, but more important, she's finally able to lay the dream of restoring her marriage to rest.

Can you think of an object in your story that can be imbued with emotional significance and mentioned at least twice in the course of your story's events?

☐ Your theme: sometimes I get to the fifth draft and find myself struggling to come up with a simple theme for my story. So I ask myself—what, other than plot, is my story about? Love? Sisterhood? Friendship? Forgiveness? Once I can detach myself from the plot and come up with a one-word answer, then I look for ways to work in dialogue, symbols, and interior monologue that pertain to my theme. I don't want to drive the theme home with a sledgehammer, but I do want to make sure it is highlighted in some way.

What's your theme? And how can you work it into your character's thoughts, words, or actions?

Don't forget the spell check. Nearly every word processing program has one, so use it well.

Consider an author's note. If you've taken liberties with geography or historical timelines, or if you'd like to thank the professionals you interviewed for your character's occupation, write an author's note in which you tell your reader everything he needs to know. Lavishly praise the folks who helped you out, mentioning them by name—and be sure to spell their names correctly. Don't forget that last important line: "If there are any errors in my depiction of a herpetologist, the mistakes are mine alone."

Consider discussion questions. Book clubs are wonderful, and people who lead book clubs appreciate authors who put discussion questions at the back of the book. I've had a book club in my home for nearly thirteen years, and feedback from those intelligent ladies has helped me grow as a writer—and no, we don't discuss my books. (Not as a rule, that is.) Even if the average reader doesn't belong to a book club, discussion questions can help your reader explore some of the ideas you've presented in your story. So go ahead and come up with ten or twelve questions for your novel. They just might prompt a reader to suggest your novel for the next meeting of her book club.

☐ Consider a bibliography. I'm aware that most novelists don't include a bibliography, but when I rely heavily on other people's books and articles, I want to give them credit. Plus, some readers may be so fascinated by a concept that they'd like to read more about it, so a book list would be appreciated. Adding a bibliography doesn't hurt anything, and it may help prove that you did your homework, especially if you're writing about a complicated topic or historical era.

☐ Consider a note to your reader, inviting him or her to leave a review on Amazon.com or other retail website. This is a relatively new idea, but certainly worth investigating. Publishing is not what it was ten years ago, and most authors, even those who are traditionally published, find themselves responsible for most of their own marketing. So why not ask your reader to share a review if they enjoyed the story?

Don't worry—if they didn't like it, they won't need encouragement to post a review.

☐ Check your manuscript formatting. Your manuscript should be formatted in the traditional manner—no fancy fonts, no colored inks, no odd layouts. If you are sending the manuscript off to an agent or publisher, you should lay it out for an 8.5 x 11 page with one-inch margins at the sides and bottom. Allow a 1.5 inch margin at the top. Double space. Begin a new chapter on a new page. Use a standard font like Garamond (the font you see here) or Times New Roman. Make sure the font is 11 or 12 point—any more and you'll strain your reader's eyes.

Your name and address should be in the upper left corner. You might want to add the manuscript's word count beneath the page number in the upper right corner.

The title should be in the center of the middle of the page, with your byline beneath it. (Hint: don't write "**by** Your Name." Just write "Your Name.")

If you have an agent, place his or her name, address, and phone number in the bottom right corner of the title page.

Formatting details aren't nearly as important today as they were before everything went digital. Fonts and sizing can now be changed with a couple of keystrokes, so this emphasis on proper formatting may seem trivial.

But if you use the proper formatting, any editor will know that you know how formatting should be done. If you use bizarre formatting, your manuscript will reek of inexperience. That may be a good thing in some situations, but not many.

☐ If you are going to self-publish, you may think you need to format for publication at this point—whoa. Please, please have your manuscript edited first, and format your manuscript as explained above to before sending it to an editor. Wait until your manuscript is ready for publication to format for publication.

Your personal final draft checklist:

SUBMISSION CHECKLIST

You are now the proud possessor of a manuscript. Perhaps it's printed and sitting on your desk as a neat stack of pages, or it's on your computer, ready to venture forth. What do you do with it?

Unless you wrote it for a specialty or niche market, you'll probably want to consider a traditional publisher first. If you can interest a traditional publisher, your book will receive professional editing, design, cover design, marketing, and sales support. You should also receive an advance against sales, a check you can enjoy any way you please (just don't forget to save some for taxes and remember that you won't see another check until you've sold enough books to actually earn that advance check).

The downside? You can expect to receive a royalty of anywhere from ten to twenty percent of the sales price—and in some instances, it may be the *net* sales price, the retail price minus forty or fifty percent.

I love speaking to children in schools, and I'm always tickled by their honest questions. I remember standing in front of one group of elementary kids. One little boy raised his hand, and when I nodded at him, he said, "So, are you like *swimming* in money?"

I laughed. "No, I'm not," I told him. I then held up one of my picture books and told the kids that it sold in stores for about

$14.99. "Of that fifteen dollars," I said, "how much do you think I get?"

"Six dollars?"

"Five?"

"Ten dollars!"

"Seven!"

You should have seen their crestfallen faces when I told them that I received about twenty-five cents from the sale of each book. "Lots of people were involved in making this book," I explained. "The artist had to be paid. And the editor. And the designer. And the printer. And the salesmen. And the marketers. And the publicity person. And the truckers who hauled it to stores. And the bookstore who bought it to sell, and the clerk who sold it."

So a writer who publishes with a traditional publisher has a great support team—but he or she has to pay them all, and we do it through lower royalties.

But something else comes with traditional publishing—credibility. When a book is traditionally published, almost everyone realizes that the book has hit a home run in the literary world, whether it's a best seller or not. That title has made it through vetting by an agent, an editor, a publisher, and a review committee. At least that many people considered it to be worthy of publishing, and that's no small matter.

Traditional publishing means your book has an opportunity to be carried in honest-to-goodness brick bookstores. They don't *have* to order your book, of course, but if the sales and marketing teams have done a good job, bookstores may order a copy or two. And replace them when those copies sell.

Perhaps the greatest advantage to traditional publishing is the fact that *they pay you,* and you will usually earn more through a traditional publisher because they have the tools to sell *thousands* of books.

I've had people ask me how much I had to pay to have my books published, and in the past I was always surprised by the question, though not so much any more. But for a writer who's trying to earn a living through publishing, that advance may be enough money to carry the family through a few months, and that's not a small consideration.

Getting a book published traditionally today isn't easy. But it may be the route you want to take. Unless your book is aimed for a specialty market, I would urge you to at least try the traditional approach. Not only will it give you an appreciation for how the process works, but you may get some good editorial advice.

Should You Hire an Editor?

I'm frequently asked this question at writers' conferences, and I have mixed feelings about it. The answer is yes and no.

Yes, you should hire an editor if the editor is going to work with you on the manuscript and give you a *substantive* (or macro) edit. In other words, he or she is going to write a long letter and tell you where the story line could be beefed up, where certain scenes should be cut, and how characters could be better developed. Any good publishing house will have editors who will do the same thing, and two good substantive edits never hurt anybody's book.

On the other hand, you should not hire an editor if this editor is going to come in and do a *line* (or micro) edit, cleaning up your prose and rewriting your book for you. I'm sure this happens on occasion, but I don't believe it's fair to the publishing house that is considering your manuscript. They want to see *how you write*, and if someone else has gone over your book and cleaned everything up, that's not a true representation of how you write, is it?

I believe it's better by far to get involved with a critique partner or a critique group who can help you learn how to clean up your writing yourself. I hope this series of writing lessons will serve the same purpose. Where do you find these critique groups? Start by asking your local librarians. Join an online writer's group. Search around, and you'll find writers by the dozens.

Bottom line: **You need to be the best writer you can be.**

Getting an Agent

I'd be remiss if I didn't tell you about an important step required by most traditional publishers: since they will only accept manuscripts from agents, you will have to get one. And getting a good agent can be as difficult as finding a publisher who's willing to buy your manuscript.

Hundreds of books and articles have been written about how to get an agent, so I'm going to boil the advice down to the basics. First, do not sign with any agent who requires money from you up front. If they charge a reading fee, or review fee, or even ask you to pay for coffee, say thank you and walk away.

Second, remember that you are the employer, the agent is the employee, though the situation may feel quite the reverse. You may feel as though you are auditioning for Julliard and lucky even to get an appointment, and truthfully, you may be. But you will be paying the agent if and when your manuscript sells, so do not allow yourself to be cowed. Neither, however, should you be bossy and demanding, as the author-agent relationship requires mutual respect in order to work.

The names of agents and agencies are easy to find on the Internet, and as you read those websites and listings, pay particular attention to the types of manuscripts this agent represents. If he or she doesn't handle children's books, don't send them a picture book manuscript. If they sell a lot of titles to Harlequin and you don't write romance, perhaps this isn't the agent for you.

I sold seventeen books before I ever got an agent, but times have changed since then. Some smaller houses will consider unagented manuscripts, but most larger houses won't. Agents provide another layer of vetting or "winnowing out" for busy editors, and they appreciate the service agents provide.

If an agent tells you your manuscript isn't ready for publication, he or she may be right. You can always get a second opinion from another agent, but you should also consider going back to the drawing board. Do not, I repeat, do not decide to self-publish this manuscript.

If you self-publish a less-than-stellar manuscript, you may be shooting yourself in the foot. A slew of bad reviews on Amazon isn't going to help your future in publishing, and bad sales will only hurt your prospects. Far better to consider that manuscript a learning experience and move on, or, better yet, take it apart piece by piece and start over, making it the best story it can be.

What if an agent or publisher tells you, "This is a good manuscript, but we simply can't find a place for it in our program?"

That's when you are free to consider another traditional publisher who perhaps can find a place for it, or consider self-publishing. If an agent or publisher tells you the manuscript is good, then you have a green light for self-publishing.

You should consider self-publishing if your book has been vetted and:

--it's a title aimed at a niche market

    --it has limited geographic appeal (i.e., a book about Florida law)

    --it's an unusual format (like these short writing lessons)

    --it's so unique that no publisher knows what to do with it.

Publishers look for books that have the potential to sell thousands of copies—books that have wide appeal in a traditional, cost-effective format. If your book doesn't fall into that category, perhaps self-publishing is your answer.

Before giving up on the idea of traditional publishing, ask yourself:

☐ Have I truly made this book the best it can be?

☐ Have I worked on it with a critique group or critique partner for honest feedback?

☐ Have I done the work—multiple drafts, careful self-editing, thorough research, attention to plot, theme, and characters?

☐ Have I sent it to a test reader or two (not family members) for their honest feedback?

☐ Have I sent it to at least three carefully selected agents? Have any of them offered encouraging comments?

☐ Am I self-publishing only because I want to say I've published a book, or am I convinced this book has the best chance for success through self-publishing?

SELF-PUBLISHING CHECKLIST

Self-publishing (also known as *indie publishing*) isn't what it used to be.

When I was in high school, my English teacher told us about vanity (or *subsidy*) publishers. Her disdain was plain to see. "These operations will publish a book by anyone, whether it's good or not," she said. "They charge people thousands of dollars, and most folks end up with a garage full of books they can't sell."

Vanity presses still exist, but today they often operate as part of a traditional publisher's program. Publishing is in a tough place today —revenues are down, costs are up, and a lot of publishers are looking for ways to increase their revenue stream.

How do they do that? They solicit manuscripts. When a manuscript comes in, they say that it "doesn't quite fit their regular publishing program, but there are other options for this book. For only $X,ooo, we can offer a package that will give you professional editing, design, printing, and sales support. You'll be listed in our catalog and your book will be sold on Amazon.com and Barnes and Noble.com, just like John Grisham's."

And lots of people will believe that their book might do quite well with this kind of support.

Well . . .

These programs are subsidy publishing programs. They will take your money and produce books, but your book will be one of millions on Amazon.com. Yes, you will be listed in the company catalog and on their website, but how many people will visit your book's page?

Not all of these programs accept every book; some *do* have editorial standards, but those standards vary from program to program. Many of them, however, will take almost any manuscript, do very little editing, produce a perfunctory cover, and produce a book that will sell a few copies to your friends and family.

If you're going to self-publish, I believe there's a better way—which I will fully describe in a bit. But first, you need to be very aware of the stigma attached to self-publishing.

I have been involved in several book fairs and literary contests, and many of them prohibit self-published books from participating. Why?

Ron Charles, editor of *The Washington Post's* Book World, explains:

At *The Post*, we're getting about 150 books a day. *A day.* And these are books that had to find an agent. And then a publisher. And then were professionally edited. And now are being professionally marketed by people with money on the line. Many of these books, of course, are bad, but many — *far more than we can review* — are interesting, engaging, informative, moving, timely and/or newsworthy for various reasons.

All the winnowing and editing work that went on before a galley ever arrives at our door make this job possible. The idea of dumping several hundred thousand additional books on our small staff every year is terrifying.

Are there great, truly *great* self-published books being produced — and ignored — every year?

I'm sure there are, and that's a tragedy. But it's not a tragedy that I can solve by reading 25 pages of every one of the 300,000 self-published books that would land in our office if we opened the door.

Independent Publishing

Self-publishing is so easy now that nearly everyone's doing it. This is both good and bad.

It's good because writers who would have found it difficult to place their unique manuscripts with traditional publishers can now take their work directly to the market—if they can figure out how to do that.

It's bad because writers with no training whatsoever are now flooding the market with inexpensive, mediocre books. They are practically giving their books away, and this practice has driven down the price of books, bringing financial hardship to those who rely on book sales for their living—publishers, writers, and agents.

And how is a reader supposed to find the rare self-published jewel among so many unpolished rocks?

Publisher's Weekly, the trade magazine for publishers and book sellers, recently reported that 450,000 books were self-published in 2013.

Although it comes with a number of caveats, Bowker's newest report on the number of self-published titles rose again in 2013, increasing 16.5%, to 458,564. The increase was due entirely to the release of new print books which rose 28.8% to 302,622 offsetting a decline in self-published e-books which fell 1.6%, to 155,942.

The totals are based on self-published titles that have an ISBN registered with Bowker as of August 6, 2014 with the year referring to the year of publication provided by the publisher. The report also does not include titles published through Kindle Direct Publishing since books created there do not need an ISBN, and also does not include titles from Nook Press. In addition, it is likely some titles are double counted as self-published authors who do both print and e-books often give different ISBNs to the same title. Beat Barblan, Bowker director of identifier services, explains that the counts are ISBNs, not titles, "and indicate trends rather than absolutes. We're consistent in the way we calculate this each year, making the reports accurate reflections of trends."

Dozens of platforms for independent publishing have arisen over

the last five years, and among the better-known servicers are Book-
Baby, Lulu, and Smashwords. These online companies will take your
digital book, translate it into files for all the digital book platforms
(files that end in .mobi, or .epub, for instance) and place them for
you in the major (and some minor) digital and/or print book sales
sites. Others like Nook Press and Amazon's Kindle and Create Space
will make your book available on their sites alone.

Because this is a free country, you're welcome to plunk down
money and try those sites, but before you do, consider this:
according to the Tech CheatSheet, as of March 2014, Amazon had
"the largest share of the e-book market . . . with 67 percent. As for
print, Amazon controls 64 percent of sales of printed books online."

Millions of people are selling books on Amazon. How well they
sell depends on the book, but self-published titles can move thousands of copies on Amazon.com: "A new Author Earnings report
suggests that self-published books now represent 31 percent of e-
book sales on Amazon's Kindle Store, and self-published writers earn
almost 40 percent of the store's royalties."

So . . . write a good book, get the word out, and it can sell
online. Getting it into brick bookstores may be tough (for some of
the same reasons cited by Ron Charles of *The Washington Post)*, but
millions of people are now accustomed to reading digital books.
And Amazon has made it doggone easy to publish an ebook
online.

After you have taken a few steps, you can publish your book in
the major markets. But don't skimp on these steps, because the same
customer review that could sell your book to others could also drive
people away.

If you want to self-publish:

☐ Have your book professionally edited . . . and I'm not saying
you should hire an English major to do it. The creative writing we
learned in high school English is not professional writing. If you
don't know any professional editors, don't worry—I do.

Most of the following folks are friends of mine and great writers.
They are also great professional editors.

Jeff GerkeJeff@jeffgerke.comwww.jeffgerke.com
Steve Rzasasteverzasa@gmail.com steverzasa.wordpress.-
com/editing-services
Deborah Raney debraney@mac.com
Sharon Hinck s.hinck@comcast.net
Jerry Gramckow jerrygramckow@rocketmail.com
Kathy Tyers kmtyers@hotmail.com
James Coggins jrc@coggins.ca

This is so important, maybe I should say it again. In caps: HAVE
YOUR BOOK PROFESSIONALLY EDITED. You won't want
someone to rewrite your book; you want someone who will help your
book be the best it can be.

☐ Have a professional design a cover for your book. Don't simply
call on someone who knows how to work in Photoshop. You need
someone who has studied the basics of design and typography
because nothing says "self-published" faster than a bad cover.

For an ebook you will need a front cover image in jpeg format.
For a paper book, however, you will need a full spread—back cover,
spine, and front cover. Pay a designer to do a complete cover,
because you're going to want one if you produce a paperback.

Where can you find a professional designer? One of my favorite
options is www.99designs.com. This site features the work of graphic
artists from around the world, and it's a good way to find good work
for reasonable prices. Many professional artists don't like 99design-
s.com because they believe it severely undercuts their prices—and it
does. But after studying both sides of the argument, I realized that
giving work to a beginning artist in Indonesia might well feed his
family for a week. And we all have to start somewhere, don't we?
When I opened my photography business, I gave away several free
shoots because I needed images in my portfolio, plus I needed the
experience. I think the same principles apply to 99designs.com.

How does it work? You come up with a project (for instance:
book cover) and prize money (a good price would be $200-$300), but
search for completed book cover contests, see how much those

contests awarded, and make your price competitive. If you offer too little, you won't get many artists to compete in your contest.

Go online, create an account, and start your contest. You will pay the money up front (the website administrators hold the prize money for you until the contest is finished), and then you will write a design brief, explaining exactly what you're thinking of. It will be helpful if you can upload a cover template in the size of what you envision as your finished book. You can find these templates at Kindle Direct Publishing, the Amazon company that produces paper versions of self-published books. More about KDP later.

In your design brief, the more information you give, the better your artists' designs will please you. You might even upload some already published covers and say, "Not exactly this—but I like this idea (or style or tone)."

You will be asked if you want to guarantee your contest—meaning that you promise to choose a winner. If you don't guarantee your contest and you don't see any designs you like after a few days, you can close your contest and get your money back. But many artists won't compete in a contest that's not guaranteed, because they don't want to invest a lot of work with no guarantee of a payoff for anyone.

You will also be offered a choice to have a "blind" contest. In a blind contest, the artists cannot see each other's work, so you will receive some very creative and different ideas. If a contest is not blind, the artists will begin to copy designs that you've indicated you like, so all the designs may begin to look similar.

Some artists love blind contests. Some don't. Not much you can do about their preferences, but I tend to like blind contests because I want originality, not copies of whatever I awarded four stars.

Next, you publish your brief. You will then want to look through other artists' portfolios. If you see some you like, you can invite them to participate in your contest.

After a couple of days, artists will begin to submit ideas for your cover. As they come in, you will be asked to give feedback in two ways: you can rate each image from one to five stars, with five stars meaning "this is almost the winner!" and one star meaning "um, back to the drawing board." You can also leave comments such as "Nice drawing, but the colors are too dark. Can we lighten it up a bit?"

The more detailed you can be in your comments, the better results you'll get from your artists.

After a few days (the contests run for a week or so), you will select five finalists. At this point you can create a poll with your finalists' designs and post them on your Facebook page. Invite people to tell you what image they like because, after all, it's John Q. Public who will be buying your book. Take those comments into consideration.

And after a few more days, you'll be asked to choose a winner. After you do, you will have a little time to have the winner make tweaks, if necessary. Also tell the artist what file type(s) you need. (Kindle requires a jpeg of the front cover; the print option requires a .pdf of the full cover, so get both.)

When you have received everything you need, you indicate that the contest is finished, and the website administrators pay the artist the prize money—all but about thirty percent, which goes to support 99Designs.com.

I have used 99 Designs for book covers, illustrated picture books, business cards, and a logo, and I've been very impressed with the work I've received. I've had nice working relationship with these artists, many of whom live in other countries, and it's an experience and service I heartily recommend.

Publish Your Book in Paperback

Should you create a paper version of your book as well as an ebook? Absolutely.

Digital Book World explains that sales of self-published books are up, and print book sales have increased more than ebook sales:

Print books have strong value to self-published authors, enabling them to reach a broad audience, often via independent bookstores.

A handful of companies continue to dominate the publishing services sector for independent authors. More than 75 percent of self-published titles with ISBNs came to market with support from just three companies: Smashwords, Amazon and Lulu.

If you're going to create an ebook, you might as well create a paperback version of it as well. Many choices are available on the Internet, but for ease of use and cost, no one beats Amazon's KDP program. This is the service I usually use to make copies of my self-published books.

The easiest way (by far!) to *format* a manuscript is through the software program **Vellum**. You simply open Vellum, open your Word manuscript in Vellum, and then choose your formatting options. Check to be sure the chapters are correct, and you're done. (If you have not formatted your Word document with styles, you may have more work to do, as your chapters may have been divided into separate files.) But Vellum is a self-published writer's dream. If you're going to write more than one book, it is well worth the investment. https://vellum.pub .

☐ If you'd rather not purchase Vellum, go to kdp.amazon.com and create an account. Once you have an account, you can download templates—one for your cover and another for the interior of your manuscript.

Before you can download the cover templates, you'll need to decide on a trim size for your book. This is completely up to you, but I'd advise looking at other books similar to the one you want to create. Measure them, and use those measurements as a guide.

If the trim size is odd, some sales outlets may not carry it or it may be more expensive to produce. So you're better off choosing a standard trim size like 5 x 8 or 5.5 x 8.5.

☐ After you've chosen your trim size, download your templates and begin to prepare your manuscript. I've found that it's easiest to download the formatted manuscript file, then I simply cut and paste my finished chapters into the formatted file. If you know how to use styles in Microsoft Word, you'll find that the typical Kindle Direct Publishing manuscript primarily uses four styles, all of which are in the KDP formatted file:

CSP—Chapter Body Text
    CSP—Chapter Body Text—First Paragraph
    CSP—CHAPTER TITLE
    CSP—Front Matter Body Text

Just make sure your first paragraph in every chapter has *CSP—Chapter Body Text—First Paragraph* showing in the style window. Other paragraphs, of course, will have *CSP—Chapter Body Text* showing in the style window.

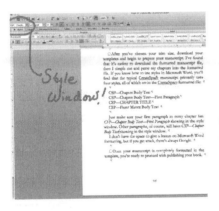

☐ Once your edited manuscript is completely formatted in the template, you're ready to proceed with publishing your book.

    The first page is easy to understand—you enter title, subtitle, author, illustrator (if any), etc. If you're not ready to publish, enter what you can and leave the rest to fill in later. The the title cannot be changed, so do not enter it until you are sure you won't want to change it later.

    ☐ The next step is obtaining an ISBN, the international code by which all books are identified. Kindle Direct Publishing gives you several different options. Once you choose one and get your ISBN, you are locked in. So choose carefully.

KDP has recently added the option to give publishers (you) a free ASIN: an Amazon stock number.

You can choose to have KDP be listed as the publisher—that's fine, but I'm still keenly aware of the prejudice against self-published books, so I've never been wild about that option. I created my own imprint, Hunt Haven Press, so I selected the "use own imprint" option. I also purchase my own ISBN from Bowker.com.

When you purchase an ISBN through KDP, you're getting a bargain—if you were to purchase an ISBN from the clearing house, you'd have to pay a couple of hundred dollars for at least ten ISBNs —fine if you want to do that, but you don't have to.

If you are going to create your own imprint, you should create a logo for this and any other books you plan to publish under your imprint. Again, 99Designs.com can be a lifesaver. Or you can pay a graphic artist to design a logo just for you.

Once you have your book's ISBN, you're ready to move on.

KDP frequently makes changes as to how books are uploaded, so the following information may not be exact. But most of the elements remain the same, though they may appear at different points of the process.

☐ When KDP asks for a description of your book, enter a brief, accurate, and persuasive description of your book—this is the sales copy that will appear on your book's page, so choose your words carefully. If you followed my instructions for your second draft, you should have an effective paragraph for back cover copy—use it here.

You will also choose a category for your book—in which category do you think you'll find the most promising book browsers?

You will then enter an author biography, with the language of your book, the country of publication, and keywords. Keywords are important: what terms would people use if searching for a book like yours? The Amazon search engine wants to know.

KDP also wants to know if you book has "adult content" or "large print" (a book in at least 16 point type).

☐ Next you will select your book's trim size, interior color, and paper color. Be aware that "full color" is expensive—both for you and for your customer. Personally, I don't think it's worth paying a full color price unless you have a color illustration on practically every page. For a children's picture book, yes. For an illustrated chapter book? Probably not. For a novel? Definitely not.

Paper color is up to you; personal choice. Cream is nice for novels; it's clean and elegant. White may work better for nonfiction.

Once you've made those choices, you're ready to upload your book file—and not just any book file. Make sure you're uploading a formatted manuscript on the KDP template.

After you've uploaded your file, the online computers will do their work to make sure there are no obvious errors in your manuscript. In a moment or two you will see a preview pane, and any formatting errors will be highlighted. Don't worry if this happens, most of the errors can be easily fixed and then you can upload your file again.

☐ Once you have uploaded your interior file, it's time to upload your cover. KDP offers an almost instant option to create your own cover—if you use it, your book will look completely generic. I would advise against it.

If you hired a cover artist, your graphic designer should have given you a .pdf file created on the KDP template for your trim size and page count—yes, you must know the number of formatted manuscript pages before your cover can be finalized. Why? So the spine can be the correct width. If your book has very few pages, you won't be able to fit any type on the spine, and that's okay.

You are also given a choice as to your cover finish—do you want a matte or glossy cover? Your choice. This choice will be offered again after the pricing page.

Now locate your cover file and upload it. For the Kindle edition, you will upload a front cover .jpeg file. For the paper edition, you will upload a full cover (back, spine, front) .pdf file.

After your book is published, you can go back any time to make changes in the interior text or the cover without penalty. You will simply go through the process again. I make changes all the time—whenever anyone finds a typo, or when I decide that a cover could be improved. The ability to make changes easily and quickly is one of the greatest advantages of print on demand publishing.

□ Once you have uploaded interior and exterior files, you'll come to a page where you're asked to submit all your files for review. Click that button, and an actual human will check your files to make sure they are printable. If they find a problem, they'll send you an email so you can take care of it. If they don't find a problem, they'll send an email saying that your final proof is ready for viewing.

Click on the link in the email to be taking to your proof page. You have two choices—either view the final book online, page by page, or pay a few dollars to have a copy of the book printed and mailed to you. (I always choose the digital option because it's free and fast.)

□ Once you approve the proof, your book will be published. Within days you'll see it available on Amazon.com and other markets —depending upon what you choose on the distribution page.

□ At one point you will choose which channels you'd like for your book's distribution. Most people choose all of them, of course, but if you publish under your own imprint, your book may not be eligible for libraries and academic institutions.

Each channel, by the way, offers a different royalty rate. You earn the greatest royalty through the most direct route, Amazon.com. Any other retailer will take a percentage, so your royalty will be lower.

□ On to the pricing page. You have limited options here—the minimum price you can charge (to cover Amazon's costs and still pay you a royalty) is stated beneath the first option box. You can use the check boxes to charge the equivalent amount in British pounds and euros. The chart to the right tells you how much you will earn on each sale through those channels.

Don't forget that the rise in self-publishing has actually brought about a decrease in the price of many books—especially ebooks. (The more plentiful a thing is, the less it costs). You don't want to overprice your book when similar books sell for less.

After you select "save and continue," you are practically finished.

☐ After you complete the process for a paper book, you will then be offered an opportunity to sell your book on Kindle. If you choose this option, KDP will take the interior and cover files you've already submitted and create Kindle files from them. Everything "transfers over," so it's an easy process.

At some point, you may be offered the option to have your book available for preorders. Why do this? Because if you garner many sales in a short time, you boost your book's ranking. And books with higher rankings can be featured in some of Amazon's lists, such as the "hot new releases" list, which only serves to increase sales.

If you want to select a future publication date, you'll still need to upload all the information (description, cover, and even a partial manuscript) and choose a publication date. Be sure to finish your book and upload the finished manuscript by the deadline Amazon sets for you, or you will be penalized.

Entire books have been written about how to format ebooks, but Amazon makes it simple. Simply visit this web page and follow the directions: https://kdp.amazon.com/help?topicId=A17W8UMoMM SQX6

Will Your Self-Published Book be Carried by the Neighborhood Bookstore?

When you publish a book on KDP, it can be available to all the major online retailers, but most brick-and-mortar stores prefer to work with the distributors (companies that furnish products from many different publishers) they've used in the past, and many bookstore managers simply don't want to deal with another account when they can get almost everything from a single source.

When I've spoken to local bookstores , I have offered to buy books at my cost and then sell them to the bookstore at a price halfway between retail and my cost. That way we both profit equally, though their profit is not nearly what it would be if they ordered direct. As always, if there's a middleman, you have to pay him.

Many local bookstores, however, simply refuse to carry self-published books. Why? Reread Ron Charles's article from *The Washington Post*. Unless your self-published book has already sold thousands of copies, been optioned for a movie, has strong local interest, or the bookseller is a dear relative, be prepared to hear "no" when you ask if they will carry your self-published book.

If, however, you can make a good case for your book, a local independent bookstore may be willing to carry a few copies—and if they hesitate, you might offer to leave them in the store on consignment. If they don't sell after a certain amount of time, you can pick up the copies and the bookstore will owe you nothing.

Try to be creative in your approach. For instance, I wrote a children's book on the true history of pretzels . . . and while it doesn't sell particularly well in the Christian bookstore (even though there is a Christian message), it sells very well at a pretzel shop in Pennsylvania.

Should Your Ebook be Exclusive to Amazon?

The Amazon Kindle program has an option that is frequently debated among indie published authors. Should you sign up for the KDP Select program?

Authors who sign up for this program have several advantages:

They receive 70 percent royalty payments in most situations

Their book is available free to subscribers of the Kindle Unlimited program, but authors are paid for each download that is at least 10 percent read.

Every 90 days, KDP Select authors can promote their book by giving it away free for five days or by creating a "Kindle Countdown" deal—the book is a low price on day one, and rises incrementally over a certain number of days. This rewards readers who purchase quickly.

Authors are also paid a fee for each book read through the Kindle Lending Library.

Once you realize that Amazon Kindle is by far the largest seller of ebooks, this program looks attractive, and it does have undeniable advantages. Customers love free books, and offering the first book in a series free can boost sales of the entire series.

The downside? Your ebook book cannot be offered on any other online retail site: not at Barnes&Noble.com, not at Kobo.com, not at Smashwords. Nowhere else. And believe me, Amazon folks check to see if you are in compliance with that rule.

You will therefore lose potential sales at other sites, but would those sales be greater than the benefits you'd receive at Amazon? Only you can determine that answer.

☐ My suggested strategy: I suggest that when you first make your book available, publish on Kindle alone and enroll in the KDP Select program. Use social media (Facebook, Twitter, email) to spread word of your book's release. Schedule five free days and let people know how they can get a free copy of your masterpiece.

☐ Many websites are dedicated to announcing free and low-cost ebooks, so search for those and have your book promoted on the days when it is free. Your goal is to garner positive reviews for your title. Don't ask your friends and family to write glowing reviews for you, especially if they haven't read the book. Amazon has begun to indicate whether or not the book was actually purchased at Amazon, so books without that verification are highly suspect, especially if they give the book five stars while everyone else gives it three.

☐ After your three-month exclusive period ends, you are free to un-enroll your book from KDP Select if you wish. You could then list it at Nook Press (which sells online at BarnesandNoble.com), Kobo, or any of the other ebook retail sites. It's your choice—you're the publisher.

What have I done? While you're perfectly free to do whatever you like, I've realized that Amazon and BarnesandNoble.com are the two biggest sellers of ebooks. Plus, Nook books are not compatible with Kindles, but a Kindle book can be read on any iPad, smart phone, or computer. So I always have my books on Amazon, and I've also enrolled many of them at Nook Press because some of my readers have Nooks . . . and I don't want them to feel slighted.

I do have a few self-published books for sale at other sites, but the sales at those sites haven't been significant enough that I would recommend them.

Update: In early 2020, I moved most of my books from all other online sales sights in order to participate in the KDP Select program. I find that nearly half of all my Amazon income each month comes from readers in the Kindle Unlimited program—and that would not be possible if my books were not in the KDP select program.

You may be surprised to realize that a multi-published author would consider indie publishing after publishing more than 100 books traditionally, but I'll say it again—publishing has changed. For the most part, I love being able to publish my own books—especially those that have gone out of print in their early editions and are now mine to do with as I please. I've taken classes in graphic design to learn how to do book covers; I've carefully weighed the pros and cons of traditional versus independent publishing. I do both now—some of my books are with traditional publishers who do a great job of marketing and distribution, areas that are difficult with self-publishing. For my more unusual projects, I choose self-publishing.

And one thing has become clear to me: every book is different, and each book deserves its own best chance to be the best it can be. Some books will do better in independent channels; others will be better served at a traditional publishing house.

And if that's not a wonderful situation, I don't know what is.

Your personal self-publishing checklist:

RECOMMENDED RESOURCES

☐ Books:

> *The Breakout Novelist*, by Donald Maass.
> *Stein on Writing*, by Sol Stein.
> *How to Grow a Novel*, by Sol Stein.
> *Self-Editing for Fiction Writers*, by Renni Browne and Dave King.

☐ Writing Programs:
Angela Hunt's video writing course: http://write-and-publish-a-great-book.thinkific.com/courses/write-and-publish-a-great-book

Jerry Jenkins's Program:
http://www.jerryjenkins.com

☐ Websites:

Formatting your book with Vellum: http://Vellum.pub.
Writer Beware: a site to protect writers from unscrupulous agents, agencies, publishers, etc.
http://www.sfwa.org/other-resources/for-authors/writer-beware/

AAR: Association of Author's Representatives, a list of agents who have agreed to uphold a standard of ethics
http://aaronline.org

☐ Self-publishing:
http://bookbaby.com
http://smashwords.com
http://kdp.amazon.com
http://www.kobo.com
http://nookpress.com

☐ A program to convert documents into digital publishing formats:

http://calibre-ebook.com

☐ Audio Book Production
   For self-published titles:
   http://www.acx.com

Marketing:
   http://bookmarketingtools.com
   For $29.00, at this site you can submit your free or low-cost ebook to dozens of sites and newsletters.

Chapter Ten

WRITING THE PICTURE BOOK

By 1987 or so, I had been a freelance writer for nearly five years. I wrote magazine articles mostly, when my small children were napping. I was content, because I became a writer in order to help my husband pay the mortgage. I had been told I had "a way with words," and I wanted a job I could do from home. Having worked very hard to bring children into our lives, I wanted to enjoy them while they were small.

So in 1983 I printed up business cards and declared myself a freelance writer. I began to read everything I could about the business of writing (which was not what I learned as a college English major), and soon I was writing magazine articles, catalog copy, almost anything people would pay me to write. I was a little amazed at how many people felt insecure about writing something as simple as a business letter. They hired me because I knew where the commas were supposed to go.

The more I wrote, the more I learned. And every time I got a new gig—for a new kind of writing—I would go to the library (this was pre-Internet) and get a book on how to write XYZ. I quickly discovered that being a writer is like being a builder. Once you learn how to use the tools properly—how to write a strong sentence, how to structure a paragraph, etc.—you can write anything from an essay to a novel, *as long as you follow the blueprint.* Every type of writing has its own blueprint, and setting out to write without knowing the blueprint is like a builder deciding to move from doghouses to Victorian mansions without knowing the first thing about Victorians or mansions.

One day I saw an ad in the back of *Writer's Digest* magazine. The ad was promoting a contest sponsored by Abingdon Press. They wanted to honor one of their writers, Lorna Balian, by finding a new picture book writer and publishing the newbie's book. Any unpublished picture book writer could enter if he or she sent in a manuscript and three sketches.

Well. I was an unpublished any-kind-of-book-writer, so I definitely qualified. I went to the library and got a book on how to write picture books, and studied the blueprint:

- Most picture books are 32 pages.
- Most picture books are less than 1,000 words.
- In a picture book, the pictures do half the work—they also tell the story, eliminating the need for many adjectives and descriptive phrases.

I'd been writing long enough to realize that *"most"* means *"industry standard."* Deviating from the standard is risky because it almost always makes your book more difficult and expensive to publish.

So I sat down and wrote a story in about twenty minutes. Because I do not draw anything other than stick figures and horse heads, I found Diane Johnson, a local woman who had painted some beautiful murals at a nearby college. I visited her, explained the contest, and she agreed to do three sketches to submit with the manuscript. She put our package our package together (quite professionally!), and we sent it off before the deadline.

A couple of months went by, then I received a phone call from the children's editor at Abingdon Press. Mrs. Etta Wilson was happy to inform me that our book won first place and would be published. They would pay us an advance, too.

I was over the moon. We later learned that Abington had expected 100 entries, but over 455 came in from all over the U.S., Canada, and the Virgin Islands. Those were narrowed down to 25, then to 13, then to six. Etta told me that when there were only two entries remaining, the judges let a nine-year-old boy choose the winner. He chose our book, and *If I Had Long, Long Hair* became the winner.

Why did *Long Hair* win? I don't think Diane and I were any more talented than any of the other finalists, but we did follow the blueprint. I'm willing to bet that the 430 entries immediately eliminated did not.

If I had a nickel for every person who has come up to me and said they'd written a children's story, I could go live on a cruise ship and sail the world. Most folks say, "I made up this story for my grandkids, and they love it, so here it is—can you help me publish it?"

I know without reading a word that the story in front of me is not publishable. Why? Because the earnest man or woman offering it probably doesn't know there is a blueprint to follow.

People think that writing for children must be easy because children are simple, the books are short, and how hard could it be?

Honest answer? Very hard. Because a picture book has so few words, every word must be GOLD. Every word must pull its weight.

Picture books are costly to produce because color printing is expensive, so publishers do not buy picture books unless they are certain the book will sell. Mediocrity or merely *good* does not pass muster. So a picture book is one of the hardest types of books to sell.

You can always self-publish, but if you want your book to sell more than 100 copies, it had better be the best you can make it.

So that is why I've written this book. If you want to write a picture book, first you have to learn what you don't know . . . so you'll know what you need to learn. You have to understand the blueprint. You have to come up with a strong plot. And you have to know how to delight children.

Writing is both an art and a science, with both creative and mechanical aspects. You supply the creativity, and this book will supply the mechanics.

Like all of the **Writing Lessons from the Front** books, this book is brief. There are other books with philosophies and backgrounds and lots of full color illustrations on glossy pages, and this isn't one of them. This is a simple, practical book that will give you the nuts-and-bolts information you need to write a good picture book. Combine that with inspiration and your imagination, and you should be good to go.

Let's get started.

WHAT IS A PICTURE BOOK?

Let's begin by making sure we understand the definition of a picture book: it is a book designed to be read to a child, usually thirty-two pages long and less than 1,000 words, in which the art is an integral part of the story telling. Picture books are designed to be read in one sitting and they should delight children and the adults who read them.

A picture book is not an early reader, in which all words are chosen for their ability to be mastered by a beginning reader. Early readers often use words which come from word lists approved by education experts.

A picture book is not a story book, which is usually longer than 1,000 words and in which the illustrations, if any, supplement the storytelling. Most story books are designed to be read to a child, or by an older child alone, in small bits—a chapter a night, for instance. Charlotte's Web is both a children's novel and a story book.

I have seen many storybooks that aim to be picture books, but fail miserably on several counts: they are too long, too preachy, and clearly designed to appeal to well-intentioned adults rather than children.

When you write your first draft of what you hope will be a picture book, run it through this checklist:

- Is the manuscript less than 1,000 words? Fewer is better.
- Have you cut all **unnecessary** adjectives so the art can provide those details?
- Have you written it with page breaks in mind? Would the action in your story require more than 14 1/2 double page spreads? Do you have enough action to fill those page spreads? (More on this later).
- Would this story delight a child and the adult reader?

If your story does not meet those criteria, or if those things sounded like gobbledegook, keep reading.

PICTURE BOOK GENRES

Not all picture books are the same, or even the same type. There are three broad categories, and genres within those categories. I once read a how-to book that gave the reader a personality quiz, then directed the would-be writer to a certain kind of picture book based on his or her responses. But you can write any type of picture book, as long as you know what the types are and follow the blueprint (sound familiar?) No need to limit yourself to one category.

The three broad categories are fiction, nonfiction, and concept books.

Fictional picture books are story books. They spin a fictional story to delight, entertain, and sometimes educate a child, in that order. No child wants to read an educational book that isn't fun, and no adult does, either. So if a story is intended to teach something, make sure the lesson is a by-product, not your primary intention. If you really want to teach, opt for nonfiction.

Nonfiction picture books aim to teach the reader about something—the history of pretzels, all about anacondas, or how farm animals live.

Conceptual picture books are often among a child's very first books. The classic *Pat the Bunny*, for instance, is neither fiction nor nonfiction, but teaches the concept of actions and textures. Many concept books encourage the child to interact with the book. A quick search on Amazon leads us to the following concept books: *Baby Touch and Feel Bunny, Never Touch a Porcupine!, See Touch Feel, My First Colors and Shapes*, and *Noisy Baby Animals*, complete with a button that plays recorded animal sounds. Other interactive books include flaps that lift up or fold out, to encourage the child to participate in the reading experience.

Many concept books are more expensive to produce because of their nonstandard formats and added features like buzzers, fabrics, and textures. Keep this fact in mind when you are considering the sort of book you want to write. Expensive books are harder to sell because a publisher takes a greater risk in producing them. If you have a concept book in mind, make sure it is unique.

Picture Book Genres

This list is not exhaustive, because genres move in and out of favor every day. Some books may fit into more than one genre, but when you are starting out, make sure your book fits into at least one of the following:

1. Wordless books: the art carries all the work of telling the story.

2. Bedtime/nighttime/dreaming books: When do most people read picture books to their children? At bedtime. We shouldn't be surprised that bedtime books are a genre unto themselves, as they tend to quiet and calm children, preparing them for bed. These books often start off with a bang and then draw down to a satisfying ending. Example: *Goodnight Moon*.

3. Generational books: These books are about the link that binds children to parents, parents to grandparents, and all family members. They demonstrate the circle of life and family love. These books may even appeal more to adults that to children. Example: *Calico Bear, Love You Forever*.

4. Adventure/monster/dinosaur books: What child doesn't love a monster? Combine a monster with adventure as in *Where the Wild Things Are*, and you have an amazing story any child will love.

5. Religious books: religious books can be overt or subtle, but will contain elements that reflect a particular faith. Many are retellings of Bible stories; others illustrate biblical or spiritual truths and values. Most explain religious lessons in simple ways a child can understand. But whatever your subject matter, make sure the book is delightful, not overly preachy or pedantic.

6. Counting books: Counting books teach children to count and illustrate the concept of numbers, including zero. Make certain, however, that the number of items pictured on a page matches the number being featured. If you're discussing the number 100, you'd better have 100 somethings in the illustration!

7. The folk/fairy tale: These books may be retelling of stories in the public domain, or new stories featuring fairy or folk tale conventions. They usually take place long ago in a nameless land far away, with larger than life characters that may have supernatural or magical powers.

8. Alphabet books: A is for alligator . . . B is for bumblebee. Alphabet books teach children the letters of the alphabet and usually feature spectacular art to complement the simple text. Many center around a theme, such as an alphabet book about animals.

9. Animal books: books about animals. I wouldn't put stories with animal protagonists in this category because animal protagonists are frequently employed when a writer wants to approach an uncomfortable topic (An animal protagonist provides a certain amount of emotional distance). No parent would read his child a book about a boy who is nearly murdered for trespassing on his neighbor's property, but *The Tale of Peter Rabbit* entertains us with a story about a bunny who nearly ends up in a pie—like his father!—because he didn't obey his mother.

Animal books teach children about farm animals, chickens, dogs, cats, etc. They illustrate the animals, show the animals as babies, and discuss what the animals do and where they live. These are usually nonfiction, or story books that teach while telling a good story.

10. Mash-up books: Combine two popular elements and create a new idea: Example: *Dear Santasaurus*.

11. Poetry books: I am referring to poetry collections like Mother Goose rhymes or stories that are music to the ear. Rhyme can be used in a fiction or nonfiction book, but the rhymes and meter had better be good, otherwise the result will be weak. I'm always surprised to see how many beginning writers work hard on their rhymes, but ignore the meter. It is just as important, because the rhythm is important to a child. Examples: Dr. Seuss books.

12. Books about ordinary life: These books deal with situations in a young child's life: getting dressed, going to the dentist or doctor, getting a pet, the arrival of a new sibling, losing a tooth. These may sound like humdrum topics, but the challenge is making these events fun, exciting, and fear-free! Example: almost any of the Mercer Mayer books.

13. The tale for all ages. Some books are enjoyed by adults as much as or even more than children. *Love You Forever* is an example, and *The Tale of Three Trees*. They are stories that appeal to children on one level, and to adults on another. These books have the potential to become classics, and sell year after year.

The next time you go to the bookstore or library, sit down in the children's section, pull out some picture books, and read them. What genres do they belong to? Why do you think the publisher chose to publish those books? What makes them work? Learn to read picture books critically . . . when you're reading for yourself. When you're reading to a child, enjoy them!

EVALUATE YOUR IDEA

Earlier I mentioned that before I begin to plot or write, I evaluate my idea. I do this for all my books, from adult novels to picture books, because this little acronym works wonders: WAGS. In order for your idea to work, your idea needs to have four elements.

W stands for *world*. Your story should take the reader to a world different from his own. In an adult novel, that means I would write a story that involves an unusual occupation, situation, or place. In my novels I've taken readers to the rain forest canopy, the world of the mortuary, medieval Ireland, and first century Jerusalem. The reader is interested in the story because he is visiting a world different from his own.

With children, the job is easier, because a child's world revolves around his room, his parents, and his home. Therefore virtually *everything* is a different world to him. The younger the child, the more true this is. For babies and toddlers, anything outside his home is a new world. For older children, anything outside the daily routine is new and different.

Fairy and folk tales carry readers to strange and distant lands. Daily life stories, in which a character goes to the dentist or doctor or library, explore those places and concepts. Animal stories illustrate the world of different animals—through fictional eyes. Rabbits don't wear jackets and sleep in beds like Peter Rabbit does. Bottom line: make sure there is something new in your story, a place or situation your child reader has not encountered before.

The A in WAGS stands for *active character.* Have you ever noticed that adults are usually absent or rarely seen in most children's stories? That's because the child protagonist must be the main character, not one of his parents. That why the adults in Charlie Brown cartoons sound like *Wonk wonk wonk,* because what they say doesn't influence the story. The story is perceived and driven by the children.

In other stories, the parents are away or dead or missing. Pippi Longstocking's parents are absent. *The Wizard of Oz*'s Dorothy lives with her aunt and uncle, and she is separated from them at the point of the inciting incident. Alice falls through the rabbit hole and finds herself in a strange world without adult guidance. The children in the *Chronicles of Narnia* have been separated from their parents by war.

This absence of adults prevents the adults from doing what we parents usually do—taking over and taking power from the child. Children's books are all about giving power to the child, allowing him to make his own mistakes and learn his own lessons. So in your story, make sure the adults are offstage most of the time.

The G in WAGS stands for *goal.* Your protagonist should have a definite desire or goal that drives the action. She can state this goal up front, or she can state it after the inciting incident, when she has entered a different world. That's what happened to Dorothy when the tornado dropped her house in Oz. She stepped out, looked around, met some Munchkins, and proclaimed, "I want to go home." Then she spent the rest of the story working to fulfill her desire.

Finally, the S in WAGS stands for *stakes.* High stakes. Something should be at risk in your story. It may not be life or death, because we are dealing with children, but that's not far-fetched in a story for older children. If Dorothy doesn't meet her goal to go back to Kansas, she doesn't die, she simply lives apart from her loved ones for the rest of her life, and that would make her unhappy. What's at risk? Her happiness and the reunion with her loved ones.

In *A Gift for Grandpa*, the boy wants to give his grandpa a watch chain. If he doesn't succeed, he doesn't die, nor is he punished, but he fails to come up with the gift he wanted to give Grandpa. What's at stake? Grandpa's happiness and the boy's delight.

In *If I Had Long, Long Hair*, Loretta wants long hair that trails behind her, but eventually she realizes that having such long hair would be messy, inconvenient, and even invite rats and gerbils to make nests in her hair. So though her happiness—having long hair—is at stake, she abandons her desire because she realizes that she'll be happier if she remains just as she is.

Not every picture book will have these elements—for instance, *Good Night Moon* doesn't because it doesn't have a protagonist. It's not a story, it's a bedtime ritual designed to soothe children to sleep. Like *Pat the Bunny*, it's a concept book. But *Where the Wild Things Are* certainly does—Max wants to be a wild thing, so he's sent to bed without supper, where he dreams and travels to the island of the wild things where he leads the parade and is immensely popular, but he misses his family, so he wakes up (and abandons his desire) and finds himself in his own bed with his supper waiting for him.

WAGS. If your story idea meets these four tests, you are ready to begin plotting.

PICTURE BOOK PLOTTING

Years ago I was asked to teach plotting to third graders. I came up with a "plot skeleton," and the concept was so simple, so visual, that now I teach it to adults and use it to plot my own stories.

As you saw in our unit on plotting, using the plot skeleton is simple: we come up with story bits for the "bones" of the story, beginning with the skull. Note: since picture books are so short, all of the story "bones" are usually present, but may be hard to spot—and sometimes they don't appear in the order listed below. But for a story—any story—to work well, it should be supported by a solid plot skeleton.

The **skull** represents the main character, the protagonist. A lot of beginning writers have a hard time deciding who the main character is, so settle that question right away. Even in an ensemble cast, one character should be more predominant than the others. Your child reader wants to place himself into your story world, and it's helpful if you can give him a sympathetic character with whom he or she can relate. Ask yourself, "Whose story is this?" That is your protagonist.

At the very beginning of your story, this main character should be dealing with two situations, which I represent in the skeleton by two yawning eye sockets: one obvious desire, one hidden need.

Usually the first few chapters of a novel are involved with the business of establishing the protagonist's world, his needs, and his personality. In a picture book, you rely on the art to set the story time and world because you only have a few pages to introduce the reader to your main character. So keep it brief, but put all the elements in place.

Your story kicks into gear when you move from the skull to the spine, a connection known as the *inciting incident*.

In a picture book, the inciting incident is often signaled by two words: "One day . . ." Those two words are a natural way to move from setting the stage to the action. As you plot your story, ask yourself, "One day, what happens to move my main character into the action of the story?" Your answer will be your inciting incident, the key that turns your story engine.

Your character stated or showed us his driving desire in the first few pages. After the inciting incident, your character sets out to achieve his goal.

In my book *The Singing Shepherd,* we learn that Jareb is a shepherd who lacks courage. His unspoken desire (shown, not told) is to be brave. Then one night something happens . . . an invitation is issued, but Jareb is too afraid to accept it.

The inciting incident in *Peter McPossum's Wiggles and Giggles* occurs on page one. His parents receive an invitation, but Peter is too wiggly, so the opening pages are all about him learning to control his wiggles and giggles.

In *Too Many Tutus*, Lola Li loves tutus. The inciting incident occurs when she receives a box from her Nana—and it's filled with tutus! So she makes a plan to enjoy them all.

In *The Chicken Who Loved Books,* Little Red loves it when Henry brings books to the coop and reads them to the chickens. But (inciting incident), one day Henry doesn't bring a book, so Little Red makes a plan to turn that situation around. Her desire is to get books back to the coop!

What would happen if your protagonist achieved their desire right away? That would result in a boring book! So you need complications that prevent the protagonist from getting what he wants, represented by the curving ribs in your plot skeleton. A novel might have 100 complications, but a picture book only needs three.

Why three? Because even in the shortest of stories three complications works better than two or four. I don't know why three gives us such a feeling of completion, but it does.

The complications are a good place to inject humor and surprise.

In *If I Had Long, Long Hair,* Loretta dreams of having long hair . . . until she realizes it could cause serious problems.

If I had long, long hair
and tried to pile it on top of my head,
I couldn't get through the doorway!

If I wore my long, long hair in braids,
my friends might tie me to a tree
and leave me there.

In *A Gift for Grandpa*, the boy wants to buy his grandpa a watch chain . . . But even though Grandma promises that God is faithful, they seem a long way from getting the watch chain.

After lunch, Grandpa went back to the fields. Grandma and I were resting on the porch when we saw the farmer coming from town. "My pig won a ribbon at the fair," he called to Grandma, "and I've brought you a present."

Grandma blinked. "A present?"
"My pig had babies!" said the farmer.
"And I'm giving the whole passel of pigs to you. Pigs are too much trouble. I'm going to raise goats instead." Grandma didn't want a passel of pigs, but the farmer insisted and left us with a big prancing pig and three little dancing pigs. The pigs scattered and rooted around in the front yard, probably looking for more Smith's Miracle Vitamin Tonic. Grandma sighed. "Lord, You know I don't need pigs. I need a watch chain."

Your third complication should be the worst complication you could think of (that would be suitable for children)—something the protagonist cannot solve on his own. It will lead your main character to his or her bleakest moment.

At the bleakest moment, your character needs *help*, but be careful how you deliver it. The ancient Greek playwrights had actors representing the Greek gods literally descend from a structure above in order to untangle their complicated plots and set things to rights. This sort of resolution is frowned upon in modern literature. Called *deus ex machina* (literally *god from the machine*), this device employs an unexpected and improbable incident to bring victory or success. If you find yourself whipping up a coincidence or a miracle after the bleakest moment, chances are you've employed deus ex machina. Back up and try again, please.

Avoid using deus ex machina by sending a helper, represented on the plot skeleton by the thigh bone. Your character obviously needs help; if he could solve the problem alone, he would have done it long before the bleakest moment.

So send in the cavalry, but remember that *they can't solve the protagonist's problem*. They can give him a push in the right direction, they can nudge, they can remind, they can inspire. But they shouldn't wave a magic wand and make everything all right. Whatever you do, do not send in an adult to solve the problem. Children are on a continual journey to become less and less dependent on their parents, so having an adult solve the problem is antithetical to their growth process. Let your protagonist solve the problem himself.

In *A Gift for Grandpa*, the boy and his grandma needed a new horse, but since they only had a dollar, they wanted to buy a watch chain. Through a series of events and Grandma's willingness to help others, they end up with a horse . . . but no watch chain. In my original draft, I had Grandma run out and cut off a portion of the horses's tail to braid a watch chain, but my editor wisely and correctly told me the *boy* should be the one who supplies the gift. Indeed he should! I changed the text, and learned a lesson from the experience —children's stories are about empowering children, and helping them learn to solve their own problems. Incidentally, the same principle holds true in all stories. In *The Wizard of Oz*, the good witch doesn't send Dorothy back to Kansas; Dorothy sends herself to Kansas once she realizes that there's no place like home.

You may be hard pressed to cite the lesson you learned from the last novel you read, but your protagonist needs to learn something. This lesson is the *epiphany*, a sudden insight that speaks volumes to your character and brings them to the conclusion of their inner journey.

James Joyce popularized the word *epiphany*, literally *the manifestation of a divine being*. (Churches celebrate the festival of Epiphany on January sixth to commemorate the meeting of the Magi and the Christ child.) After receiving help from an outside source, your character should see something—a person, a situation, or an object—in a new light.

When the scarecrow asks why Glenda waited so long to explain the power of the ruby slippers, the good witch says, "Because she wouldn't have believed me. She had to learn it for herself."

The scarecrow then asks, "What'd you learn, Dorothy?"

Without hesitation, Dorothy announces that she's learned a lesson: "The next time I go looking for my heart's desire, I won't look any farther than my own back yard."

What does your protagonist learn in the course of his trial? What has he realized about his life, his past, or his future? Does he appreciate something or someone he used to take for granted? Write down what your character has learned, then show us how he can put this knowledge into action. Armed with this new realization or understanding, what does your protagonist do that he could not do before?

The boy in *A Gift for Grandpa* learns that God supplies our needs and even our wants in unexpected ways.

The birthday horse waited outside for Grandpa as we took the silky horsehair into the house. Grandma helped me braid it into the most beautiful watch chain we had ever seen.

Then we wrapped Grandpa's gift and waited for him to come home.

In *The True Princess,* after spending a long time living as a commoner, the princess learns that it's not jewels and satins that mark a daughter of the king, but love.

Your story should end with a changed protagonist—he or she has gone through a profound experience and has changed as a result, hopefully for the better. When he reenters his ordinary world, he has a new understanding to share with others.

How will you visually illustrate your character's change?

Plot Dissection: Brandon takes a Bath

To illustrate how simple plotting by skeleton is, let me present the script to one of my picture books. It should be easy to see how it all comes together in even a simple little story like this one.

I've put my comments in brackets.

[The opening: the protagonist's (Brandon's) ordinary world:]

p. 5: Yesterday I spent the day at my cousins' house. Aunt Molly, Uncle George, and my cousins Sam and Tricia are calm, quiet people, but Brandon is something else.

p. 6-7: Brandon played outside in the mud and wrote on himself with colored markers. At dinner, he put spaghetti on his head. It was a messy, dirty day. [Obvious need: a bath. Hidden need: like all little kids, Brandon needs to know he's loved.]

p. 8-9: After supper Aunt Molly asked, "Brandon, are you ready to take a bath?" [The inciting incident: Mom's invitation.]
Brandon shook his head. "No," he said. "I'm not ready to take a bath." [Brandon's goal: avoid the bath! Bathtime signals an end to the day, an end to his fun.]
[We move into the Story World: the bathroom.]
p. 10-11: "But Brandon," Uncle George said, "if you take a bath you will be clean and sweet-smelling." [He's urging Brandon toward the tub.]
Brandon made fish faces at Tricia. "I'm not ready to take a bath." [Brandon counters by doing something else. This pattern will be repeated many times.]

p. 12-13: "Brandon," Aunt Molly said, "I'm giving the bath water a squirt of bubbling super soap. You can soak in mountains of bubbles."
Brandon twirled on his toes and said, "I'm not ready to take a bath."

p. 14-15: "Brandon," Sam said, "I'm putting my toy boat in the tub. You can sail it."
Brandon stood on his head and said, "I'm not ready to take a bath."

p. 16-17: "Brandon," Tricia said, "I'm putting toy dishes in the tub. You can pretend to pour milk and coffee."
Brandon somersaulted across the floor. "I'm not ready to take a bath."

p. 18-19: "Brandon," Aunt Molly called, "I'm putting your beach bucket and shovel in the tub. You can scoop up bubbles and put them in the bucket."

Brandon marched like a soldier and said, "I'm-not-rea-dy-to-take-a-bath."

p. 20-21: "Brandon," called Uncle George, "I'm blowing up your swimming ring seahorse for the tub."
Brandon started pulling the laces out of his dad's sneakers. "I'm not ready to take a bath."

p. 22-23: "Brandon," Sam said, "I'm putting Howard in the water. You can swim with your pet turtle."
Brandon found the day-old lollipop he'd stuck under the table. "I'm not ready to take a bath."

p. 24-25: "Brandon," I said, holding up a bottle from the kitchen, "I'm squirting green drops in your bath water. You can play in colored bubbles!"
Brandon hopped like a rabbit and squeaked. "I'm not ready to take a bath."

p. 26-27: Uncle George sighed and turned to Aunt Molly. "I suppose we could skip bathtime and move straight to bedtime. Because Brandon simply doesn't want to take a bath." [The opposition closes in, leading to Brandon's bleakest moment—though, because it's a children's story, it's only bleak to a child.]
"Now I do," Brandon shouted. "But there's no room for me in the tub!" [Cornered, Brandon takes the most favorable option.]

p. 28-29: "No problem," said Uncle George. "We'll make room."
Uncle George took out the seahorse.
Aunt Molly took out the bucket and shovel.
Sam took out the turtle and the boat.
Tricia took out the toy dishes.
But I couldn't take the green drops out of the water. [The unseen narrator acts as helper. She has inadvertently provided Brandon with a means of escape.]

p. 30-31: Brandon took off his dirty clothes and climbed in the tub. He splashed and played, and played and splashed. Finally he called, "I'm ready to get out!"

"Oh no!" Aunt Molly said, peeking at him. "He's green!"
    "Brandon," said Uncle George, "Wouldn't you like to take a nice, clean bath?"

p. 32: Brandon shook his green hair and climbed out of the tub. "Not now. I'm not ready to take a bath!" [Resolution: Brandon runs out of the bathroom, heading back to his ordinary world of play and fun with two easy-going parents and siblings.]

See how the bones of the story come together? Sometimes you may not find it necessary to represent every "bone" of the story, because many times that element can be implied. But once you get a sense for how the bones fit together, you are well on your way to constructing any kind of story you please.

———

Now you're ready to begin writing. Put your major story elements on note cards, if you like, and number a blank sheet of paper from one to 32. These are the pages in your picture book.
    Pages 1 and 32 are half-page spreads.
    Page 2 is usually dedicated to the copyright notice.
    Page 3 may have a dedication.
    Page 4 may be blank, or it may be combined with page 5 to open the book with a double page spread.
    From this point on, put brackets around each even and odd number: 6 and 7, 8 and 9, etc. Those are your double page spreads. You may use them as one unit, or you may use each page as a separate unit, depending on how much action is in your text. The child reader expects to see each major action playing out.
    If you write, for instance.

Zeke rode his bike until he met Tom. Then he and Tom went to the fair.

The reader will expect to see a bike, Tom, and a fair. You could do riding the bike and meeting Tom on one page, and going to the fair on another, or you could do them together on a double page spread. Just be certain that the text goes on the page where the action is illustrated.

Consider your story, and assign each element and/or major action to a set of bracketed pages: for instance, "Brandon dancing away from daddy, page 8-9."

Do this for all 32 pages, and when you have finished, you will have laid out your picture book plot. You've conquered the biggest hurdle. Now work to polish your prose and make certain the story works.

Whenever I find myself bogged down in a story or something seems out of place, it's invariably because I've gone down a rabbit trail or become unfocused. Whenever that happens, I pull out my plot skeleton and remind myself of what it is my characters are working toward. What is their hidden need, and how are they changing so it will be met? What is their desire or goal, and how do their current activities either push them toward their goal or pull them away from it?

With a little reminder from my scrawny plot skeleton, I am back on my way within minutes.

Now it's your turn. Go plot something wonderful.

DELIGHT

In the introduction, I told you that a picture book should delight children . . . and the adult reading the story. How do you do that?

Humor delights. What do children find funny? Funny words and sounds, funny situations, and the unexpected.

Rhythm delights. Many picture books delight children because they have a repeating refrain the child can repeat as the story progresses. Like "I'm not ready to take a bath" or "If I had long, long hair, I'd . . ."

As an adult I was absolutely delighted by Joyce Maxner's *Nicholas Cricket*, a book that can turn any reader into a musician. The book is poetic and rhythmic, and you can't help but fall into the cadence of the words and rhythm. The story is simple—at night, the bugs come out to play in the Bug a Wug Band, and the other bugs dance—but the magic of the story is in the rhythm of the words. Try saying "Moonlight glows and summer wind blows" as "peep-peep-peepers come dancing through the vines" and "rabbits come dancing on tip-tippy toes" because

"the music is just so grand.
The music is just so grand.
The music is just so grand."[1]

Art delights. Whether you or the publisher chooses the art, make sure it fits the tone and text of your story. One of my stories, *The Singing Shepherd,* was first published in 1992, and the art was rather formal and still. I had previously released *The Tale of Three Trees,* and I think the publisher wanted to "brand" the second book in a similar style and format.

But *Shepherd* is not the same kind of story as *Trees.* It features humor and exaggeration, so after the book went out of print, I republished the book and hired my own artist. The second edition is much more suited to the story of *The Singing Shepherd.*

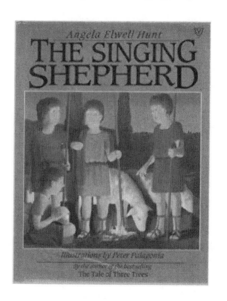

How can you tell if a book will delight children? Find some children and read it to them. Go to your public library and read it to some children at story telling hour (ask the librarian for permission first). Read it to children at your church. Read it to your grandchildren. But don't take the grands' word for it—they're biased.

Notice where the children laugh (or don't laugh), and where they fidget. Not every child will react the same way, of course, but look for the overall responses. Do a blind test—mix your story in with other books, and see how they react to yours compared to how they react to others. When you read the other stories, notice what the author does to elicit responses from the children. How can you incorporate that technique into your work? (Don't steal the author's words or ideas, but notice and use his or her techniques).

The best way to remember how children think is to spend time with them. It's good for the soul. And the best way to learn how to write a picture book is to read lots of them. They're good for the soul, too.

---

1. Joyce Maxner, *Nicholas Cricket*. New York: Harper Collins, 1989.

CUT THE WEASEL WORDS

So you've written a story and it's two thousand words. Too long. How can you shorten it without losing the gist of the story?

First, take your manuscript and a yellow highlighter. Read through the story and highlight any adjectives. Ask yourself, "Can the art supply these details?" If it can, cut the unnecessary words. But sometimes you want adjectives for artistic or rhythmic purposes, and that's okay. My book *If I had Long, Long Hair* just wouldn't be the same if I cut the adjectives and it became "If I Had Hair."

Second, you may have too many complications in your plot. Did you fit everything into the page spreads on your numbered page? If you have more story than you have page spreads, you probably need to cut some actions or complications. Keep it simple.

Perhaps you have too many characters. If two characters are serving the same purpose, delete one. If your protagonist Sam has two best friends, give him one.

Make sure you don't have a paragraph of preaching at the end of the story. Children are more intuitive than we realize. You don't have to explain the moral or point of the story; the child will figure it out.

Aside: I wrote a book called *The True Princess*. It's a Christian parable disguised as a fairy tale, about a beautiful princess who wears fancy clothes and lives in a palace. One day her father has to go away, but he leaves her with Nana, who teaches her how to live like a normal village girl. When the princess is lonely, Nana comforts her until her father the king returns.

One day I read the story to a group of kindergarten children at a Christian school. I asked them who the king represented, and they knew: God! Then I asked who Nana represented. The teachers were surprised when a little boy raised his hand and said, "The Holy Spirit!"

He was right. Children are clever, and you don't need to spell things out. Let them learn the lesson for themselves.

Because picture books are so lean, every word must work. Cutting weasel words is never more important than when writing for children.

Perhaps you've written too much in the first act. You don't have to give us the protagonist's life story or any backstory at all. Just start the story and move forward. A sentence or two of introduction is usually enough. The art will show us who he/she is, where they live, and what era the character lives in.

Now let's tackle the weasel words. What's a weasel word? It's a word that clutters up your manuscript. Some of them are common to almost everyone who speaks English; others are unique to each writer. For instance, after I handed in one of my adult novels, the editor called and said I was using *pull* too much.

I was flabbergasted. "Pull?"

"Yes," she said. "You have people *pulling* into driveways, *pulling* onto roads, *pulling* things from their purses and pockets. The word is all over the place."

I shook my head. "I didn't realize."

But I went back and did a search for the word *pull* in my manuscript—and there it was, sprinkled like paprika every few paragraphs. I deleted some, changed some to *turned*, others to *took*, others to *tugged*. But now I'm much more aware of my use of the word *pull*.

Tools for Tracking

The best tool for tracking down your weasel words is your word processing program's search and replace feature. If you write in any of the standard programs—Word, Word Perfect, Scrivener, Pages—you will find *search* (or *find*) and *replace*. When you're searching for a particular weasel word, ask your program to search for the word with spaces before and after it (unless it's a word likely to be used several times at the end of a sentence. In that case, you'll want to omit the last space).

For instance, if I was searching for *it*, I would enter [space]it[space] in the search box. Then I'd enter [space]IT[space] in the *replace* box. If you forget to add the spaces, the program will capitalize every instance of *it* in your book, and you'll have to manually change them back to what they should be.

That's what I do for every weasel word on my list. I use search and replace to find the word or phrase (with spaces), then I replace it with the exact same word or phrase, except in all capital letters (also with spaces before and after). This doesn't change any of my prose, but those weasel words now LOOM on the page and catch my attention as I work through subsequent drafts. And every time I see one, I stop and ask myself if I can make the sentence better without that word. If I can, great. If I can't—or if it would make the sentence too convoluted—the sentence remains as it was.

Identifying the Weasel Words

The first weasel word is one I first noticed the year I taught high school English. I'd never thought of it as a weasel word, but suddenly there it was, all over my students' papers. I grew weary of circling it with my bright red pen, and over and over again I drew little weasel faces in the margins of their papers.

A very small, very overused word. Can you guess what it is? Yes! IT!

It is so common we really don't think about it, but sometimes we fall into patterns that result in what I call "vague its." This particular species of *it* has infested many a sentence. When you find one of these, the best thing to do is shoot it and start over by asking, "What am I really trying to say here?"

Example: Mary wore a blue dress with flowers on *it*.

Does that *it* cause you to stop or slow down in any way? Can you tell immediately what *it* represents?

Yes, the blue dress. You shouldn't have to think too long about that *it*, so it's a good *it*. You could keep it, though you cut even more words by writing:

Mary wore a blue flowered dress.

The *it* that weakens your prose is found in sentences like this:

It is hard to get a drivers' license.

Hmm. What does that first *it* stand for? You have to think a moment, don't you? *It* has no apparent connection to anything else in the sentence, the paragraph, or the world.

So back up and say what you're really trying to say:

Getting a driver's license is hard. Or complicated. Or whatever you really meant.

What about this example:

"You don't understand," Mom said, sniffling. "*It's* so hard to live without your Dad."

In the second example, the questionable *it* is found in dialogue, and we loosen up when considering dialogue because people talk in all kinds of ways. If your character doesn't use proper grammar when she's crying and upset, she's just like the rest of us. Welcome her to the human race, and let her keep her undefined *it*.

Pardoning Reasonable Weasels

Please understand that the principles I'm presenting here are not hard and fast rules. I'm not saying every *it* should be condemned. Writing is part craft and part art, and I would never want to infringe on anyone's art . . . as long as they knew what they were doing. But when people make a word mess and call it art, well . . . I'm not likely to read it.

Doesn't mean everyone will feel the same way.

So if you want to write *It's the way he smiled that made me love him*, no one's going to demand that you be tarred and feathered by the writer police.

But as you sit down to revise and edit your manuscript, it's a good idea to search for *[space]it[space]* and replace it with the same term, but in capital letters. Look at each of the *its* you find in your manuscript, and see if each one is clearly related to the word it represents. If so, fine, no problem. But if you have a disturbing number of the noisome vague *its*, perhaps you should consider their eradication.

Passive Verbs

We are a video generation. We have grown up with film and television and instant-everything. We microwave and keep the Internet at our fingertips. We Google for information, we call up maps in our cars, and we can even send emails through our refrigerators.

So why wouldn't you want words that move at the speed of life?

You're probably familiar with the *to be* verbs: *is are am was* and *were*. These are passive words, and sometimes they have their place. Sometimes you want to say "The sky was a blue dome overhead" and be done with it.

But at other times we pull out the passive verbs when other perfectly active and visual words are within arm's reach.

If I write *the cat was on the table*, what do you see the cat doing as the sentence plays out in your mind? You're not really sure, are you, because the verb *was* is a wimpy little verb that doesn't pull much weight. If you do a search/replace and replace every *was* with *WAS*, you'll be able to go through your manuscript and replace every wimpy *was* with a hunky anything else.

You could write:

The cat yawned on the table

The cat reclined on the table

The cat retched on the table

The cat curled itself on the table
The cat lay on the table
The cat died on the table
The cat stretched on the table
. . . the possibilities are endless.

I always search for *was* and *were* in every draft and replace them with capitals because I want to see if I can find something better. Sometimes I stick with the simple *was*. Most of the time I find a better, more active way to write my sentence.

If I'm writing in present tense, of course, I search for *am* and *is* as well. I won't replace every active verb, but at least I *consider* its replacement. That consideration is what teaches us to write tighter.

Weak Adjectives and Enabling Adverbs

An adverb, by definition, is employed to support a verb that isn't doing its job. So be brave and search for ly[space], replace it with LY[space], and you should corral a small herd of shifty adverbs. For each of them, either see if you can replace the weak verb with something stronger, or simply cut the adverb. You'll do your manuscript a big favor.

Someone once reminded me that Jesus taught people by using nouns and strong verbs . . . and we all know how long people have been repeating *His* stories.

Cut the Obvious

My high school English teacher told us we should pay ourselves a quarter for every word we can cut. Cutting makes a manuscript stronger.

True story: on at least two occasions I have taken novels that had gone out of print and sold them to another publisher. But before I handed in the old manuscript to a new publisher, I asked if I could edit it again. Why? "Because," I told one of my editors, "I write tighter now, and I want to improve it."

On those two occasions, I took the manuscript and without deleting a single line of the plot, I cut over nine thousand words from the book. How? By cutting out statements of the obvious like She stood ~~from her chair~~. Three words, three quarters.

He clapped ~~his hands~~. (What else is he going to clap, unless he's a walrus?)

They ~~all~~ stood ~~to their feet~~. (Ditto. Unless they stand on something else, lose the unnecessary words.)

She nodded ~~her head in agreement~~. (A nod means agreement.)

He stood ~~up~~. She crouched ~~down~~. (You can almost always get rid of *up* and *down*.)

She scratched her head ~~with her hand~~. (Unless she's using her ballpoint pen to take care of the itch.)

She ~~reached out and~~ accepted the trophy.

Do you see how quickly those unnecessary words can add up? So spare a few trees and develop a sense for spotting extraneous verbiage. Then cut, cut, cut.

The Thing about That

I overuse *that* all the time. It slips into my language, my thoughts, and my writing. So whenever I start to cull the weasel words, I do a search for *that*, replace it with THAT, and then carefully consider every THAT I come across. I don't know a test for it except to read the sentence without it—if the sentence makes sense without the THAT, I take it out. If the sentence seems to be missing something important, I leave the *that*. Simple.

Miscellaneous Weasel Words

Other weasels on almost every list of overused words are *just, very, rather, began to, started to, some, "of the," "there was,"* and *suddenly*.

Just is used too much. You may want to leave it in dialogue, because people do use it in casual conversation, but in nonfiction writing or narrative, you'll probably want to omit *just*. Or replace it with *simply* where applicable.

Very often comes off as amateurish unless it's in a character's dialogue. Remember—the more concise the writing, the stronger the writing, so your sentence will probably be stronger without words like *very*.

Why write *he began to run* or *he started to eat*, when you could write *he ran* or *he ate?* Unless you purposely want someone to be in the process of beginning an activity, the simple past tense will do. But if you want to write:

As he began to eat, a shot rang out, shattering his pasta bowl,

Then *began to* is best.

"Of the" is often used in formal titles (The Sword of the Lord and of Gideon), but if you find yourself writing *he hid inside the cloak of the knight,* then ditch the *of the* and write *he hid in the knight's cloak.* Much, much cleaner.

"There was" is a passive verb linked to a nothing word. So if you find those constructions in your book and you didn't write it for a purposeful reason, cut the nothing words and figure out what you're trying to say. Instead of

There was a peaceful haze over the valley . . .

write

A peaceful haze hovered over the valley.

Suddenly: In fiction, if you are writing and a shot rings out, to your characters it has rung out *suddenly* whether you use the word or not. See for yourself:

She bent to breathe in the scent of the sweet flowers. "Thank you for the lovely bouquet," she told the little girl. She pressed a kiss to the child's forehead and slipped her fingers around the beribboned stems, ready to hand the flowers to her waiting attendant—

A shot rang out.

She turned, saw horror on her attendant's face, and felt a dull pressure in her back, but that had to be the result of walking all day, from bending to receive dozens of little bouquets, from kissing children and shaking hands and smiling until her jaws ached like they ached now, but no, the pain was lower, but it wasn't pain exactly, it was pressure, and then she heard a splatting sound and felt something splash her shoes, probably the children, maybe a child had spilled a bottle of water, but as she looked down she saw that the water was red, as red as her dress, as red as the single rose the prince had left on her pillow this morning—

Sorry—I got a little carried away with my sinister fairy tale that is clearly NOT a picture book.

Do you see how you don't need *suddenly* to write a sudden action? If it occurs unexpectedly, it will *feel* sudden.

Unless a character's house is on fire or he's running for his life, you will probably want to **lose the exclamation points**. Too many comes across as amateurish—as though you're working too hard to convey an emotion or sense of urgency. So reserve them for truly dire circumstances, if you use them at all.

Find more elegant ways to convey emotion or urgency through dialogue, interior monologue, or action. And remember—sometimes an emotion is stronger if it's understated.

Quiet can be intense.

Those suggestions are a few ways to help you whittle down your word count. Remember who will be reading this story: a tired adult, home after a busy day, putting the children to bed. The adults don't want to read a long story.

Think of the artist—he or she has to fit a lot into a page spread or two, plus leave room for the text. Too much text means too little space for the art.

And think of the child—he's tired, he's ready to sleep, and he wants to hear a story, not a word salad. So choose the words that count, and lose the rest. Your story will be the better for it.

THE OTHER HALF: THE ART

A picture book is half text, half art. The artist does a lot of hard work, and if you negotiate a shared royalty deal, they deserve half the royalties.

Remember when I told you that my first picture book won a contest and was published as a result? I mentioned that Diane Johnson did three sketches to send in with the manuscript, and on the basis of my text and her art, we won. First prize was publication and an advance, which we split 50/50.

But at that point, my work as a writer was done, and Diane had to do the hard work of illustrating the entire book, including cover and title page. She worked a day job as a graphic artist, so she had to do the work in her free time on evenings and weekends. She would work hard on a sketch, paint it, and send it in . . . and many times she had to make adjustments to suit the editorial board. (This was before we could send things with a click of a computer key!)

Diane did a beautiful job on the book, but when I sold my second picture book to Abingdon Press, they asked Diane if she wanted to illustrate it and she said no. Working a full time job and illustrating books on a deadline was just too much (and I don't blame her for turning the job down).

Never think art is easy—it's every bit as demanding as coming up with a good idea and writing a story.

So once you have your picture book text ready to go, how do you find an artist?

If you are seeking to be traditionally published, where a publisher buys your manuscript, gives you a contract, and pays you an advance, you don't have to worry. That publisher should have an art/design department, and they will design your book and find an artist to do the illustrations. Lots of beginning picture book writers think they need to submit art with the text, but don't do it! They could not like the art and reject your book, so that practice cuts your chance of acceptance by 50 percent. The only occasion to submit both text and art to a traditional publisher is if YOU are a professional artist and you are submitting an entire package. Some people have the talent to do both. I don't.

If, however, you want to self-publish your book, you need to find your own artist. Trust me—do not ask a friend. You may think your friend is a great artist, but most artists have a distinctive style, and you ought to compare several artists' styles to see which one best suits your book.

For years I have used the talented artists at 99designs.com to illustrate my self-published picture books. Artists from around the world have samples of their work on 99designs.com, and you can look through the different illustrators' work and find the ones you like. Then you can invite those artists to participate in a contest or work one-on-one with you to illustrate your book.

I held contests for several of my books, creating a brief stating exactly what was required: illustrations for an 8x10 picture book that would be published and available on Amazon. It would require 13 double page spreads and two single page spreads, as well as a cover and title page. I would supply the manuscript, and I wanted to have the work done by (date). I always added this: *I would like to have the work submitted by the deadline, but I would rather have good than fast, so please consider that date flexible.*

I understand that life happens. The last artist I worked with was working on her way to meeting the deadline, but then her daughter was struck by a car, which put her behind schedule. Of course I understood. I would rather have a mother care for her daughter than go crazy trying to meet my deadline.

Not every illustrator on 99Designs has done picture books, so I always remind them of several things:

- the illustration needs to conform to the text. Don't draw five pigs if the text says there are four.
- Keep text and important visual elements away from the page edges and the gutter (the space in the center of a double page spread). These areas may be cut off during the printing process.
- Place the text on a separate layer so the font can be changed or the text edited without harming the art.
- I always ask the artist to send me the files in Photoshop format. Some people may prefer InDesign, but I don't have that program and Photoshop lets me do everything I need to do.

You'll need to set a budget for your project and let the artists know what that is. I'm hesitant to put a number here because such things change, but I can tell you this: let it be at *least* $1,000. That is a lot of work. Artists who accept deals on 99designs and other such sites sign a release when the work is done, giving all the rights to the owner/author. Technically, it is a work for hire, and you will be the owner of the illustrations when all is done. This will be a relief for you when you are publishing your book—you won't have to keep track of dividing royalties and paying the artist her share every year.

I know that some professional graphic artists frown on sites like 99designs and say that those artists don't earn a living wage. Not an American living wage, perhaps, but I did some research and learned that the amount I paid an artist in Indonesia was enough to feed his family for a month. And don't all writers start out writing for pennies a word? I did. As a newbie, I was grateful for an opportunity to write and enlarge my portfolio. So I believe in programs like 99designs, and have used artists from Indonesia, Britain, Germany, Slovakia, and the U.S. All of them were super-talented and I have been delighted with the results.

PUBLISHING YOUR PICTURE BOOK

Which is better, traditional or self-publishing?

Without a doubt, traditional publishing is best. If you sell your book to a traditional publisher, they will handle the publishing, the artwork, the design, the editing, the sales, and the distribution. That last one is HUGE. They will see that your book is placed into brick-and-mortar bookstores, and that is where people pick up picture books, read them, and buy them for their children and grand-children.

Beware of subsidy or vanity publishing. These folks ask YOU to pay while they edit, sell, and distribute your book. But their distribu-tion consists mainly of listing your book on Amazon.com and other online sites, so no one is hand-selling your book. Most bookstores will not purchase books from subsidy publishers, so you book will be one title in a sea of other self-published books. Unless you are hand-selling your book, reading your book in schools, and spending your own money to promote it, it will sell maybe one hundred copies.

Did I say I have self-published several picture books? Yes—but I do the editing and designing myself. I took a few basic classes in graphic design and I learned how to use Photoshop, so I can take the digital files I receive from the artist and adjust the text, size a cover to certain specs, and upload the files to sites like

Amazon.com and BarnesandNoble.com. Several of my self-published picture books were originally traditionally published, so I hired artists to do new illustrations (because the old illustrations were owned by the publisher) OR I asked the original artists if they'd give me permission to use their art and I send them a royalty check every year.

So why don't I try to traditionally publish my new picture books, if traditional publishing is so much better? Several reasons:

- Time. It takes months to sell a picture book, and about a year to bring it to publication. I'd rather not wait because I have already developed a readership, though most of my books—and readers—are for adult novels. Picture books are a lovely distraction for me.
- The market. When publishing hits upon hard times, children's books are often the first to be eliminated. As I mentioned before, they are expensive to produce, and the market is smaller.
- Selling. Not many agents represent children's books (for the above reasons), and I don't want to deal with selling it myself.
- Control. I'm not a control freak, but it *is* nice to be able to arrange, write, and publish a book on my own terms.
- Money? Actually, money is not a primary consideration. A traditional publisher would probably give me an advance, and that's always nice, but the royalty would be only about 6 or 7 percent because the other half of the typical royalty goes to the artist. Still, a traditional publisher should sell more copies than I could as a self-publisher.
- Self-publishing can bring a royalty ranging from 35-70 percent, but you need to remember that a color book is going to be more expensive to print than a paperback novel. The retail price is going to be higher (thus handicapping sales), so your total royalty is going to be lower.

How Do You Self-Publish a Picture Book?

The process isn't complicated, but it can be a little tricky when you're first getting used to it. I like to keep things simple.

Picture books today are primarily sold in three formats: ebook, hardcover, and paperback. I would recommend ebook and hardcover. Color paperbacks can be nearly as expensive to print as hardcovers, and as a parent, I would want all my kids' books to be tough because kids can be hard on books! I still have the picture books I bought for my kids, and now my grandkids read them.

To publish a hardcover version of your book, I recommend the program at IngramSpark.com. You can publish an ebook (ePub format) and a print version by entering the basic information and uploading a cover and a pdf file containing the entire book.

If you are not skilled with Photoshop, you might want to hire a graphic artist to create PDFs of your individual book spreads, then combine all of them into one file.

Ingram Spark will provide a cover template, so you or your graphic artist will need to fit your cover onto the template and upload it in CMYK format and high resolution. Ingram Spark has details on their website.

Note: CMYK format (refers to the color mode of an image) is for printing on paper. Your pages for the print edition should all be saved in CMYK format.

RGYB format works best for the jpeg files you'll use for your ebooks. This format looks best on digital screens.

Your ebook will be in a fixed layout format—the text won't be resizable on an ebook reader. To create a book for Kindle, download the free **Kindle Kids' Book Creator** and load your book pages into the program. It's easy to use—just drag and drop the pages in the correct order, enter the appropriate information, and click. Within seconds you will have a mobi file, which you can upload to the Kindle Publishing Program as your Kindle ebook. Amazon KDP also will allow you to turn that ebook into a paperback if you want, but that's up to you. Amazon KDP does not offer hardcovers at this time.

I have not covered every detail—you'll need to learn about ISBNs, pricing, etc. —but you can find that information online at whichever publishing outlet you choose. An ISBN is the international book number—every edition of a book has its own number. Amazon Kindle will give you a free ISBN for your Kindle book, and you can purchase one at Ingram Spark.

Why Write a Picture Book?

If there's not a lot of money to be made, and if the work is exacting, then why write picture books at all? For love.

I love kids, I love the way they think, and I love explaining the world to little ones through story. I love writing those stories, and using humor to illustrate deep truths. Picture books are an art form I enjoy, so that's why I do it.

(And to be completely honest, after paying an artist, it takes a *long time* for me to actually make a profit on self-published picture books.)

If you don't love reading picture books, you should probably write something else. You can write chapter books for older kids, middle grade books for ages 10-14, or young adult books for teenagers. You can write anything . . . as long as you study the blueprint and know how to use the tools.

But if you love children, and writing, and art, picture books might be your perfect niche. You may have such a gift that you can easily sell to traditional publishers, so please follow your heart. If you are serious about pursuing the art of picture books, you should join the Society for Children's Book Writers and Illustrators, the largest organization of children's writers and illustrators in the world. You can find more information about them at their website: https://www.scbwi.org.

I wish you every success on your journey of creating art and wonder for children.

PICTURE BOOK EXERCISES

1. FIND SOME CHILDREN AGES 3-8. ASK THEM ABOUT THEIR favorite stories. What sort of things do they like to hear about? Monsters? Aliens? Transformers? Make a list.

2. Using the list you've just made, come up with three different story ideas with WAGS. Stories that will take the hearer to a different world, with an active character who has a definite goal that involves high stakes.

3. Write out your three stories—don't worry about editing, just write out the stories and let the words flow.

4. Find some more children in your target age group. Tell them your stories and see how they respond. If they are less than delighted, ask them how the stories could be improved . . . and then make those changes. Chose the best of the three stories to polish and consider for publication . . . but only if you're getting really strong feedback from children (who are not related to you).

ABOUT THE AUTHOR

Angela Hunt writes for readers who have learned to expect the unexpected from this versatile writer. With over four million copies of her books sold worldwide, she is the best-selling author of more than 165 works ranging from picture books (*The Tale of Three Trees*) to novels and nonfiction.

Now that her two children are grown, Angie and her husband live in Florida with Very Big Dogs (a direct result of watching *Turner and Hooch* too many times). This affinity for mastiffs has not been without its rewards—one of their dogs was featured on *Live with Regis and Kelly* as the second-largest canine in America. Their dog received this dubious honor after an all-expenses-paid trip to Manhattan for the dog and the Hunts, complete with VIP air travel and a stretch limo in which they toured New York City. Afterward, the dog gave out pawtographs at the airport.

Angela admits to being fascinated by animals, medicine, unexplained phenomena, and "just about everything." Books, she says, have always shaped her life— in the fifth grade she learned how to flirt from reading *Gone with the Wind*.

Her books have won the coveted Christy Award, several Angel Awards from Excellence in Media, and the Gold and Silver Medallions from *Foreword Magazine*'s Book of the Year Award. In 2007, her novel *The Note* was featured as a Christmas movie on the Hallmark channel. She recently completed her doctorate in biblical literature and another in Theology.

When she's not home writing, Angie often travels to teach writing workshops at schools and writers' conferences. And to talk about her dogs, of course. Readers may visit her web site at www.angelahunt books.com.

Made in the USA
Columbia, SC
18 July 2024

38828630R00262